UNDERSTANDING EDUCATION
An Overview

UNDERSTANDING EDUCATION

An Overview

O.P. Dhiman

PUBLICATIONS

KALPAZ PUBLICATIONS

DELHI-110052

UNDERSTANDING EDUCATION
An Overview of Education

Rs. 750

ISBN: 81-7835-674-0

Published in 2008 in India by
Kalpaz Publications
C-30, Satyawati Nagar,
Delhi-110052
E-mail: kalpaz@hotmail.com
Phone : 9212729499

Printed at : Excel Prints, Naraina, New Delhi.

To

Student-Teachers

and

Teacher–Educators

Contents

O.P. Dhiman
M.A. (Philosphy & Pol. Sc.), M.Ed.
Hony. DIRECTOR
Formerly Principal
Multani Mal Modi College
PATIALA – 147001

Mobile: 0-98887-73537
Tel. (R) : 0175-6543009
Residence :
Ashiana, 49 - Raghbir Nagar,
PATIALA – 147001

Foreword

It is heartening to learn that my former colleague, worthy Sh. O.P. Dhiman has penned the book 'Understanding Education : An Overview of Education.' Well organized in a coherent manner in eight chapters, the contents reflect the aurhor's deep understanding of the issues taken up. The subject matter has been examined in a logical and reflective way.

In the recent years, we are witness to a phenomenol expansion of teacher-education. All kinds of education institutes, teacher educators and books on teacher-education abound the big bazar of teacher education. Very many text books on Education written by pseudonymous authors and published by fly- by- night publishers adorn the shelves of the college libraries.

Given the situation as is today, I think, this book of Shri Dhiman will fill the vacuum created due to lack of quality books on Education. I am sure, the book will be indispensable for B.Ed., M.Ed & M.A. (Education) students of different universities. For educational administrators, planners and the serious readers, it will be a useful compendium on education—its basis, processes and products.

(Dr. Kanwarjit Singh)

Preface

The present book *'Understanding Education :* an Over-View of Education', as the name suggests, is designed as an introductory text on Education for the student-teachers, teacher-educators and others interested in the pursuit of Education. This book is the result of my unique experiment of teaching different papers, covering different aspects of Education to my M.Ed. and B.Ed. students for more than 26 years. Every year, in the beginning of the session, before starting teaching different papers alloted to me, I used to devote at least seven or eight lectures to give an over-view of Education to my students. I found that these lectures helped the students in understanding the specific papers in a better way.

The book has been divided into eight chapters, namely:

1. Meaning, Nature and Bases of Education
2. Aims of Education
3. Educational Aims in India
4. The Curriculum
5. Methods of Teaching
6. Teaching Devices
7. Audio-Visual Aids
8. Evaluation.

Education is a purposeful activity having certain specific aims and objectives. For the realization of these objectives, learning experiences are provided through various methods of teaching. To make the methods of teaching interesting and effective, different teaching devices and audio-visual aids are used. Last of all, evaluation is done to find out if the desired objectives have been achieved. All these aspects of Education are logically integrated to form ONE UNIT to make an understanding of Education in totality.

Thus, this book is an earnest endevour to give an Over-View of Education in a comprehensive but comprehensible way that will serve as a foundation for better understanding of various papers of M.Ed., B.Ed. and M.A. (Education) Courses.

I do not claim any originality in the subject-matter. I only seek to examine, analyse and present all the aspects of Education integrated into logical sequence to give an Over-View of Education. However, for opinions expressed and for whatever inadequacies and shortcomings there might be, I alone am responsible.

I hope, this compact book of eight chapters will help the M.Ed., B.Ed., and M.A. (Education) students, Teacher-Educators, and Educational Administrators and Planners to understand all the aspects of Education in a better way.

I will be happy to receive the comments and suggestions, if any, from the readers for the modification and improvement of this book.

ASHIANA **O.P. Dhiman**
49, Raghbir Nagar
Patiala-147001
(India)

Acknowledgements

Any accomplishment requires inspiration, help and guidance of many people and this book is not an exception. During its preparation, I have been inspired, helped and guided by a number of well-wishers.

I cannot but remember with profound feeling of piety and gratitude my mother, Late Mrs. Maya Dhiman who created in me a burning passion for democratic ideals and critical-objective thinking.

Formal though it may look, I must acknowledge my grateful appreciation to my wife, Mrs. Manorama Dhiman, Former Head, Deptt. of Home Science, Govt. College for Women, Patiala for her inspiration and devotion but for which, the present work would have been well-nigh impossible.

I must appreciate my grand children—Shivam, Anish, Chahat, Muskan and Ayush, from whom I have learnt a lot to refresh my thinking on Education.

I acknowledge the co-operation extended to me by several friends and colleagues in the preparation of this book. I am especially thankful to my friend and colleague, Dr. Harcharan Singh, Lecturer, Multani Mal Modi Post-Graduate College, Patiala for reading the manuscript of this book and giving me valuable suggestions.

I take this opportunity to put on record my deep sense of gratitude to all the Principals of Govt. College of Education, Patiala with whom I have worked, who always loved and inspired me despite my habit of being critical and independent in my views and exposition.

The acknowledgement will remain incomplete without thanking my students who were instrumental in clarifying some of my thoughts and stimulate me to think always a new on different aspects of education. They have taught me more than they may realise.

I must be thankful to all the authors on whose work I have drawn freely.

Most of all I wish to express my deep sense of gratitude to my esteemed friend and colleague Dr. Kanwarjit Singh, Director of Public Instruction (Colleges), Punjab.

Last, though not the least, I am grateful to my publishers, especially Shri Amit Garg for his enthusism in the publication of this book.

March 6, 2008 **O.P. Dhiman**

1

Meaning, Nature and Bases of Education

What is education? This fundamental question has been exercising the minds of philosophers and thinkers from Socrates and Plato to Gandhi and Dewey. The word 'Education' has a very wide connotation and it is very difficult to give its precise definition. A biologist, a psychologist, a priest, a philosopher, a statesman, a teacher, a merchant, a shopkeeper and even an artisan will give widely different definitions. Definitions—whether naive or serious – lead us nowhere. Those seldom reveal the real meaning and nature of Education.

Let us discuss, in this chapter, what education is or what it implies.

ETYMOLOGICAL EXPLANATION OF EDUCATION

The first step in any systematic attempt to understand the nature of Education should be to trace its sources of derivation. Etymologically, the term 'Education' is traced to different sources.

Education as Bringing up Process

According to one view, 'education' has been derived from the Latin word *'educare'* which means *'to bring up'* or *'to raise.'* According to this view, education is a process of imparting, to an individual, certain information and knowledge which society deems necessary. Education implies modification of the behaviour of the individual by imposing standards of society upon him. Thus, education is a process of external imposition rather than growth from within. This derivation gives us the concept of teacher-centred rather than child-centred education.

Education as a Drawing out Process

There is a group of thinkers who believe that the term 'education' has been derived from the Latin word *'educere'* which means to *'lead out'* or *'to draw out.'* Education, they think, means to draw out something and not to put in something.

These theorists who hold that education is a drawing out process, give a slightly different explanation of the word 'education'. They believe that the term 'education' has been derived from two Latin words, *'e'* meaning *'out of'* and *'duco'* meaning *'to lead'*. Education, therefore, means to lead out or draw out the best in man. It is the process of 'drawing out from within' rather than 'imposing from without.'

Education, from this point of view, is considered as a process of the development of what is innate in the child. It is an agency of, or an instrument for, the transformation of the potential into the actual. This explanation presumes that all knowledge is inherent in children. Education, therefore, implies growth from within rather than imposition from without. Education is a process of the development of talent inborn in the individual and not conveying to an individual a body of information or knowledge. A large number of eminent educators and philosophers have endorsed this interpretation. "By education", says Gandhiji, "I mean an all round drawing out of the best in the child and man—body, mind and spirit."

Education as a Bringing up as well as a Drawing out Process

The two viewpoints of education, discussed above, cannot be isolated from each other. The view that education is a drawing out process can be accepted with a pinch of salt. In this interpretation, an important aspect of education has been disregarded. Can it be possible that everything which forms part of education was already inherent in the child's mind? Is it possible to draw out everything? Can it be established that everything— ideas, ideals, beliefs, opinions and attitudes —was potential in the mind of the child? It is true that certain inherent capacities do form part of the natural endowment of the child, but the factual knowledge acquired, skills learnt or the habits and sentiments developed, during life time, were not innate in the child's mind. Therefore, it can be said that in the absence of poured-in knowledge or suitable foundation laid through learning under environmental influences, drawing out will be out of question. Unless knowledge or experience is given to the child, we cannot draw out, the best in him. Education, therefore, is not only a drawing out, but also a bringing up process, whereby the educand is trained for certain types of social behaviour—democratic living, worthy citizenship, international understanding and is developed into a full man or woman with a well integrated personality. "True education", says Gandhiji, "is that which draws out and stimulates the spiritual, intellectual and physical faculties of the children."

Indian Synonyms of Education

The words 'Shiksha' (शिक्षा) and 'Vidya' (विद्या) are the Indian synonyms of 'Education'. Shiksha is derived from the Sanskrit verbal root (धातु) 'Shas' (शास) which means to 'discipline', 'to control', 'to instruct' or 'to teach'. Similarly the word Vidya is derived from the Sanskrit verbal root 'vid' (विद्) which means 'to know'. Thus, it refers to acquisition of knowledge. Hence disciplining the mind and acquisition of knowledge have always been the dominant theme in Indian approach to understanding education.

NARROW AND BROAD MEANING OF EDUCATION

Narrow Meaning of Education

Education, in its narrow sense, is regarded as equivalent to instruction, imparted in a school or college. Education is believed to begin with the entrance of the child to a school and end with his departure from the university. The amount of education, thus received by the child, is measured in terms of the number and the grades of examinations passed by him. There is deliberate effort, on the part of the educator, to inculcate certain habits, attitudes or influences in the learner, which by tradition are considered to be essential and useful to him.

In the narrow sense, therefore, education includes those specific influences which are brought to bear upon the child with a definite purpose, in pre-planned, suitable and methodical manner by parents, teachers and the community, and which are for the welfare of the younger generation and perpetual preservation of the cultural heritage. For the achievement of this end, in addition to home, a special institution, called the school, is created and a particular person, called the teacher, is appointed. According to this view, education is mostly limited to class-room teaching of ready-made materials.

"In the narrow and more definite (or specific) sense", says T. Raymont, "in which the term is used in common speech and in legal enactments, education does not include self-culture and the general influences of one's surroundings, but only those special influences which are consciously and *designedly* brought to bear upon the young by the adult portion of the community, whether through the family, the church, or the State." These influences or modes of influences are deliberately planned, chosen and employed by the community for the welfare of the members of the rising generation. The purpose of these influences is to modify the behaviour of the child in such a way that he may become different from what he would have been without education. It is to affect change which makes possible a better adjustment of human nature to the surroundings and to change the surroundings so as to harmonise with human nature. It is restricted to that function of the community which consists of passing on traditions, its background, its knowledge and its attitudes to the members of the rising generation through specialised people, instruments, and methods.

Broad Meaning of Education

In its broad sense, education is a life long process, which starts with the conception and ends with the death. Education, in its wider sense, includes all the influences which act upon an individual during his passage from the cradle to the grave. An individual goes on increasing his knowledge and learns through his experiences and contacts with environment. Education, as such, is not teaching or learning of 3 Rs—reading, writing and recurring. It consists of development of 4 Hs—head, heart, hand and health.

Education, in the broad sense, includes all the knowledge and experiences, acquired during infancy, childhood, adolescence, youth, manhood or old age through any agency of education—the school, home, church, society etc. In this way, one's whole life and all life activities become a real source of education. Thus, education becomes the sum-total of all experiences that the child receives in the school or outside, through the study of different subjects, through various activities, through the library, the playground, the workshop or through other agencies. Lodge in his book *Philosophy and Education*, while explaining the nature of education in the wider sense, says, "In the wider sense, all experience is said to be educative. The bite of a mosquito, the taste of a water-melon, the experience of falling in love, of flying in an aeroplane, of being caught in a storm in a small boat—all such experiences have a directly educative effect on us. The child educates his parents, the pupil educates his teachers—Everything we say, think or do, educates us, no less than what is said or done to us by other beings, animate or inanimate. In this wider sense, life is education and education is life. Whatever broadens our horizon, deepens our insight, refines our reactions, and stimulates thought and feeling, educates us."

In the broad or non-specific sense, education means the process of development from infancy to maturity. In other words, it is the process, whereby a human being gradually adapts himself in various ways to his physical, social, and spiritual environments. Thus, education is a lifelong process. "It is really life that educates," says T. Raymont. "One is educated by one's vocation, by home life, by friendship, by marriage, by parenthood, by recreation, by travel, and so forth."

Broadly viewed, education is life and life is education. Education, in the broader sense, is transmission of life by the living, to the living, through living and for living.

Synthesis of the Two Meanings

Viewed separately, these meanings of education hardly serve the desired ends. There is a need of reconciling the two meanings. Education must include knowledge and skills along with the factors necessary for the modification of child's behaviour and development of his personality. Both the meanings have to play an appropriate and significant role in the education of the child.

Decidedly, education is more than schooling and instruction, although these are its significant features. We may say that education consists of acquiring knowledge, skills and attitudes which assist one in maintaining good health, a reasonable amount of economic security and genuine happiness in life. We can conclude with the remarks of Dr. S. Radhakrishnan, when he says, "Education, to be complete, must be humane, it must include not only training of the intellect but also the refinement of the heart and the discipline of the spirit."

FORMAL AND INFORMAL EDUCATION

Education may be formal or informal. Informal education is incidental—the education which a person receives from living with others. It is important and natural, but it is not deliberately planned.

Formal education is consciously and deliberately planned for the purpose of training the child. It consists in direct schooling or tuition. Let us now discuss these two types of education in detail.

Formal Education

Formal education is that which is consciously and deliberately planned for the modification of behaviour with a particular end in view. Formal education is undertaken in schools or institutions specifically established and maintained for the purpose. It therefore, takes the form of schooling, tuition and instruction. As the child goes to a school, he has to be formal and act according to the discipline of that school. He is conscious of the fact that he goes to that school for getting education. He is aware of his presence in the school throughout the day. Similar is the case with the teacher. He too, is aware of all these things. Thus, both the pupil and the teacher deliberately engage themselves in the process of education with predetermined objective in view. In a school, not only the atmosphere is formal, but the curriculum and methods of teaching are also formal. These are fixed in advance with clear-cut ends in view. All teaching is formal.

It may, however, be maintained that any process of teaching, which involves supervision, instruction, set plan, definite aim and principles, amounts to formal education, no matter whether given in a school or a workshop. As such, it also includes vocational or general education imparted by parents in a formal way.

Informal Education

Informal education is not pre-planned or deliberate. It is incidental and takes place consciously as well as unconsciously. Child learns many habits, manners, and patterns while living with others or moving in different spheres like home, society and groups etc. Actually, such education is not given by any specialised agency or institution, although this forms the essential feature of all education.

In an informal way, child imitates the elder members of the community and thus inbibes certain virtues, most essential for life. He is in this way getting education. Such an education is gained through experiences and actual living in the family or community. There is no prescribed course, no fixed time-table and no formal means of education. The transmission of cultural heritage and life-experiences takes place in a natural way. Such an education becomes life long process and is called informal education.

Difference between Formal and Informal Education

Formal and informal education can be differentiated as follows :

Formal Education	*Informal Education*
1. End : Formal education has formal end.	1. Informal education has no formal end.
2. Means : It has formal means.	2. It has no formal means.
3. Teacher : There are qualified teachers who impart education.	3. There are no specified teachers in informal education. Whosoever imparts knowledge is the teacher.
4. Conscious : Both, the educator and the educand are conscious about the process.	4. Neither the educator nor the educand is conscious about the process.
5. Curriculum and time-table; It has some prescribed course and fixed time-table.	5. It has no prescribed course and no fixed time-table.

Formal Education	*Informal Education*
6. Body : There is some organising body behind it. It is given in school or college.	6. There is no organising body behind it. There is no fixed place for it.
7. Examinations : In formal education, examinations are given and certificates or degrees are awarded.	7. In informal education, there are no examinations. Such type of education is never completed.
8. Agencies : Agencies of formal education are school, library, museum, art gallery, laboratory and books.	8. Agencies of informal education are family, community, religion, state and playground.
9. Period : It starts and ends at a particular stage.	9. It continues throughout life. It is a life long continuous process.
10. Strain : It leads to mental strain because serious efforts are made.	10. Informal education, being natural, does not strain the learner.

From Informal to Formal Education

During the primitive times, all educatior was informal. It was limited to activities like hunting, fishing, workshopping, protection from the natural calamities, and so on. The child could learn such life activities by direct participation in the day-to-day life of the community and in an informal way from the more experienced members of the community. At that time life was very simple. So was the social order and culture. A son was to follow the profession of his father, and the daughter of her mother. With the advancement of civilization and growing complexity of social order and culture, education began to lose its informal nature. With the growth of civilization and advancement in the filed of science and technology, the accumulated knowledge and the skills became more and more complex, which created the need for formal education. It necessitated the selection of educational experiences and consequently, education progressed from the incidental and the informal aspects of life towards the conscious formality of school. Hence, formal education became differential from the informal, and school became a specialized agency of Education.

Synthesis of the Two Types

As we have already noted, both formal and informal types of education try to prepare the child for life. However, as teachers, we are mostly concerned with formal education and, therefore, consider this type of education to be more important. Whereas, the influences of formal education are systematic, definite and permanent, those of informal education tend to be vague and indefinite. That is why in the case of formal education we can predict results to a certain extent which is not possible in the case of informal education. It is through formal education that we can train and educate the immature child according to the demands of society.

All this may be quite true, still we cannot ignore the important role played by informal education in the life of a child. For formal education, a child stays in the school for five or six hours while the rest of the day is spent in the home, community, church, playground etc., outside the school. The environment where the child spends the major part of his day, must therefore, have much more effect upon him than the school. Therefore, the importance of informal education cannot be ignored.

Education in its 'totality' includes both, formal and informal education. In the modern structure, both types of education play important roles. The difference may be of quality or quantity, but each is implied by the other. Both are independent, but inter-connected. We cannot minimise the essential virtues like social, moral, spiritual values etc.

in human life that the informal education imparts. Similarly, we cannot ignore the significance of schooling, instruction and training that the formal education provides. Granted, that education is modification of human behaviour, a process of social change and transmission of cultural heritage, it is evident that formal as well as informal education should essentially form the basis of all educational organisation and planning. The two types of education are complementary to each other.

FORMAL AND NON-FORMAL EDUCATION

A new concept, which has developed recently after the publication of the report of International Commission on the Development of Education entitled 'Learning to Be', is the Non-Formal Education. The Commission feels that inspite of the vast financial resources being spent on education, vast majority of the people do not get the desired education. Some of them find it difficult, due to their pre-occupation in earning, while others desirous of admission in Schools, Colleges and Universities fail to get admission, because of shortage of seats and a very large number of aspirants for admission.

The Commission, therefore, suggests that alternative arrangements should be made for those who cannot attend formal institutions, because of one reason or the other. As a result, Distance Education Departments have been started by many Universities and also a number of Open Universities have been started Now, those who fail to get admission in formal Educational Institutes can get education through correspondence programmes, contact programmes, vacation programmes, satellite instructional programmes, teaching machines, programmed lessons and the like, through Distance Education and Open Universities. Such education is known as Non-Formal Education.

Formal, Informal and Non-Formal are not three types of education, as it is mostly misunderstood. There are only two types of education. Formal and Informal from one angle *i.e.* contents of education or 'what education' and Formal and Non-formal from another angle *i.e.* method of education or 'how education'. Thus, formal education can be formal or non-formal. If a student passes an examination from some formal educational institution, it will be Formal Education. If he passes that examination through distance education programme, it will be to some extent Non-formal education because in this case, as compared to the former, somewhat less formalities will be there. But if he passes that examination as a private candidate, it will be still more Non-formal Education, as in this case very few formalities will be there.

Non-formal education, as a system, is supplementary or parallel to formal education. Open Schools, Open Universities and Correspondence or Distance-Education departments of the Universities are coming to stay as important instruments of education. Whether they are capable of achieving educational excellence of the order of formal education system, is a big question? However, they are of unique importance in this modern world.

EDUCATION AND OTHER TERMS

Education is generally confused with literacy, instruction, schooling and training. In the interest of clarity, therefore, education should be distinguished from these terms, though a distinct line of demarcation is ruled out. A brief explanation of the meaning of each of these terms will, however, give us a better insight into the real nature of education.

Education and Literacy

We often hear the people saying, "He knows reading and writing." "My wife is not educated." In both of these sayings, education means reading and writing. Thus we have not made distinction between reading, writing and education. A literate wife may be less educated than an illiterate wife. There is a difference between education and literacy.

Knowledge of reading and writing is literacy. No doubt literacy is a part of education, but it is not education. "Literacy," says Gandhiji, "is not the end of education, nor even the begining. It is one of the means whereby man and woman can be educated. Literacy in itself is no education."

Literacy lays more emphasis on the subjects and tools rather than on the personality of the educand, which is the main concern of education. Education is an all-round harmonious development of all the aspects of human-personality—body, mind and spirit.

The following tables will make the difference between Education and Literacy more clear:

Education	*Literacy*
1. Education has wider scope than literacy. Literacy is only a part of education.	1. Literacy means knowledge of 3Rs only i.e., reading, writing and arithmetic.
2. Education is the all round development of personality i.e., body, mind and soul.	2. Literacy helps in development of mind only and that is also to some extent.
3. Education humanizes humanity. It makes the man social being.	3. Literacy does not humanise humanity. A literate person may not be social.
4. Education is a continuous and life-long process.	4. Literacy is not a life-long process.
5. Education means all round drawing out of the best in child and man i.e., body, mind and spirit. Even the illiterate may be educated persons.	5. The person with the knowledge of 3Rs is a literate person. A person without the knowledge of 3Rs is not a literate person.

(*Contd.*)

Education	*Literacy*
6. An educated person is competent to solve the complex problems of life.	6. A literate person may not be competent to solve various problems of life.
7. Education is not mere teaching. All formal and informal, active and passive agencies provide education to a person.	7. Literacy is the end product of teaching. Only formal and active agencies make a person literate.
8. Education is formal as well as informal, planned as well as unplanned, organised as well as unorganised.	8. Literacy is only formal, planned and organised enterprise.
9. Education is deliberate as well as incidental.	9. Literacy is always deliberate.

Education and Instruction

Sometimes the term *'education'* is used to indicate day-to-day teaching of lessons in school. The process of imparting knowledge and skills in the class room or laboratory may be called instruction, but not education. Whereas instruction is the process of conveying to an individual a body of information or knowledge, education is a process of development of the powers which are inborn in the child, at a rate and in a manner, determined by the capacity of the child. Whereas instruction implies external imposition, education implies growth from within. Thus, instruction is only one of the means of education and not education. Education is the complete development of the student's personality.

The following table will make clear the difference between Education and Instruction.

Education	*Instruction*
1. The scope of education is very wide. Education means all-round development of innate potentialities of the individual. It helps in physical, intellectual, emotional, social, aesthetic, cultural, moral and spiritual development of the individual.	1. The scope of instruction is narrow. Instruction means to impart knowledge of specific subjects through teaching. Instruction is generally related to intellectual development only. It is always imparted by an expert.
2. Education is a continuous and life-long process.	2. The period of imparting instruction is limited.
3. Education aims at many sided development of the individual *i.e.*, physical, intellectual, emotional and social etc. It aims at preparing the individual for life.	3. Instruction aims at intellectual development of the individual which is one sided. The aim of instruction is to prepare the individual for passing the school or college examination.
4. Education is imparted in home, educational institutions, religious and political groups, library, cultural and social institutions.	4. Instruction is generally confined to the class-room. It is generally imparted in educational institutions i.e., schools and colleges.
5. Both formal and informal agencies provide education.	5. Instructions are provided by formal agencies of education.
6. Education, in the broadest sense, does not follow systematic and rigid approach.	6. Instructions are generally imparted in a systematic manner, in a certain framework of rules and regulations.

(Contd.)

Education	*Instruction*
7. In education, child is more important than the educator. The place of child is central, pivotal and of prime importance. Teacher's role is subsidiary.	7. In instruction, teacher is more important than the child. Teacher occupies the central place.
8. In education, child's abilities, interests, aptitudes, developmental level and other potentialities are given special consideration.	8. In instruction, child's abilities, interests, aptitudes, developmental level and other potentialities are ignored. Readymade knowledge is forced into his mind.
9. Curriculum of education is very comprehensive. The person's entire life is the curriculum.	9. Curriculum of instruction is narrow and fixed. It is based upon various subjects.
10. The range of methods of imparting education is very wide.	10. Limited methods are used for imparting instruction. Instructions are generally imparted through lecture and notes-giving methods.
11. In education importance is attached to social discipline.	11. In instruction, discipline is through command.
12. In education all the members of society, depending upon the situation can play the role of teacher.	12. In instruction, teachers are professionally trained and fixed.
13. Knowledge acquired through education can be permanent. It can be	13. In instruction, cramming is encouraged. It is soon forgotten. It cannot be

(*Contd.*)

Education	*Instruction*
applied to solve various problems of life.	applied to meet the challenges of life successfully.
14. Education is formal as well as informal, planned as well as unplanned, organised as well as unorganised, deliberate as well as incidental.	14. Instructions are always formal, planned and deliberate.
15. In education, behaviour is more important. Degree or certificate may not be given.	15. In instruction good marks are the motivating factor. Degree or certificate is awarded after the successful completion of the course.
16. Education ends with life.	16. Instruction ends in class-room.

Education and Schooling

Education is sometimes confused with schooling. The concept of schooling is similar to that of instruction, but it is a wider concept. It includes academic activities and programmes, other than class-room instruction. Co-curricular activities, community work, hobbies, educational trips and social service camps form part of school, though they are excluded from the limited sphere of instruction. The venue of schooling may be the school or its neighbourhood—even environment taken as a whole. If education is considered as schooling it means that the child is educated only for five or six hours a day and not for the remaining time. Again, this means that he is educated only for six days a week and not on Sundays and other holidays. Perhaps he is educated more when he watches movies, listens to radio, chats with friends and members of his family. Education is more comprehensive than schooling which is confined to a certain function only. Education is a life-long continuous process.

The following table will make clear the difference between Education and Schooling.

Education	*Schooling*
1. The scope of education is very wide. Education is a life-long process. It starts from the womb and ends with the tomb *i.e.*, it starts when the child is born and continues up to death.	1. The scope of school is narrow and limited. Schooling is confined to the period for which the child remains on the rolls of an institution. Schooling includes academic activities and programmes, other than classroom instruction of communicated information. Co-curricular activities form an important part of schooling, but they are not included in the scope of instruction.
2. Education is a life-long process.	2. Period of schooling is confined to childhood and adolescence.
3. **Aspects** : There are formal, informal and non-formal aspects of education.	3. School has only formal aspect.
4. **Atmosphere** : The atmosphere in education is natural as well as artificial.	4. The atmosphere in schooling is artificial.
5. **Aim** : The aim of education is all round development of personality *i.e.*, physical, intellectual, emotional, social, aesthetic and moral development of the individual.	5. The aim of schooling is also all round development of personality of the individual, but major emphasis is on intellectual development.

(*Contd.*)

Education	*Schooling*
6. The places of education are home, school, as well as social, cultural, political, religious and business institutions.	6. The place of schooling is confined to four walls of the school.
7. Agents of education are parents and other family members, friends, neighbours, preachers etc.	7. Agents of school are primarily teachers.
8. Agencies of education are family, school, peer group, places of worship, state, radio, television, press etc.	8. School is the only agency of schooling.
9. Curriculum is as wide as life. It includes the whole life.	9. Curriculum of schooling is limited to some specific subjects and activities.
10. The range of methods of imparting education is very wide.	10. Only fixed methods of teaching like lecture, notes-giving, demonstration, experimental, project and discussion methods are used.
11. There is social discipline and social control.	11. Emphasis is on strict discipline.
12. All members of the society, depending upon the situation, can play the role of teacher.	12. There are specific teachers for every subject and co-curricular activities.
13. Formality and informality between the teacher and pupil go side by side.	13. Formality is observed between the teacher-pupil relations.

(Contd.)

Education	*Schooling*
14. There is important place of practicality in education.	14. More emphasis is placed on theoretical aspect in schooling.
15. There may be no definite time of evaluation. It may continue throughout life. It may be direct as well as indirect.	15. There is definite time of evaluation. Evaluation is essentially done at the end of each class. Theoretical and practical knowledge of the subjects and the activities is evaluated. It is direct and by fixed methods.
16. Certificate may or may not be given.	16. Certificate is given in schooling.

Education and Training

In the opinion of some thinkers, education is an act of training, meant to enable a person to take his proper place in the life of the community. Man is basically animal. Hence, he needs training in emotional adjustment, in controlling his impulses and aspirations and in modifying his behaviour so that he may not face maladjustment when he participates in a group. Education, no doubt, provides training for adult life. But, training itself is not education. Animals are also trained by imitating the action of others, but in their training the purpose is neither conscious nor well designed. In education, on the other side, the purpose is clear and well designed. Education is a conscious process to train the individual so that he should make correct responses to the problems of life. If a child bows automatically while he is in the company of others, his response is physical and he may be called a trained child. If the child bows out of respect, he may be called educated, because this is a mental response. In training, the desired outer action is secured; in education, the desired inner attitude, the mental and emotional disposition of behaviour are secured. True education means training the individual to discriminate between good and evil, both on the level of physical response as well as mental response. However, in popular sense, training is associated with preparation for professional career, or technical education. Education is a comprehensive term and training is only a part of it. It is only because of this distinction between education and training that the names of all the Teachers' Training Colleges in India have been changed into Colleges of Education.

The following table will make clear the difference between Education and Training.

Education	*Training*
1. The scope of education is very wide. Education includes teaching and training. Education refers to overall growth and development. It takes care of man's development in cognitive, affective and psycho-motor domain.	1. (*i*) The scope of training is limited. Training is confined to teaching only. Training is only a part of education. It implies development and perfection of skills and competencies of the learner. It is primarily concerned with developing tricks of the trade and professional competencies; the psycho-motor dimension of man's personality.
2. Education is a life long process. It continues from birth to death.	2. Period of training is fixed. It may be for a few days, a few months, a year or a few years.
3. The aim of education is the all round development of a person.	3. The aim of training is the development of one or more specific skills.

(*Contd.*)

Education	Training
4. Places for imparting education are home, school, college or university, religious institutions, social centres, cultural centres, neighbourhood, political groups and community.	4. Training is imparted in training institutions, like school, college, hospital, workshop, factory, office or any other training centre.
5. Both formal and informal agencies provide education.	5. Training is provided only by formal agencies of education.
6. Education in the broadest sense does not follow rigid and systematic approach.	6. Training has rigid and systematic approach. It is given in a systematic manner, in a certain frame-work of rules and regulations.
7. Education is both, theoretical as well as practical.	7. In training, more emphasis is placed on practical aspect.
8. Curriculum of education is broad and indefinite as in informal education. It is definite, fixed or determined in formal education.	8. The curriculum of training is usually fixed or determined in conformity with the skills to be learnt.
9 In education, the range of methods used, is very wide.	9. In training, limited and fixed methods are used. Methods change only from one skill to another.
10. In education, importance is attached to social discipline. Education socializes an individual.	10. In training, discipline is usually strict and authoritarian. Training may not socialize an individual. Many intellectually trained persons are not social in their behaviour.

(*Contd.*)

Education	*Training*
11. There is flexibility in the provision of teachers. There are no teachers in informal education.	11. There are fixed teachers or instructors.
12. Means of evaluation are very wide. Both direct and indirect means are used. Certificate or degree is awarded in formal education but not in informal education.	12. In training, proficiency in the skill of the profession or field is tested. Means of evaluation are direct. Certificate or degree is given on the successful completion of the training.
13. There are various sources of inspiration in education. Social frame is the important source of inspiration.	13. Economic aspect is the main source of inspiration in training.

Education and Indoctrination

Indoctrination means education by authority, imposition, strict discipline, regiment and controlled instructions. Authoritarianism is the hallmark of indoctrination. Everything, including aims and objectives, content and subject-matter, activities and programmes of education of the pupil are selected and settled by authorities. Indoctrination is one-sided, with the sole purpose of forcing information, ideas and practices from outside, as part of education. There is no freedom to the pupil to learn by himself or to direct the process of learning according to his own needs, interests and aspirations. He is a passive recipient of learning experience. It kills his initiative, freedom and curiosity. It follows the technique of cramming and makes learning dull, mechanical and monotonous.

Indoctrination ensures that behaviour is changed in a specific direction without rational thought, reflection or even willingness. Indoctrination may be used for developing, in the students, a particular set of beliefs, values and moral principles. It should be noted that indoctrination is a part of education. Education is as broad as ocean, indoctrination is a tank.

The table given below will make clear the difference between Education and Indoctrination.

Education	*Indoctrination*
1. The scope of education is very wide.	1. The scope of indoctrination is limited and narrow.
2. Education is a continuous and life-long process. It continues from birth to death. It is needed at every stage *i.e.*, childhood, adolescent and adulthood stage, including old age.	2. The time of indoctrination is fixed. Indoctrination is much needed in junior classes, because at this stage child's mind is not mature and he receives dogmas without arguments. As the brain of the child develops, he starts reasoning.
3. Education has formal, informal and non-formal aspects.	3. Indoctrination is all formal.
4. Atmosphere in the process of education is natural as well as artificial.	4. Atmosphere in indoctrination is artificial and dominated by authority.
5. Education aims at all round development of the person.	5. Indoctrination aims at changing some beliefs and attitudes and developing, among the student, a particular set of values and principles. Indoctrination aims at emotional development of the child.

(*Contd.*)

Education	*Indoctrination*
6. Education may be person-centred.	6. Indoctrination is dogma-centred, thought-centred, authority-centred or teacher-centred.
7. The activities of the whole life form curriculum in education.	7. Curriculum, in indoctrination is confined to beliefs, ideas and dogmas-religous, political and moral.
8. Various methods are used to impart education.	8. Lecture methods is emphasised in indoctrination.
9. Education may provide freedom to a person.	9. There is no freedom to the child to learn by himself. Everything, including aims and objectives, curriculum, programmes and activities, are directed by the authority.
10. All the members of society can play the role of teachers in informal education.	10. Professional teachers impart knowledge.
11. Evaluation may be done by observing social adjustment of the person.	11. Evaluation of the person is done on the basis of the criteria of changes in his thoughts and beliefs.

The following table will throw more light on tho terms – Schooling, Instruction, Training and Indoctrination.

The above table shows that the aim of education is all round development of personality. Schooling helps in achieving the aim of formal education. Instruction helps in development of knowledge (*i.e.*, cognitive aspect). Training helps in developing skills. Indoctrination helps in bringing about changes in affective aspect (feeling aspect) of behaviour *i.e.*, thoughts, beliefs and values. Schooling, instruction, training and indoctrination play an important role in achieving the aim of education.

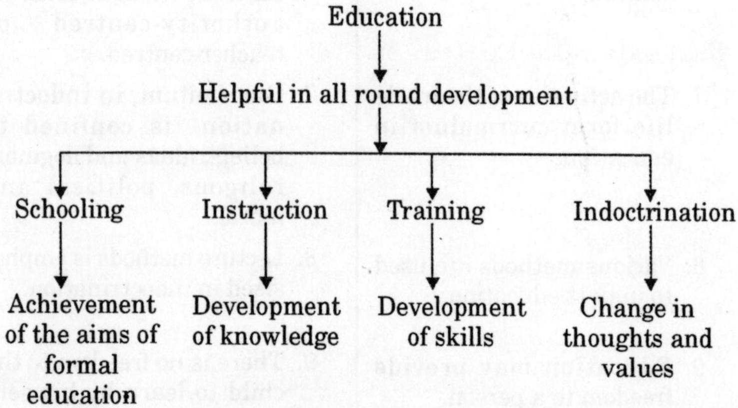

Education cannot be equated with Literacy, Instruction, Schooling, Training or Indoctrination

In the light of above discussion, we can say that education cannot be equated with literacy, instruction, schooling or training. It is a comprehensive and continuous process. It is planned as well as unplanned, formal as well as informal. Literacy, instruction, schooling and training, however, are confined only to planned and organized enterprises. Education, no doubt, does include literacy, it does have instructional aspect, it implies schooling and it involves training of body and mind. However, education is growth from within rather than an imposition from without. Education is related to life, it is life itself.

IMPORTANT FEATURES OF EDUCATION

The best way to understand the nature of a thing, consists in enumerating some of its important features. Let us now try to understand the nature of education by describing its salient features.

Education is a Human Enterprise

Education, it is clear, is for the human beings and for the inanimate objects, plants, or animals. We may train a dog, but we cannot educate it. Educative capacity of man distinguishes him from other objects—animate or inanimate. It is only man who can be educated. Therefore, education is a human enterprise.

Education is a Process and not an Object

Education is not an object which persons possess or which is a part of them. One does not have education in the same way as one might have a thousand rupees or brown hair. Even knowledge or skill or good character are not in themselves education, but only an evidence that one has been educated. Education is not an object, it is a process, a kind of activity in relation to human beings. To educate is to engage in a process and to 'have education' is to be someone who has undergone a process.

Education is a Purposeful Process

Education is a deliberate process, undertaken by the teacher and the taught, for reaching a definite destination. It is inspired both by immediate and remote goals. The central problem of education is educational aims. Methods and curriculum are determined in conformity with the educational aims. Aims are relative to a number of variables—socio-economic structure, political ideology, philosophy of life etc. The interpretation of educational aims by educational thinkers has varied from one thinker to another and from age to age. However, the individual and the social aims are the two broad categories under which the various aims can be subsumed. These aims are complementary to each other and not contradictory.

Education is a Continuous Process

Education is not a process which, after starting at one time, comes to an end at a definite time. We often say, "He has finished his education" or "he has now started education." In fact, education commences at birth and continues upto death. There is no end to this process. It goes on throughout life without any break or barrier. Education is not only the school, but the educand receives it by his participation in his environment—physical and social, specially through the informal agencies of home, the play group, the profession, the community, the church, the state, the press, the cinema, the radio, the television etc. Thus, education is a comprehensive, life-long and continuous process.

Education is a Triangular Process

Education was considered a uni-polar process in the past. It was Adams who first pointed out that education is a bi-polar process. "Education" says Adam, "is a conscious and deliberate process in which one personality acts upon another in order to modify the development of the other by the communication of knowledge." In the bi-polar process two persons are involved. At one pole we have the educator and at the other the educand. The one speaks, the other listens; the one teaches, the other learns; the one directs, the other follows. Their activities are inter-related and inter-dependent. If the educator does not come down to the level of the educand and if the educand is not stimulated to rise to the level of the educator, the work of imparting and receiving education cannot proceed. Thus, it is a conscious and deliberate process in which there is subject-object relationship.

Unlike Adams, Dewey considers education as a tri-angular process. Dewey recognises the importance of psychological side of the process which includes the study of the child's needs, interests, capacities and talents, and which forms the basis of this process. Yet he lays a greater stress on the sociological side. "All education", he says, "proceeds by the participation of the individual in social consciousness of the race." Thus, Dewey believes that society plays a very vital role in the process of imparting education.

Therefore, we can say that education is not a bi-polar, but a tri-angular process. It involves inter-play of three elements—the educator, the educand and the social forces. The social forces, provided by the social environment or society, supply the material to the teacher and it is taught in the form of curriculum. The curriculum is framed in the light of the needs and demands of the society. Hence, we can say that education is a tri-angular process. It is a social process with social functions.

Education is Conservative as well as Dynamic

The social aspect of education includes cultural aspect. Education creates social order and it also stabilises it. It ensures and facilitates the community of social life by preserving and transmitting the cultural heritage from generation to generation. Education is the instrument whereby culture is transmitted from the adult section of the community to the younger section, from one generation to another, and from one period of history to another.

Culture is not only transmitted but also preserved and developed further. Conservation and further development are implied in the process of transmission. We do not inherit culture in the way we inherit parents' property. Culture is not static, it is dynamic. It is in a state of constant flux. Thus, education, which acts as an agency for the transmission of culture, also serves as the means by which it is not only conserved, but also reconstructed, re-organised, transformed and expanded. Education is, thus, both conservative as well as a dynamic force.

Education is both—a Science and an Art

In the past, education was considered as an art. We thought that a man having perfect knowledge of his subject and interested in the process of teaching, turns out to be an efficient teacher by practice of teaching. This is true to some extent. It is said that teachers are born and not made. It is also said that doctors and engineers are born, and not made. But that does not mean that medicine and engineering are arts. These are, undoubtedly, sciences. Education, is undoubtedly an art, but it is also a science. Education, like other sciences, undertakes a systematic study of certain facts and principles. It employs the usual scientific method of observation and experimentation. It classifies its data into certain categories, makes use of the analytico-synthetic method, proceeds from particular to general, and tries to explain facts and discovers principles underlying the various educational problems and finally establishes a number of generalizations about its methodology, motivation, learning, curriculum construction and evaluation. Education is a science in itself, and it has established its own existence, as an independent subject.

In 'education' we discuss subjects like Educational Principles, Educational Psychology, Educational Administration, Teaching Methods, Guidance, Evaluation etc. But, while we are saying that education is a science, we should not forget that education is an art also. In spite of the knowledge of educational science, one cannot become a successful teacher unless one puts it into practice. We have to put the principles into practice which is the artistic feature of education. Thus, education is both—a science as well as an art.

BASES OF EDUCATION

The process of education is based upon certain fundamental aspects of human life. It is actually man, who needs education and as such education is concerned with the various phases and stages of his life, right from his biological inheritance to social heritage. The whole process of education consists of transforming the animal being into social being, in the light of his instincts, urges, needs and temperament.

In order to realize this supreme aim of education, we require the study of man – his biological, psychological, social and ethical life.

Thus it is clearly realised that education has its roots in human society, individual capacity and responsiveness and it looks upward for human excellence. Therefore, the form, process, content and objectives of education essentially have a base on which its theory and practice is to be erected.For systematic understanding of education, in its entirety, we must understand its various bases.

Classification of Bases

The bases of education may broadly be classified as under :

1. Biological
2. Psychological
3. Social
4. Philosophical

Since education aims at something, it represents a learning process. Taking into consideration the nature of the learner, it tries to socialise the learner, enabling the learner to understand his social milieu and ultimately it leads the learner to realise his aspirations. This sort of involvement of man with education may be represented diagrammatically in the form of a triangle.

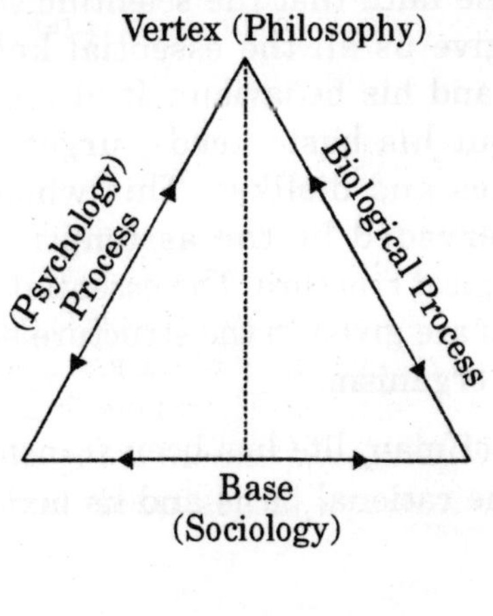

Thus the major aspects of education are inter-linked and there takes place a two-way interaction amongst them. Each one is affected by the other and contributes to the formulations and intensity of the other. All such interactions will be elaborated in the succeeding pages.

Here it will be enough to make explicit that education, as a social process, has its direction and content and all these are determined by its linkage with Biology, Psychology, Sociology and Philosophy which provide an adequate base for educational edifice.

Biological Bases of Education

Man often is looked upon as animal being. No doubt, he has affinities with the lower order, but he is superior to other creatures due to intelligence and mental powers. Man is a patential being and creates his own environment. He does not adapt himself to nature, but adapts nature according to his needs. He eats to live and not lives to eat. Biological aspect of his life is the starting point. From biological existence man has to attain his sociological, cultural and ethical existence.

Biologically it is believed that man is the product of evolution. For the purpose of evolution, biological nature of man is human nature. Its conception of educational research is based upon the faith that the scientific study of human organism can give us all the essential knowledge about human nature and his behaviour. It also provides us the knowledge about his basic needs, urges, instincts and powers; his likes and dislikes. This whole approach to education is pervaded by the assumption that man is basically a biological creature. The essential characteristics of human beings are given in the structure and functioning of the biological organism.

In the case of man, life has been transferred from the instinctive to the rational basis and he becomes amenable to education. In the case of other animals, nature helps by adjusting them to the environment. But man has to acquire experiences which will later function in modifying action and it is possible because of the nervous constitution of the man that makes him an eminently educable being. His adjustment is on the mental plane.

As compared to other animals, the infancy period of human child is quite longer. During this period child needs care, nourishment and help. He is dependent on others. If we leave him unattended, bring him up in isolation, his future will not be better than Ramu, the wolf boy (died a few years ago). This prolonged period is meant to prepare the child for the complex human life. Without this, he is very much like a savage or a beast. All these factors provide essential bases to education.

Psychological Basis of Education

Every child is born with certain natural and inherited endowments. These endowments are modified and sublimated for making the individual child a useful member of society. The process of such modification of endowments or change of animal behaviour, is known as 'education'. For the ultimate success of this process, we have to base it on a scientific plan which depends upon the scientific study of the child's mind. This scientific study of the child's mind or behaviour is known as *'Psychology'*. Thus the psychological basis is an important basis of education.

A teacher has to deal with the child as material. Therefore, unless he thoroughly understands the natural inclinations of the child, his heredity, environment, desires, aptitudes, habits, feelings, likes and dislikes, he cannot succeed in imparting good education. All this is the knowledge of Psychology. It exhorts the teacher that "when the rule of thumb fails, the laws of Psychology can bring fruitful results." With this knowledge, the teacher is saved from committing blunders and from learning at the cost of his pupils.

As we have already noted, education is a process of controlling and modifying behaviour and Pshycology seeks to discover the general laws which explain the behaviour of living organisms. It, therefore, follows that the theory of education must base itself, very largely, on the science of Psychology. The knowledge of human behaviour is of great help to the teacher in the formulation of the policy on education. Great educators like Rousseau and Pestalozzi had realized that teacher's primary concern is the overall development of the child. With an accurate knowledge of the child's mental process a teacher can accomplish his task successfully. Later on, Froebel developed this very idea in his Kindergarten scheme of child education.

"The teacher must know both Latin and John, in order to teach well." While the knowledge of Latin is the mastery of the subject-matter, the knowledge of John is Psychology. It, therefore follows that a teacher, to be a good and successful teacher, must know the subject-matter as well as the child or Psychology.

The Sociological Basis of Education

"Man cannot be human, unless he learns to live, think, feel and behave like men." Great individuals who have contributed a lot to the progress of mankind, could not do so in a social vacuum, but only after assimilating the rich heritage of their society. Sociological factor, therefore, plays an important role in the education of an individual. According to John Dewey, "All education proceeds by the participation of the individual in the social consciousness of the race. This participation moulds his powers and personality to fit him in the society, for which and in which, he has to live."

Every individual child is a creature of the culture of his community or society. His personality, to a great extent, is a product of the cultural influences that his society brings to bear upon him. Aristotle says that man is a social animal. He is born physically, developed mentally and educated in society. Different social agencies react upon his individuality and then transform it into personality, enabling it to lead a useful and worthwhile life. As educators, therefore, it is essential for us to know how the individual lives and behaves in the society to which he belongs. Education must help the individual in his social adjustment to the total cultural milieu. It is only after we have gained this knowledge, we can plan his future education. Herein lies the importance of sociological basis of education.

The child is to live in and for the community to which he belongs. Hence true education comes through the stimulation of the child's power by the demands of the social situation in which he finds himself. John Dewey has also directed our attention to the social function of education which is carried through school, as a special environment. It is through and in the school that the development of desirable attitudes and dispositions, which is so essential for the continuous and progressive social life, takes place. Thus school is an important social institution which according to John Dewey, "purifies and idealises the existing social institutions and customs and which is a living society for the children."

Philosophical Basis of Education

Education is a purposeful social process and it has its aims and objectives. It is not an undesigned process, mechanically operating on man. It has its why, what and how dimensions with clear-cut force of action. Priority-wise, what and how of Education take their inspiration from the why aspect. It makes quite evident that this 'why' is explained by philosophy alone and by no other human discipline. This normative dimension of education is a privilege of philosophy alone to determine. Therefore, a philosophic base of education is its first essentiality.

All the Bases of Education are Complementary to Each Other

After discussing all the bases of education separately, we can say that there is a need for synthesis among these bases. Education develops the whole man. All these bases have their distinctive features and the common factor of all the bases is the man—his total development. It is a truism that biological factors of human life discuss man only on the physical plane. Psychology studies an individual as a learner. All this keeps an individual in isolation. In the absence of sociological and ethical factors, human life is incomplete and education is only a half-way. Hence, for the complete development of human personality, there is a need to study these various factors. Man is essentially a social-being and a moral being. His biological heredity remains meaningless in the absence of social heredity. He can achieve social perfection only by cultivating ethical values approved by the society. To conclude, it may once again be emphasised that all these bases must be studied together in order to establish harmony between the individual and the society.

SOME DEFINITIONS OF EDUCATION

From the earlier times to the modern era, various thinkers and educators, in order to make the concept of education clear, have defined education in their own characteristic way. These definitions throw a flood of light on various aspects of education and its essential features. A genral survey of some of the definitions by Western and Indian thinkers reveals to us a multiplicity of definitions of Education.

Definitions by Western Thinkers

Modern progressive education owes most to the West. The views of some of the Western thinkers are as under :

1. "I mean by education that training which is given by suitable habits to the first instincts of virtue in children." The end of education is "to develop in the body and the soul all the beauty and all the perfection of which they are capable." —Plato

2. "Education is the creation of a sound mind in a sound body." It is, "to develop man's faculties, especially his mind so that he may be able to enjoy the contemplation of the supreme truth, goodness and beauty in which perfect happiness essentially consists." —Aristotle

3. "Education is unfoldment of what is already enfolded in the germ. It is the process through which the child makes the internal external." —Froebel

4. "Whatever helps to shape the human being, to make the human being, what he is, or to hinder him from what he is not—is part of his education." —J.S. Mill

5. "Education is a natural, harmonious and progressive development of man's innate powers." —Pestalozzi

6. "By Education I mean the influence of the environment upon the individual to produce a permanent change in his habits of behaviour, of thought, and of attitude." —G.H. Thomson

7. "Education is the development of good moral character." —Herbart

8. "Education is the complete development of individual so that he can make an original contribution to human life, according to his best capacity." —T.P. Nunn

9. "Education is a conscious and deliberate process in which one personality acts upon another in order to modify the development of the other, by the communication and manipulation of knowledge." —Adams

10. "Education is the development of all those capacities in the individual which will enable him to control his environment and fulfil his possibilities." —John Dewey

11. "Education is the influence of a person who holds the vital belief brought to bear on another person, with the object of making him also hold that belief." —Ross

12. "Education is the deliberate and systematic influence exerted by the mature person upon the immature, through interaction, discipline, and harmonious development of physical, intellectual, aesthetic, social and spiritual powers of the human being, according to individual and social needs and directed towards the union of the educand with his creator, as the final end." —Redden

Definitions by Indian Thinkers

Education, being an important social activity, its meanings have been changing through the ages, due to change in social and physical conditions. Different educationists, therefore, interpret it differently, at different times. Some of the most popular definitions, given by Indian educational thinkers, are given below:

1. "Education is something which makes a man self-reliant and self-less." —Rigveda

2. "Education is that whose end-product is salvation." —Upanishads

3. "Education is that which makes a man of good character and useful to the society."

—Yajnavalkya (the famous legislator)

4. "Human education means the training which one gets from nature."

—Panini (the famous grammarian)

5. "Education means training for the country and love for the nation." —Kautilya (the famous politician)

6. "Education means development of self-contentment."

—Kannada (the famous philosopher)

7. "Education is the realization of the self."

—Shankaracharya (the famous Vedantist)

8. "Education is the manifestation of perfection already in man." —Vivekananda

9. "The highest education is that which does not merely give us information but makes our life in harmony with all existence." —Tagore

10. "By education, I mean an all-round drawing out of the best in child and man—body, mind and spirit."

—Gandhiji

Various Features Emphasised by Different Educators

The scope of this short treatise on 'Understanding Education' does not permit any detailed discussion, explanation and comment upon the definitions enumerated above. What seems to be possible or expedient under the present limitations, is to indicate and stress various features that have been emphasised in these definitions. These are:

1. It's unilateral, bi-polar or tri-angular in nature.
2. It's a drawing out or a bringing up process.
3. It's being knowledge or experience.

4. It's the development of some particular aspect of human personality or a harmonious integrated growth.

5. It's being conducive for the good of the individual or the welfare of the society.

6. It's being a liberal discipline or a vocational course.

7. Its being stabilizer of social order and conservator of culture or an instrument of change and social reconstruction.

CONCLUSION

Although comparisons are often arbitrary, the conclusion seems to be irresistible that education, it is universally admitted, whatever else it may be, is a means for the development of full man or woman—a balanced all round harmonious development of personality. But the precise analysis of personality is, unfortunately, controversial in nature. Educators have somehow, been victims of 'this' or 'that' philosophy. Many of them have been influenced by a partial view of human nature. No definition can be adjuged satisfactory, if it is not determined by the proper synthesis of the two main factors of human personality—the animal and the spiritual or the rational self.

It is generally admitted in the West that personality constitutes body and mind, and it is the function of education, therefore, to bring about a harmonious development of all these aspects of human personality. This explanation is perhaps based upon an inadequate understanding of human nature, because it neglects the most important aspect of human personality—namely the spirit. Personality constitutes body, mind and spirit or soul. Any definition or concept of education that puts exclusive emphasis on one of these aspects of human personality militates against the basic principle. Most of the ills of our educational system from the dawn of civilization can be traced to undue emphasis laid on the one or more of these aspects and indifference to the others. An evil of the present day education, all over the world, is the neglect of the spiritual aspect of human personality. Gandhiji revolts against this evil of the modern education and emphasises on all the aspects of human personality. Thus, his concept of education tends to remove the inadequacies of modern education and his definition of education seems to be more suitable than any other, when he says, "By education, I mean an all-round drawing out the best in child and man—body, mind and spirit". In other words, "true education is that which draws out and stimulates the spiritual, intellectual and physical faculties of the children."

2

Aims of Education

Education, as we have already discussed in the previous chapter, is a purposeful activity. It is undertaken, both by the educator and the educand, for the sake of a clear-cut objective. Therefore, every system and process of education, in order to be worth anything must have some aim, which should reflect the philosophical aim of human life. If there is education without an aim, the educator is unable know where he has to lead his pupil to and what the learner has to become as a result of his education. Unless there is a clear aim before education, it would be impossible to measure the achievement of the educand. Therefore, the first consideration in any discussion on education must be a statement of its aims.

NATURE OF THE AIMS OF EDUCATION

In order to know the aims of education, it is necessary to understand the nature of these aims. Are the aims of education fixed, final, eternal and universal or are they flexible, adaptable, changeable and relative? Let us discuss this problem in the light of two distinct philosophies of education—Idealism and Pragmatism.

Idealism on Aims of Education

Idealism stands for the superiority of mind over matter and it conceives the nature of ultimate reality in terms of mind or spirit rather than in terms of matter. The idealist believes in the existence of absolute, eternal and unchanging values and consequently defines the ultimate aims of education in terms of these values. According to Idealism, the aims of education are spiritual in nature and are pre-determined, absolute, unchanging and universal. The values of life are not man-made, but pre-existing. The aim of education is realization of these pre-existing, absolute and universal values.

According to some idealists, there are two types of educational aims—immediate and ultimate. Whereas the immediate aims are changing, flexible and adaptable; the ultimate aims are eternal, absolute and unchanging. In determining any hierarchy of values, the immediate objectives must occupy a subordinate position.

Pragmatism on Aims of Education

Pragmatism believes that the nature of reality is not fixed. What is true today, may not be true tomorrow. Pragmatism therefore, does not believe in absolute and eternal values. Values are man-made and constant experimentation is needed to test their validity. Thus, pragmatism requires an individual to be creative, so that he should formulate values of life on the basis of his experiences.

Criteria of Good Aims

John Dewey outlines the following characteristics of aims in his book, 'Democracy and Education' :

1. Good aims are related to real situations of life. They grow out of real life situations and they can be achieved only under those situations.

2. Good aims are flexible. Conditions of life are always changing and aims should be flexible to meet successfully the challenge of new situations appearing in society.

3. Good aims always represent a span of diverse activities. They also involve purposeful activity. They should correspond to our existing needs and should be supported by our philosophy of life.

Importance and Necessity of Educational Aims

According to *Encyclopaedia of Modern Education* "Education is purposeful and ethical activity. Hence it is unthinkable without aims." We cannot proceed in any walk of life without aim. For achieving success in activity of life, clear and well defined aim is essential. An educator, without the knowledge of aims, can be compared to a sailor who does not know his destination. This means that a system of education, which is not clear about its aims or which has undesirable ends, is bound to fail. Aims give foresight to the educational planner. All our methods of teaching, our curriculum and our system of evaluation are shaped and moulded according to our aims of education. It is the ignorance of right aims that has vitiated our educational system, its methods and its products, and has resulted in the physical, intellectual and moral degradation of the race.

There is a great necessity of aims in education because of the following reasons :

1. **To direct efforts :** If aim is known, we can direct our efforts to that end. Educational aims keep the teacher and the taught on the right track. They provide a line of action and guidance to the teachers. They give direction and zest to the activities of the pupils.

2. **To avoid wastage :** Educational aims help us to avoid wastage of time and energy. In the words of John Dewey, "To have an aim is to act with meaning." Aims help us to act intelligently and to act with a meaning. We know what is to be done and we straightway start doing that.

3. **To evaluate ourselves :** Educational aims help us to evaluate ourselves. They help us to take stock of the results of our efforts. The aim is a yard-stick with which we

can measure our success and failure. They are necessary to assess the outcomes of the educational process.

4. To provide efficient school administration : Aims are necessary for efficient school administration and organisation. They help the school authorities in organising, equipping and administering the school. Various aspects of school administration and organisation, such as proper selection of teachers, proper curriculum planning, proper library equipment, proper planning of curricular and co-curricular activities are guided by the educational aims. It is rightly said that good schools evolve out of enlightened aims. Aims are *guide-lights* in the educational process. Like the sun, aims illumine our life. The ignorance of right aims will spoil the whole educational system.

5. To evaluate the existing conditions : We, as educators, carefully evaluate the existing conditions *i.e.*, contents of education, methods of teaching, efficiency of teaching, library equipment, planning of curricular and co-curricular activities in the light of our objectives and plan for the future.

THE DETERMINANTS OF EDUCATIONAL AIMS

Even a casual survey of the history of education will reveal that there have been different aims of education in different countries in the past. Even in the same country, the aims of education have been different at different times. For example, in India the aims of education during Ancient period were not the same which were there during the British period. Again, the aims of education in the modern India are different from those which were prevalent in the British India. The aims of education in a democratic country like England or America are not the same as they are in a communist countries like Russia and China. The important determinants of the educational aims which have led to their diversity are discussed below:

The Philosophies of Life

The philosophy of life, in which the people of a particular society or time believe, goes a long way in determining the aims of education. In a materialistic society, educational aims are based on the materialistic outlook of the people. In such a society there is no place for moral ideals and spiritual values and the aim of education is self-gratification or self-expression. On the contrary, for the idealists, who believe in the spiritual basis of the universe, the aim of education is self-realization or exaltation of personality. A pessimistic attitude towards life fashions pessimistic aims of education, whereas an optimistic philosophy of life determines optimistic aims of education. In short, the different philosophies of life give rise to different aims of education.

The Socio-political Ideologies

Socio-political ideologies, too, determine educational aims. For example, different social philosophies—views about the Individual-society or Individual-state relationship had led to different concepts of educational aims. According to totalitarianism, the state is considered as an end in itself. The individual is regarded only as a means for the good of the state. Evidently, the educational aim under such a regime is to train the individual for blind obedience to the state and there is a rigid, state-controlled and stereotyped system of education. Accordingly, the aim of education is considered as self-expression or self-gratification. On the contrary, according to individualism or pluralism the individual is regarded as an end in himself and the state as a means to the good of the individual. Accordingly, the aim of education is considered as self-realization and the state adopts 'Hands off' policy in the sphere of education. Democracy strikes a balance between individual freedom and social obligations. The authoritarian and dictatorial attitude of the state is replaced by parental one. The aim of education under democratic regimes is considered to be social efficiency or citizenship.

Again, education in any country and at all periods reflects values of the ruling class. All forms of governments—democratic, fascist or communist—formulate their own aims of education to serve their purpose. In a democracy, educational aims are not fixed, absolute or eternal. They change with the changing aspirations and demands of the society. Man, in a democracy, is considered as an end in himself and not as a means to an end. Therefore, educational institutions cater to the diverse abilities and aptitudes of children. The child is educated for a life of freedom, for the fullest possible realization of his capacities and their service to the community. Accordingly the aim of education is to inculcate values like liberty, equality and fraternity. In a fascist regime, the individual exists for the state. Thus in a fascist state the individual must bow to the demands of the state and the aim of education is to inculcate values like service, sacrifice, duty and obedience. The educational aims in a communist state are formulated quite differently from those in a fascist or democratic state. As labour is the cardinal ideal of the communist society, it forms the central pivot of the educational aims. The student must feel himself a worker in a labouring society. Educational institutions are considered as deliberate instruments of State policy. To ensure the victory of communist ideals, educational aims stress the need of virtues like bravery, loyalty, steadfastness and discipline.

Hence, we can say that different socio-political-ideologies give rise to different educational aims.

The Socio-economic Problems

Sometimes social and economic problems of a country also influence the educational aims of that country. For example, India is a country of various castes, creeds and religions. Social stratification has been rigid. This has created special social problems. Education, therefore, must fight the caste-barriers. Similarly, in determining its educational objectives every country has to take into consideration its economic conditions. We can take the example of Denmark. About half a century back the country faced economic crisis. Traditional occupations did not yield income to support all the people of the country. A survey of national resources and man-power was made. The country had meagre resources, but it was close to a steady market for certain food articles. For the economic advancement of the country, it was advised to start dairy products, even though the food for the cattle was to be imported from other countries. Denmark educated its generation to meet the new requirements. The result was that Denmark, not only increased the per capita income and her national wealth, but also captured the markets of England and several other countries.

Similarly, India of today has low economic standards of living. As a large majority of the people in India have to live at an economically sub-human level, one of the most important functions of education is to improve productive efficiency, to increase national wealth and to bridge the gulf between the rich and the poor so that the dream of socialistic society may become reality. Thus, we can say that social and economic conditions of a country also determine the educational aims of that country.

Exploration of Knowledge

Educational aims are also influenced by exploration of knowledge. Because of rapid exploration in sciences, education today has become science-oriented all over the world. In India also educationists are stressing the need for science-oriented education in schools, colleges and universities. More and more stress is being laid on the study of modern sciences. The government is giving liberal grants and scholarships, by way of providing incentive, for the study of science. This clearly shows that the spreading of new knowledge is an important factor in determining aims of education.

DIFFERENT AIMS OF EDUCATION

We have already discussed the important determinants of educational aims which have led to their diversity. We shall confine our attention to some important ones and discuss them here.

The Knowledge Aim

Since the time of Sophists (400 B.C.) down to the present day, knowledge has almost been universally considered as the aim of education. There are some educators who hold the acquisition of knowledge to be the only aim of education. They emphasise the cognitive or the intellectual side of personality. Forgetting that knowledge is merely an instrument for achieving other ends, they exalt it into an end by identifying it with education. The acquisition of knowledge of different subjects is regarded as the test of successful schooling and success in examination is regarded as the criterion of such acquisition. The only aim of education is 'complete knowledge' or 'knowledge, more knowledge and yet more knowledge.'

Those philosophers and educationists, who hold the knowledge aim of education, offer a justification for their view. They argue that knowledge is indispensable for all right actions and it alone is the source of all power and happiness. Before one could feel either pleasure or pain in respect of any subject, or could make any response with regard to it, one has to know what it is. Thus knowledge is not an idle or merely ornamental possession; it is a source of complete living and progress. For example, if education is intended to help individual-environment adjustment, the individual must have the knowledge of his environment, before he can think of adjusting himself to it. Again, if education is to help the child to realize moral values, he must first have a knowledge of those values. Thus, knowledge alone is power; knowledge alone is happiness; knowledge alone is virtue; knowledge alone is progress.

Criticism of Knowledge Aim: The knowledge aim of education has been criticised by many educators who put forward a number of arguments against this aim. They argue that over emphasis on the knowledge is likely to reduce all schools to mere 'knowledge-shops' and the teacher to a mere 'information monger'. Schools are infact agencies to bring about the all-round and not merely intellectual development of the pupils. They believe that knowledge is not the only aim of education. They argue that no amount of knowledge can make a person truly educated. True, we cannot be wise without some basis of knowledge, but at the same time we may remain devoid of wisdom even after acquiring much knowledge. True, we should have knowledge of moral values to become virtuous, but we may remain immoral, even after having knowledge of all moral values. Education is partly information and partly formation. The knowledge aim ignores the later part. Knowledge aim is unpsychological because it emphasises the study of subject matter rather than the child. It reduces the child to the position of a passive learner and places the teacher on a very high level.

Conclusion: If we weigh the arguments advanced for and against the knowledge aim, we arrive at the conclusion that knowledge, though, is not the only or supreme aim of education, yet it is one of the important aims of education. Knowledge is an indispensable means for any suitable and comprehensive aim of education. But knowledge should be a 'means to an end' and not an 'end in itself.' It should be acquired for human happiness and social welfare.

The Vocational Aim

Whenever we ask any parent, "Why do you send your children to schools and universities?" The answer will always be, "So that they may get some good vocation in life." No one can deny this concern of parents for their children. Man has three basic needs—food, shelter and clothing. If education does not fulfil these, it does not fulfil its aim. The long stride by industrialization and mechanization in the modern age of science gives priority to vocational aim over all other aims. Every man, unless he is born with a silver spoon in his mouth, has to search out a living for himself. It is this aim which enables an individual to solve the problem of his livelihood. If education fails to achieve it, it is not worth its name. Therefore, the main aim of education should be to train the child for a vocation, profession, business, calling or trade. This aim is also known as 'bread and butter aim' or 'utilitarian aim'.

The supporters of this aim maintain that 'education for vocation' makes use of the habits and instincts of the educand; appeals to his interest and aptitude; stimulates his thought, skill and observation; and trains him for social efficiency. They argue that man cannot live without means of subsistence; his economic needs will have to be satisfied. If an individual is not able to earn his own living and that of the children dependent upon him, he is a parasite upon others. He misses for himself one of the most educative experiences of life. Therefore, no scheme of education can afford to neglect such basic consideration. Moreover, the vocational aim is an integral part of the general aim of education.

Criticism of the Vocational Aim: The vocational aim of education has also been criticised. It is argued that man, after all, is born not only to eat and drink but also to gain knowledge, acquire culture and develop personality. Therefore the vocational aim is not a complete aim by itself. Earning one's bread is only one part of man's life, not the whole of it. Moreover, if vocational aim is over-emphasised, education is reduced to nothing but commercialism. It ceases to be a refining and ennobling influence. It may make an individual a good doctor, a good teacher or a good engineer, but it does not necessarily make him a good man. It does make him rich, but does not inspire him for the ideals of life. It does not prepare him for complete living.

Conclusion: In the light of above discussion, it may be said that there is considerable justification for the vocational aim of education. But the fact remains that most of the evils that have crept into the life of the modern man are because of an over-emphasis on this aim.

The Moral Aim

There are some educationists, generally belonging to the idealistic school, who think that the ultimate aim of education should be character building or moral development. Character means an inner consistency or unity of personality. It means consistency, steadfastness, dependability and stability. A man of character acts because of principles or ideals within, rather than from expediency or because of pressure from without. They believe that a man of character—a man endowed with strong will, virtuous conduct, noble ideals—is the only one who can be considered really educated. On the contrary, one who lacks these qualities, however learned or cultured otherwise, is a person on whom education has been completely lost. Therefore, knowledge culture, physical development, vocational efficiency, all are secondary to moral training. The formation of sound moral character should be the primary and only aim of education. Education is the process of modifying child's original behaviour.

Criticism of Moral Aim: True, character-building is a very laudable aim of education, but it has its other side also. Morality, as pragmatists believe, is never fixed, absolute or predetermined. It is relative. Moral ideals change with a change in time and social values. Ideals valued today may not be given any importance after the lapse of a hundred years. As such, it is not possible to interpret and trace moral ideals which can be considered effective in a particular situation. Moreover, undue emphasis on moral aim throws the other aims of education to a lower level. The physical and intellectual development of the child is as important as his moral progress.

Conclusion: Therefore, we can conclude that only character-building cannot be the aim of education. Not only good moral qualities, but qualities like intelligence, creativity, health and vigour are also needed for the welfare of man and society.

The Complete Living Aim

Some educational theorists insist upon the need of an aim of education which will be all-comprehensive. This viewpoint has led to the emergence of two aims—'the complete living aim' and 'the harmonious development aim'. The former has been formulated and expounded by Spencer. Education, according to this great thinker, should acquaint us with the laws and ways of complete living. He has given a list of activities and suitable subjects. According to Spencer, training of activities of self preservation, indirect preservation of life, rearing of off-springs, social preservation and leisure can be imparted, through Hygiene, Physics, Language, Mathematics, Geography, History, Child Psychology, Home Science, Music etc.

The emptiness of this aim can be shown with the help of certain questions. What can determine the completeness of life? Is this aim an unchanging thing? It should be noted that no mention has been made of art, literature and religion in the above list. Therefore, it can be said that the aim of complete living put forth by Spencer is too vague to be held and worked for by any educator.

The Harmonious Development Aim

One serious objection to various aims of education discussed above, is that they all are one-sided or incomplete. In the opinion of some thinkers harmonious development of mental, physical and aesthetic powers is the aim of education. According to them every child is born with certain powers and capacities—physical, mental and intellectual powers, spiritual moral and aesthetic capacities and social tendencies. The aim of education is to help the development of all these powers and capacities hidden in the child. If some of these capacities are developed, while others are neglected, the result would be an unsystematic and irregular development of personality. Therefore, the advocates of harmonious development aim urge that education should aim at the development of all capacities and powers of the child, rather than that of only a few of them and neglect others.

Gandhiji is a strong advocate of the harmonious development aim. For him, the aim of education is the development of full man. However, since the essential nature of man is spiritual, Gandhiji advocates the aim of all round development of the physical, intellectual and emotional aspects of personality under the guidance of spiritual. Lop-sided development of personality is the product of modern education which neglects the spiritual aspect of human personality.

Conclusion: The harmonious development aim deserves credit for its comprehensiveness. This aim embraces all other aims discussed above, because all these together aim at the harmonious development of personality. In fact, no aim is worth persuing unless it contributes towards such development. But the critics of this aim maintain that man is one unit and this division of his personality in different aspects is impossible. And, even if we take this division to be true, what would be the measure of definite quantities of harmonious development. In their opinion this harmonious development is an imaginary ideal which cannot be applicable in life.

The Leisure Aim

Science has revolutionized human life. It has shown us how we can do a greater volume of work in shorter time and with less physical labour. It has placed at our disposal innumerable labour-saving devices. The type-writer, the computing machine, the telephone, the motor-cars, the electric fan and light, the refrigerator—all these and many others show how much work we can do with minimum labour. They save us from the mechanical drudgery of manual work. At the same time, they create plenty of liesure. Hence, the aim of education in the modern time should be to teach people proper utilization of leisure so that they add to the achievements of man in art, architecture and literature, and thus develop their culture. Teachers and organizers should pay attention to education for leisure. For doing so, reasons are not far to seek.

Education for leisure brings out the hidden talents of children and thus helps them to find their proper place in life. It trains them to participate in creative activities leading to their development and the progress of society. It makes their life richer, their tastes refined, their minds occupied. Hence, schools must make a provision of co-curricular activities, hobbies, games, sports, music, painting, dance etc. All this sounds well.

Synthesis of Different Aims

Since, the aims of education discussed above are epigrams rather than real definitions, they do not take us very far and quite naturally leave us unsatisfied. They are half truths—one sided or incomplete statements, for it is impossible to compress in one small sentence, the whole meaning and aim of an important human activity as education. But, in spite of their lack of agreement and their inadequacy, one-sidedness or incompleteness, the various aims are complementary to each other rather than contradictory. There is no real antithesis between them, but merely a difference of stress. They over-lap although they do not coincide. Since they are complementary and overlapping in nature, they can be reconciled with one another.3

INDIVIDUAL VERSUS SOCIAL AIMS OF EDUCATION

We have discussed in brief some of the important aims of education. The main emphasis of each of them is either on the individual or on the social aim. Thus, they are ultimately reducible to only two major aims—individual and social—which appear to be opposed to each other. Before we see whether they are opposed or compatible, let us discuss in brief the nature of these two aims.

THE INDIVIDUAL AIM

The exponents of the individual aim in education assert that the individual should be in the fore-front of the picture. This concept is based on the socio-political philosophy that social institutions, such as the family, the church, the school and the state, exist only for improving the life of the individual. The individual is the end and these social institutions are the means. Therefore, they justify their existence only, if they are conducive to the promotion of the individual's welfare. The schools, as one of the important social institutions, exists for the educand, and not the educand for the school. Therefore, the school should offer an environment and atmosphere that is conducive to each child's development. Rousseau, the father of naturalism, is the greatest supporter of individual aim in education.

Some of the supporters of the individual aim in education are extremists. They are against all sorts of restrictions. They advocate untrammelled and unrestricted freedom for the educand. They think that, the aim of education is self-expression. It implies unrestricted freedom for the individual to act according to his own nature, even if that action may be objectionable to others. They are against discipline, religion or morality. The purpose of educational efforts, according to Sir Percy Nunn is to secure conditions coducive to the complete development of individuality and to help him to make his "original contribution to the variegated whole of human life as fully and as truly characteristic as his nature permits." Although Nunn supports his contention by an appeal to biology, his conception of individuality is a philosophic one. It is an ideal which has yet to be attained, "a spiritual perfection that is possible to each individual." In other words, Nunn's conception of individuality is synonymous with what self-realization stands for.

Self-realization is not the same thing as self-expression. Self-expression as a meaning of development of individuality emphasizes the play of self-assertion. It implies unrestricted freedom to act as nature prompts, even if that action is objectionable and undesirable. No doubt, self-realization does necessarily imply a certain amount of self-assertion, but only if it is not undesirable for society. Moreover, in self-expression, the self is taken as ready-made, merely waiting to express itself. The self in the ideal of self-realization is not the undisciplined self which is ready-made but one that is a bundle of possibilities and potentialities. Self-realization does not always need freedom from restraint. According to Adams, the self in the ideal of self-realization cannot realize itself against society, it realizes itself in society through social-interaction.

Narrow Meaning of Individual Aim

In the narrow sense individual aim of education is given names like Self-expression, All Round Development of Child's Power and Natural Development. In this sense this aim of education is based on naturalistic philosophy. According to this philosophy, the child should be given complete freedom to develop according to his instincts.

Wider Meaning of Individual Aim

In the wider sense, development of individual as an aim of education can be described as 'Self-realization'. According to this meaning, while keeping in view needs, interests and abilities, the child should be given all those opportunities which may help him in the total development of all of his potentialities and in making him an excellent individual.

Factors Influencing Individual Aim

The following factors influence the Individual Aim of Education.

1. Effect of Biological Sciences: The biological sciences suggest that every living being is different from every other living being. Every individual has certain unique characteristics. Natural development means the development of only these unique characteristics of the individual. Thus education aims at development of the individual abilities of each child. *Sir Percy Nunn*, who takes the biological point of view, holds that the central aim of education is the autonomous development of the individual. Hence individual and not the society should be the centre of all educational efforts.

2. Effect of Naturalism: Naturalists like Rousseau, Comenius, Pestalozzi suggest that education which aims at the development of individuality is the only education 'according to nature.' They assume that the child's nature is good and any interference with its evolution would be harmful. They believe that the child is born with "trailing clouds of glory" as *Wordsworth* says, "and society simply corrupts him, for its influence is as heavy as frost." According to *Rousseau,* "Everything is good as it comes from the hands of Author of Nature, but everything degenerates in the hands of man. God makes all things good. Man meddles with them and they become evil."

3. Effect of Psychology: Modern psychology places a lot of emphasis on individual differences. All individuals differ from one another in respect of their interests, abilities, attitudes and personality. The aim of education is to develop each child in conformity with his special abilities. Consequently, education has become individual (child) oriented.

4. Influence of Progressivists: Progressivists are of the view that the progress of mankind is due to great individuals. The world has progressed only because some individuals have contributed to it according to their special abilities. They include great educationists, philosophers, scientists, inventors, social reformers, religious leaders and the like. Had such gifted individuals not existed, progress in any sphere of activity would have been impossible. Hence education should aim at individual development if it seeks to contribute to social development. According to *T.P. Nunn*, "Nothing good enters into the human world except in and through the free activities of the individual men and women and education practice must be shaped to accord with this truth."

Nunn further says that education must secure conditions under which individuality is most completely developed and should help the individual "to make his original contribution to the variegated whole of human life as full and as truly characteristic as his nature permits." If an individual is fully developed, the society is automatically developed. Hence the aim of education is to develop the abilities of men and women as individuals. This alone will produce leaders in various walks of life and make the world progressive.

5. Influence of Spiritualists: The spiritualists are of the view that the good of the society lies in the good, the "infinite value of the individual person." Since the spiritual development of the man is individual, education should produce such conditions as would be conducive to the highest development of an individual's innate powers. In other words, education should lead the individual to self-realization.

6. Effect of Democratic Ideals: Democracy emphasises the freedom of an individual. Democratic state should provide facilities for all individuals to develop in any direction they conceive to be useful to themselves. *Bertrand*

Russell has suggested, "Education of the individual is a finer thing than the education of the citizen."

Education must not only seek to produce fine citizens but also fine individuals. The educational system should be so designed that it helps to develop the individuality of the child. All educational efforts should bring into focus the individual and not the society.

Criticism of Individual Aim

Individual aim of Education has been criticised on the following grounds:

1. Encouragement of Individualism: Individual aim of education supports individualism. The opponents of this aim of education hold that if education aims at development of individuality, then it will lead to spread of anarchy. The individual may begin to exert to the extent 'Ahm Brahmo Asmi.' (I am God) and then believe "life exists for me; clear of my way. I must have what I want, and so on." It may produce persons like Hitler and Mussolini, and society will have to face harmful consequences of individualism. Thus individual aim of education is the enemy of socialism. Hence individual aim of education cannot be accepted in the socialistic state.

2. Disregard of Man's Social Nature: The supporters of individual aim of education ignore the fact that man is a social animal and his individuality or self is realised through social interaction. Raymont says, "An isolated individual is a figment of imagination." It means that only in society and because of society, he acquires a personality—otherwise he remains an animal.

3. Disregard of Environment: Criticising Nunn's autonomous development of individuality, *Rusk* says that this idea is biological and therefore, defective. Biological development is determined by the past. It ignores the influence of socio-cultural environment and stresses only heredity. Psychology has proved that environment plays a very significant role in the development of the individuality of the child. *Ross* beautifully remarks, "Individuality is of no value and personality is a meaningless term apart from social environment."

4. Difficulty in Making Social Adjustment: Under all circumstances man has to live with other individuals in the society. For leading a successful life, it is essential for him to make adjustment with others. Too much emphasis on individual aim will cause difficulty in making social adjustment.

5. Not Practicable: Theoretically individual aim of education may be accepted but it is not practicable. It is not possible at any stage to fix different types of curriculum for each student.

In the light of above discussion, we can say that the extreme individual aim is not desirable. We must admit that individual cannot develop his individuality in vacuum. He can develop his maximum potentialities in the social context alone. Self-expression is essential for the development of the individual, but it does not mean that the individual should have absolute freedom. Absolute freedom enjoyed by the individual will disintegrate society. Self-expression is desirable only when it integrates rather than disintegrates society. Similarly, self-realization is good, but it should not be achieved in isolation from the society; it should be realized while living in the society. Thus the emphasis that is now-a-days being placed on the individual aims of education does not imply total neglect of the social aims. It is in fact a synthesis of the individual and social aims. It is impossible to conceive of one in the total absence of the other. There is no human being outside society and society is made up of human beings. Hence, even if education is designed to aim at social service, it implicitly promotes the interests and the individuality of the human being.

From the above discussion of Individual Aims of Education, it is clear that there are narrow and wider meanings of Individual Aims of Education which can be summed up as below :

Individual Aim

Narrow Meaning → Self-expression or All round development of child's power or Natural development

Wider Meaning → Self-realization

THE SOCIAL AIM

The supporters of the social aim of education believe that society or state alone is the real, and the individual is only a means. They hold that an individual should be educated for the good of the society. The social aim of education, they believe, will produce social cohesion and a sense of co-operation which is necessary for enjoying the amenities of life. Its supporters cannot conceive of an individual living, and developing in isolation from society. As Raymont says, "The isolated individual is a figment of the imagination. As long as a human individual is a social animal, living in society and developing through social contacts, there will be some subordination of individuality to public or social needs of society and the curbing of individuality will go on consciously or unconsciously."

The social aim, however, is not as simple as it seems. It has two meanings. In the first sense, by social aim we mean purpose of the state. The function of education in relation to that aim is to cater consistently for the welfare of the state subordinating the welfare of the individual to that of the state. This is a narrow interpretation which is given by certain extremist thinkers. They think that the state is an "idealised metaphysical entity over and above the individual citizen, superior in every way." The state or society alone is the reality and the individual is only "a throb in the social pulse." The state is the embodiment of reason, justice and morality and the individual is inferior to it in all respects. Hence, the state is to control and direct every affair in life, including education, which is but a means of shaping its citizens to a certain mould. It is the state which is to decide the mode and type of education or training that an individual is to receive. The curriculum and methods of education are also the complete monopoly of the state and the individual has no choice to develop his powers in his own way. He is only to obey what the authorities dictate. His needs, urges and nature are completely ignored. The exponents of this school of thought believe in imparting education through social control and their watch-words in the educational process are discipline, obedience, regimentation and authority. The interpretation is best illustrated in the Spartan system of education in ancient times and by the more recent Japanese and Nazi systems of education. These systems crushed individual initiative and enterprise and brought for the misery of man such cataclysms as those of 1914 and the World War of 1939-1945.

Another interpretation given to the 'social aim' in education is the one which is applauded in Great Britain, America and other democratic countries. It finds expression in such slogans as 'education for social service' or 'education for citizenship', and aims at the good of the community laying stress on teaching citizenship in schools directly and indirectly, through various subjects in the curriculum and through various social activities. Such virtues as co-operation and self-abnegation are to be cultivated. It is true that the demands of society are to be given priority against the inclination and wishes of an individual, but the dictatorial or authoritarian attitude of state will be replaced by paternal attitude. The function of education according to this ideal is to enable the individual to develop himself fully according to the means compatible with the interests of society.

Professor Bagley and Dewey think that social aim in education attempts to bring about 'social efficiency'. According to Professor Bagley, social efficiency stands for :

1. 'economic efficiency' or ability 'to put his own weight' in economic life.
2. 'negative morality' or willingness to sacrifice those of his desires, the gratification of which would interfere with the economic efficiency of others.
3. 'positive morality', or the willingness to sacrifice his own desires when gratification would not contribute directly or indirectly to social progress.

In a broader sense, social efficiency means, cultivation of one's powers and capacities to join freely, intelligently, and fully in the shared activities of the community as a whole. Education should make each individual socially efficient and must secure social efficiency by the positive use of individual powers and capacities in social occupations and 'not by negative constraint' or imposition from without. A socially efficient individual is able to earn his livelihood. He is not a drag or parasite on any other member of society. He is a good citizen and as such possesses knowledge and intelligence enough to understand and appreciate the world. He is ready to sacrifice his own desires if their satisfaction is harmful for others or if their gratification does not contribute, directly or indirectly, to social progress. A socially efficient individual conforms to a certain standard of conduct known as the moral standard.

From the above discussion of Social Aims of Education, it is clear that there are narrow and wider meanings of

Social Aims of Education which can be summed of as below :

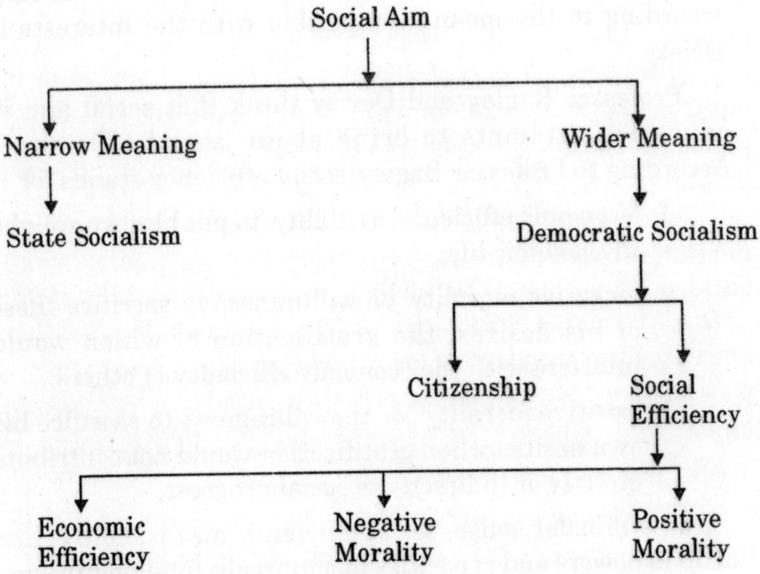

Narrow Meaning of Social Aim

In the extreme form of socialism, narrow meaning of social aim is emphasised. The advocates of the social aim in its extreme form conceive that society or state is an idealised super-human entity over and above the individual. The individual is subordinated to the state. The state is the embodiment of reason, justice and morality and the individual is inferior to it in all respects. The state or society alone is the reality and the individual is only "A throb in the social pulse." It has a mission and destiny to fulfil, which is the good and greater glory of itself. Individuals of a particular state will have to sacrifice their own interests for the welfare of the state. The good of society and the state comes to be the *summum bonum* (ultimate aim) of life and particularly of education.

Education seems to be the most powerful means for the achievement of this end. It is the state which is expected to devise and enforce a rigid system of education. The state is supreme to lay down the curriculum and even to dictate the methods. In the words of *Ross,* "The watch words are always discipline, organisation, a willing acceptance of authority, a damping down of individuality." The slogan is "Everything of the state, everything for the state, and everything by the state."

The concept of state socialism and subordinating the individual to the state is not a modern concept. Such concept was held in ancient times by Sparta and the other city states of Greece. Italy was its exponent in the medieval times. Hegel revived the same in his political theory and philosophy in the eighteenth century. Hitler, Mussolini, Stalin, Khrushchev and Mao have been its recent subscribers.

Wider Meaning of Social Aim

In democratic socialism wider meaning of social aim is emphasised. The supporters of this aim contend that the purpose of education is to prepare the individual for successful participation in activities. The development of the individual should be secured to promote the welfare of the society. Individual development, in no case, should interefere with, or restrict the welfare of the society, of which he is a component. In other words, democratic view of the social aim of education is to make the individual socially efficient for a democratic society. A socially efficient individual is one who is physically strong, intellectually enlightened, culturally refined, vocationally self-sufficient and morally well disciplined. A socially efficient individual, according to *John Dewey,* would be able to control his environment and fulfil his possibilities. He further adds, "All education proceeds by participation of the individual in the social consciousness of the race." Social efficiency becomes the measure of man's success in life. It has come to stay as the be-all and end-all of education.

Bagley and Dewey, who are the chief exponents of this aim of education have given it the names like "Social service" and "Social efficiency".

John Dewey states, "In the broad sense, social efficiency indirectly means cultivation of one's powers and capacities to join freely, intelligently and fully in the shared activities of the community as a whole. It implies socialisation of mind which is actively concerned with making experiences more communicable, in breaking down the barriers of social stratification which make individuals impervious to the interests of others."

In short, wider meaning of social aim of education finds expression in such rallying cries as "Education for social service," and aims at the good of the community, laying stress on teaching citizenship in school, through various subjects in the curriculum and through various social activities. This democratic view of social aim of education is applauded in India, Great Britain, America and other democratic countries.

Why Social Aim?

Following arguments are given in favour of Social Aims of Education.

Social Nature of Man : Man is a social animal. He cannot live without society. Hence he should give top priority to the welfare of society and should sacrifice everything if need arises.

Socialised Individual: Individual is born with certain animal tendencies. It is society which makes him cultured and civilised. Qualities like sympathy, social service, obedience, kindness, love and brotherhood are developed in the society. Social environment makes him human. He is socialised through society ; hence welfare of society should be emphasised in education.

Development of Individual: Development of individual is possible only in society. Hence every individual should be ready to sacrifice his greatest interest for the betterment of society. According to Ross "Individuality is of no value and personality, is a meaningless term apart from the social environment." Similarly *J.B. Baldwin* opines, "Personality cannot be expressed in any but social terms."

Peace, Justice and Security: Man cannot have peace, justice and security without social organisation. Hence society or state is a basic necessity. Thus education should prepare the individual for the state.

Salvation: Some philosophers believe that salvation lies in social service.

Criticism Against Social Aim

The social aim has been criticised on the following grounds :

Unpsychological: The social aim of education, in its narrow meaning, is unpsychological. In this form, personal interests, instincts and abilities of the children are ignored. Individuals are asked to sacrifice their own interests for the welfare of the state. So their natural development is blocked.

Man is only a Means to an End: In its extreme form, social aim stresses the fact that individual should sacrifice even his life for the betterment of the state. In this way, man is only a means to an end, end being the betterment of the state. Thus the social aim reduces the individual to a non-entity.

Suppression of Individual Freedom: Social aim opposes individual freedom. There is a complete regimentation of ideas and feelings. Under a totalitarian form of government, this aim makes the individual a mere puppet in the hands of unscrupulous statesmen. Thus his individuality will be crushed. It is felt that education should not stand for the suppression of individuality. It should rather work for its exaltation.

Hindrance in the Development of Art and Literature: Development of art and literature depends upon individual's devoted efforts. As we have stated that under social aim there is no place for individual freedom. Hence according to this aim of education there will be hindrance in the development of art and literature.

Hindrance in Intellectual and Character Development: Over emphasis on this aim will stand as an obstacle in the way of intellectual and character development as well as emotional integration. Horne is also of this view.

Development of Narrow Nationalism: This aim of education will develop narrow nationalism. The idea or the belief of "my country, right or wrong" will take place. Such a frame of mind will block the progress and lead to narrow-mindedness, blunt thinking and unscientific understanding. The idea of my country right or wrong, has brought about two world wars.

SYNTHESIS OF THE INDIVIDUAL AND THE SOCIAL AIMS

How far is it possible to strike a balance between individual and social aims of education? At one glance it seems that they are poles apart and that no synthesis is possible.

If social aim in education means education for 'good of the state' and individual aim in education means 'self expression', there cannot be any synthesis between the social and individual aims in education.

However, a synthesis is possible if the social aim in education implies the encouragement of social service, social efficiency, ideals of good citizenship and the individual aim in education means 'self realization' rather than 'self expression'. As a matter of fact, there is no real antagonism between the rival claims of the state and the individual. The interests of the state can be promoted by the development of good qualities in the individual, and the individuals can make the best of themselves in and through the state. The individual has no meaning apart from society. Man by nature is not self-sufficing; and he is a social creature. He must live in a social environment and have social contracts if individuality is to be fostered and elevated. Ross has summed up the whole controversy in these words, "Thus individuality is of no value and personality is a meaningless term apart from the social environment in which they are developed and made manifest. Self-realization can be achieved only through social service, and social ideals of real value can come into being only through free individuals who have developed valuable individuality. The circle cannot be broken." Gandhiji also believes that self-realization can be achieved only through social service. He says, "Willing submission to social control and restraint for the sake of the well-being of the whole society enriches both, the individual and the society of which the former is a member.

To sum up we can say that there is, in fact, no conflict between the individual and social aims of education. Individual as well as society has the same claim on education. Hence, a synthesis of the two aims is essential. And the real aim of Education is the good of the individual, as well as the welfare of the society.

CONCLUSION

There is no conflict between self-realization and social service therefore individual and social aim of education are not contradictory. They are rather one and the same. They are the suitable ideal of life and education. We can make this world a richer, nobler and happier place only by promoting both. Both are complementary and can be pursued at the same time.

3

Educational Aims in India

We have already discussed in the previous chapter, the nature and determinants of educational aims in general. In this chapter, we propose to discuss the same with reference to Indian conditions. Every society evolves its own system of education meant to prepare individuals for a particular end. In India the aims of education have been changing with changing philosophies of the people from time to time. Let us have a brief historical retrospect of educational aims in India.

A HISTORICAL RETROSPECT

In the Brahmanic system of education, the religious and moral aims dominated. Education was regarded as a means of inculcating such moral habits as strict obedience to elders, truthfulness, honesty and temperance. It enjoined on the pupils the tenets of the all comprehensive Dharma, which included the ideas of sacred law and duty, justice, religious and moral rectitude and the established practices and customs of caste and community. Later on, when the caste system became rigid, vocational aim of education also came into being. Each caste was to be given a certain type of education which would fit enable members for a certain profession or vocation in life.

Buddhistic education was primarily monastic in its outlook and content. It aimed at the religious development of the individual. Later on, Buddhistic education underwent a change in ideology and practice. It became secular in content and was given a vocational bias. Education was to pave way for royal appointments and other lucrative jobs.

Early Mohammedan education did not depart from the ancient religious ideal. The chief function of the 'Maktabs', which were invariably attached to some mosque? was to instruct the boys in those portions of the Holy Quaran which were to be memorised and was to be used by them in performing their daily rituals and at other religious functions and ceremonies.

During the Mughal period, educational aims were reshaped for the better. The emphasis was shifted from the religious aims as such to moral aims. Such moral virtues as equanimity in the face of success or failure, the ability to adjust to the surroundings and the ability to earn one's livelihood were looked up in an educated person.

The educational system implanted by the British in India, was designed only to prepare Indians, for taking certain subordinate positions, in government offices; it was not intended to develop among the people capacities to take leadership and initiative in different walks of life. The aims of education were not based on the broad foundations of national culture and did not derive their inspiration from the achievements of the past or the pre-occupation of the present or the hopes of the future. Hence, after her independence, when India transformed herself into secular, democratic republic and declared the establishment of the socialistic pattern of society, it was inevitable that the existing educational system should be reviewed and a new comprehensive system of education responding to the challenging needs of the country be devised.

To evolve such a national system of education, the Government of India appointed from time to time three commissions, namely the University Commission (1948-49), the Secondary Education Commission (1952-53) and the Indian Education Commission (1964-66). The Secondary Education Commission has formulated the aims of Secondary Education. The Indian Education Commission has also given a list of national objectives of education.

Now let us discuss the aims of education as given by these Commissions.

SECONDARY EDUCATION COMMISSION ON EDUCATIONAL AIMS

From a careful analysis of the dominant needs of India, the commission formulated the following aims of Secondary Education.

Developing Democratic Citizenship

The adoption of the goals of democracy and socialism necessitates the development of habits, attitudes and qualities of character which will enable its citizens to bear the responsibilities of democratic citizenship. Among these qualities which are to be fostered through curricular and co-curricular activities in secondary schools are :

1. The capacity for clear thinking (allied to which is the capacity for clearness in speech and writing).
2. The scientific attitude of mind.
3. Receptivity to new ideas.
4. Respect for the dignity and worth of every individual.
5. The ability to live harmoniously with one's fellow-men through the cultivation of discipline, co-operation, social sensitiveness and tolerance; and
6. A sense of true patriotism.

Vocational Efficiency

India is rich in potential resources, but at present she is actually a poor country. Therefore, one of the urgent needs of the country is to improve productive efficiency and to increase the national wealth and thereby to raise the standard of living. In this respect the Commission recommends fostering dignity of manual labour and promotion of technical skills for the advancement of industry and technology. Thus, our Secondary Education must be ridden off the purely theoretical instruction, and must lay greater emphasis on craft, productive work and diversification of courses. This will certainly result in equipping educated youngmen psychologically with better vocational efficiency, whereby they will help increasing the national wealth and improving the general standard of living.

Education for Leadership

Since the youth of today will assume leadership in different walks of life tomorrow, special function of the secondary education is to train persons who will be able to assume the responsibility of leadership—in social, political, industrial and cultural fields—in their own small groups of community or locality. To achieve success in this work, the qualities of justice, courage, discipline, tolerance, wisdom, sacrifice, initiative, resourcefulness, understanding of social issues, civic as well as vocational efficiency should be developed in the young men and women of our land.

Development of Personality

An important aim of democratic education is the all-round development of every individual's personality. This requires that education should take into account all his needs—psychological, social, emotional, and practical—and cater to all of them. It should release in him the sources of creative energy so that he may be able to appreciate his cultural heritage, to cultivate rich interests, which he can pursue in his leisure, and contribute in later life, to the development of this heritage. Hence, education should be so organized that subjects like art, craft, music, dancing, and the development of hobbies should find a place of honour in the curriculum. Only when education is organized on the basis of freedom and its scope is widened to include new subjects and new activities, the pupils will go out with more sensitive and quickened minds and will respond readily to the numerous stimuli in the world of art and nature. At the same time, they will be able not only to enjoy their cultural heritage more keenly but also help in its enrichment.

THE INDIAN EDUCATION COMMISSION ON EDUCATIONAL AIMS

The Indian Education Commission has also given a four-fold aim of our national education. According to the Commission education should aim at :

1. Increasing productivity.
2. Achieving social and national integration.
3. Accelerating the process of modernization.
4. Cultivating social, moral and spiritual values.

The Commission has also given suggestions for the achievement of these aims. Let us now discuss those suggestions.

Increasing Productivity

For the promotion of productivity the Commission emphasises that :

1. Science education should become an integral part of school courses.
2. Work experience should be introduced as an integral part of all education.
3. Every attempt should be made to orient work experience to productive processes including agriculture, technology and industrialization.
4. Secondary education should increasingly and largely be vocationalized.

Achieving Social and National Integration

It is an important objective of education. The following steps should be taken to strengthen national consciousness and unity.

1. The common school system of public education should be adopted as a national goal and effectively

implemented in a phased programme, spread over twenty years.

2. Social and national service should be made obligatory for all the students at all stages. It will prove an effective instrument for building character, improving discipline, inculcating faith in the dignity of labour and developing a sense of social responsibility, if it is organized concurrently with academic studies in schools and colleges.

3. The development of an appropriate language policy can materially assist in social and national integration.

4. A re-evaluation of our cultural heritage is needed. For this, there should be well organized teaching of languages, literature, philosophy, religion, history of India, Indian Architecture, sculpture, painting, music, dance and drama. Inter-state camps, summer schools etc. should be organized.

5. The Educational programme in schools and colleges should be designed to inculcate democratic values.

Accelerating the Process of Modernization

There has been a great explosion of knowledge during the last few decades. Education in a modern society is no longer concerned with the imparting of knowledge or the preparation of finished product, but with the awakening of curiosity, the development of proper interests, attitudes and values and the building up of such essential skills, as independent study and capacity to think and judge for oneself, without which it is not possible to become responsible members of a democratic society. The progress of modernization will be directly related to the pace of educational advance. And the one sure way to modernize quickly is to spread education, to produce educated and skilled citizens and to train an adequate and competent intelligentsia, coming from all strata of society, whose loyalities and aspirations are deeply rooted in the Indian soil. This also involves a radical change in the methods of teaching and in the training of teachers.

Cultivating Social, Moral and Spiritual Values

The expanding knowledge and the growing power which it placed at the disposal of modern society must be combined with the strengthening and deepening of the sense of social responsibility and a keener appreciation of moral and spiritual values. For this purpose, active measures should be adopted to give a value orientation to education.

1. The Central and the State Governments should adopt measures to introduce moral, social and spiritual values in all institutions under their central (or under local authority) on the lines recommended by the University Education Commission and the Committee on Religious and Moral Instruction. The privately managed institutions should also follow suit.

2. Departments of Comparative religions and philosophies of the Universities should be specially concerned with the ways in which these values can be taught widely and effectively and they should undertake preparation of special literature for the use by the students and the teachers.

3. The Commission observed that a multi-religious democratic state like ours, should also promote a tolerant study of all religions so that its citizens can understand each other better and live amicably together. For this purpose, a syllabus, giving well chosen information about each of the major religions, should be included as a part of the course in citizenship or as a part of general education to be introduced in schools and colleges upto the first degree. It would be of great advantage if common text books are prepared at the national level by competent experts in each religion.

CHALLENGE OF EDUCATION—A POLICY PERSPECTIVE ON EDUCATIONAL AIMS

The document, 'Challenge of Education—A Policy Perspective' released in August, 1985 by the Union Ministry of Human Resources Development for a nation-wide debate for evolving a new education policy, over the 1968 education policy, states that education is a complex subject with wide-ranging ramifications. A definitive view on a new policy for education has to be finalised in consultation with the decision makers in the State and Central Governments, the parliamentarians, educationists, intellectuals, teachers, parents, students, enterpreneurs etc. The document states various viewpoints in a forthright manner. It has also given Aims of Education.

Goal Orientation for Educational Planning

A recapitulation of the goals of education, emphasised by the Indian Constitutions and enunciated, from time to time, by thinkers, planners, policy makers and educationists indicates that this basic issue should be considered from three interrelated approaches.

First of all, it is necessary to define the role of the educational system in totality, since it has an institutional character of its own which goes beyond its main function of imparting education to the pupils. The system is expected to generate new knowledge in all fields within the reach of the human mind. In addition, it has to evolve principles, methodologies and guidelines for the application of knowledge for benefiting society. It is also expected to provide knowledge and skills for solving the problems of development. It must also enable the students to develop an understanding and a perspective of the physical and social environment. Research and development and extension, therefore, have to be accepted as essential ingredients of the educational process.

Secondly, emphasis has to be laid on the socio-economic well-being, competence and creativity of the individual, which encompasses :

(*i*) physical, intellectual and aesthetic development of personality;

(*ii*) inculcation of a scientific temper and democratic, moral and spiritual values;

(*iii*) development of self-confidence to innovate and face unfamiliar situations;

(*iv*) creation of an awareness of the physical, social, technological, economic and cultural environment;

(*v*) fostering a healthy attitude to dignity of labour and hard work;

(*vi*) a commitment to principles of secularism and social justice;

(*vii*) dedication to uphold the integrity and honour as well as foster the development of the country; and

(*viii*) promotion of international understanding.

In addition to develop the personal attributes listed above, education has to assume the responsibility for imparting knowledge about concepts and facts relating to different subjects and for developing skills in the area of languages and communication, as also interest in hobbies, games and sports.

Besides, in relation to economic development and employment, education has to equip the pupils with competence, in terms of knowledge and skills, in various combinations at different levels of understanding, relating to the opportunities of employment in the context of a particular pattern and the rate of development.

Education has to play an important role in integrating the individual into the social system. It is meant to inculcate suitable habits for health care, mental application, management of time and conservation of physical, mental and emotional energy.

Thus perceived, education can be the most effective means for equalising opportunities and reducing disparities between human beings. In a democratic society, it is considered a fundamental right of the citizens. In the ultimate analysis, therefore, the aim must be to enlarge the coverage and improve the quality of education in our institutions so that a person, belonging to any region, caste, creed, sex or economic strata, would have the chance of developing his or her potentials to the full.

It seems relevant to underline the fact that the goals of education listed above do not envisage the laying down of omnibus objectives for all levels of education on, a *priori* basis. Adult education would have different goals from those of school and university education. In different age groups relevant to elementary, secondary, vocational and higher education, the need as well as capacity for acquiring knowledge and skills varies considerably. Moreover, the process of learning itself is a hierarchical process and therefore, envisages different levels of inputs and outputs. Another point which needs consideration is that many students do not pursue formal education beyond a certain stage. This necessitates that, for each stage of education, discrete objectives and competence would have to be spelt out and for achieving these, integrated and holistic packages of formal and non-formal learning will have to be developed.

INDIAN SOCIO-POLITICO-ECONOMIC SITUATIONS AND EDUCATIONAL AIMS

We have achieved freedom after centuries of slavery. This freedom cannot be preserved and the vision of a socialistic pattern of society, that we have held before us, cannot be built unless we improve the quality of our education.

We have adopted democracy, socialism and secularism as our national ideals. We should keep in our mind that democracy in India has evolved in a society which, to a very great degree, is rural and agrarian, also in a society in which vast majority of the people are ignorant, where many superstitious and rigid ways of behaviour prevail; where people are victims of many prejudices and social maladies; where there are wide diversities in their modes of living, in their methods of speaking, in their customs and manners and loyalities; where people have got political freedom without having necessary resources to defend it. Therefore, no system of education borrowed from other countries can be grafted in the Indian soil. No doubt, there has been a marked progress in education in many states; the literacy figure has risen, many more schools have been opened, the number of technical and professional schools and colleges has increased; there has been a rapid growth of university education and much has been done to promote scientific research; many plans, both at the union as well as states level have been carried into execution and many of them are still on. Yet, it seems that things have not progressed in the way and in the direction in which they were intended.

What is needed now? We need a system of education which is geared to the needs of the country, which is practicable within the resources in men and material which we have; which is based on the country's traditions and social behaviour and which assures all those efficiencies to the youth.

To achieve these national goals, our education must inculcate among the pupils such qualities as respect for the opposed views, respect for freedom, respect for the dignity of man, respect for rule of law and respect for constitutional change. It must develop among them optimistic out-look, positive attitude towards work and dignity of labour, scientific and objective thinking and critical judgement. It must teach them to utilise their leisure time in a proper manner, and above all, it must promote among them emotional and national integration.

4

The Curriculum

We have already discussed the aims and objectives of education. Now we have to discuss the problem, how these aims are to be realised. In other words 'what' forms of knowledge and experience are to be given to children at school to prepare them for effective living. This brings us to the problem of curriculum.

WHAT IS CURRICULUM

Etymologically the term 'curriculum' is derived from the Latin word 'Currere' which means 'run'. Thus curriculum means 'a course to be run for reaching a certain goal or destination'. In this sense education is imagined as a race, with its aims as the goals and curriculm as the course, leading to that goal.

Curriculum is not a Race but a Chase

But such a concept of the curriculum fits in extremely well with the traditional view of Education—education being conceived as training in such skills as reading, writing, arithmetic and in acquiring mastery over certain areas of knowledge. As the trainer trains the horse to reach the target, by leading him through the course, so does the teacher train the pupils to realise the educational objectives by leading them through the curriculum prescribed for the purpose. It provides the necessary practice and indicates the necessary reading which would help the pupils in gaining the desired knowledge. The growth and the development of the pupils, which instead of resembling any set pattern, are unique individually. So no mechanical conception of the curriculum can serve the purpose of true education. The viewing of the curriculum as a 'chase' instead of a 'race' removes a good many misunderstandings. In case of a race, the goal is fixed with exactitude and the course through which the goal is to be reached, is also outlined with precision. In the case of a chase, however, the goal is fixed only in a general manner; it does not remain fixed, but varies from time to time in the course of the pursuit. The course, therefore, cannot be decided with precision, it has to vary with the variation in the nature of the goal.

The latest trend in this respect, therefore, is to regard the curriculum as flexible rather than rigid. It may differ from school to school and even in the same school and in the same grade from individual to individual. The content of education can be outlined only in a general way allowing enough scope for variation within the general frame-work. For example, "knowledge of the environment may be decided upon as an item, in the curriculum, but its scope will differ from school to school. Not only this, even the activities through which knowledge is expected to be gained, may also differ in accordance with the resources of different schools and the characteristics of the pupils, they have on roll.

THE HISTORY OF THE CURRICULUM

The present curriculum, as we see it in any country in the world, is a result of the process of accretion. Hence, a very brief discussion of the development of the curriculum through the ages will not only be relevant but also useful.

Curriculum in Ancient India

Education in ancient India, emphasised the development of spiritual values at the cost of material ones. It was essentially religious in character and it aimed at preparing the pupils for life in the other world. To start with the Vedas formed the principal subject matter for study. With the development of elaborate rituals, Ethics also came in. This was followed by the addition of music as 'Chhandas' were emphasised in the recitation of the Vedas. Grammar was also studied with seriousness in order to gain mastery over the Sanskrit language. With the development of culture, other 'liberal arts' such as Logic and Sciences like, Astronomy and Arithmetic also found place in the curriculum.

It may be remembered that this sort of education was meant primarily for the Brahmins whose profession consisted in studying, teaching and performing rituals. The Brahmins were maintained by the society to preserve its religious and philosophical heritage, to carry on research in the field, to pass on the cultural heritage to the younger generation and to help people in gaining religious merit. It is obvious from this, that though the curriculum was liberal in nature, it only provided for the vocation of Brahmins. The Kashtriyas were the next who took advantage of the educational system. Shastra Vidya or the Science of weapons was included in the curriculum meant for them with the sole aim of meeting their vocational needs and requirements.

Curriculum in Greece

The ancient Greeks were also educated for transcendental values, though they were not religious in nature. Realization of Truth, Goodness and Beauty was their ideal of human life. Hence the curriculum was so designed as to cultivate the higher aspects of human nature, it was 'liberal' in the sense that it attempted to 'liberate' the soul from the bondage of the body. The dualism between body and mind influenced the Greek curriculum to a very great extent. It was thought that the mundane everyday affairs of the life catered for the body and hence were not fit subjects to be studied—subjects which led to the development of the intellect alone were to be included in the curriculum. It has also to be borne in mind that the Greek culture was intellectual in its content and aesthetic in its bias. Thus in ancient Athens, the curriculum provided for the fullest development of the individual through 'Gymnastics' and 'Music'. As the culture became more formal, it was reduced to a study of the 'Seven liberal Arts'—Grammar, Rhetoric and Logic, later known as the Trivium, Arithmetic, Geometry, Astronomy and Music, later known as the quadrivium.

Curriculum in Rome

Curriculum in ancient Rome was very much similar to that in ancient Greece. The only addition being the Greek language which, infact, was included under the title of Grammar. It may be mentioned here that both in Greece and in Rome, education was meant for the citizens as distinguished from that of the slaves. The citizens lived on the labours of the slaves and were, therefore, able to concentrate upon the cultivation of higher values in life.

Influence of Christianity

With the predominance of the Christian church, during the Middle Ages, Greek and Roman education was viewed as pagan. Secular Idealism gave place to religious idealim and consequently the curriculum came to be dominated by theology and the writing of Church Father. Even the liberal Arts of the Greek and Roman periods were given a religious bias. As a consequence, education was intended mostly for the clergy and the curriculum catered to their special needs.

Influence of Humanism

Humanism, under the spell of Renaissance, attempted to revive the concept of liberal education held by the Greeks, and the Romans. But under its influence, the study of Greek and Latin as languages acquired profound importance in the curriculum. Moreover, the Humanists could not outgrow the influence of Christianity and as such neglected the aesthetic side of the classical curriculum. The aesthetic side of the Greek and Roman learning was realised only in countries south of the Alps where the new merchant class evolved the chief pattern of education. As their aim of education evolved, to acquire the status of a 'gentleman', training in polished manners became an important item in the curriculum.

Inclusion of Science

The development of Science in the 17th and 18th centuries opened a new vista of values for humanity. It showed immense possibility in the increase of material values, so much so that their development could be taken not only as the aim of human life but that of education also. The dualism between the body and the mind on the one hand and between the material values and the spiritual or moral values on the other, began to vanish. As a result of this, there was pressing demand for the inclusion of Science. But this claim was not recognised till the success of the Industrial Revolution which led to its inclusion in the curriculum on utilitarian grounds.

The scientific age not only resulted in the acceptance of science as a school subject but it also brought about a new outlook, the scientific outlook in the curriculum construction. People became conscious of its importance and wanted to be definite about the purpose of introducing a particular subject in the curriculum. As such, the humanistic curriculum became the subject of much criticism. The defence of humanism was found in the Faculty Theory of Psychology, which postulated the division of mind into a number of faculties such as Intelligence, Memory, Imagination, Reasoning etc. It further believed that education consisted in the training of mental faculties and it was argued that though Latin and Greek had little relevance to life in the modern world, they were instruments of rare utility in training the mental faculties. This made the study of these languages extremely formal. They were studied as disciplines for the mind.

Neo-Humanism

Though the disciplinary view of the curriculum held the ground for a long time protests against it were heard from both the idealistic and realistic thinkers. Milton, for example, not denying the claims of classics, insisted that selection should be made of the curriculum on the basis of their functions, bearing on the times in which the pupil lived. The viewpoint is designated as 'Humanistic Realism' in educational theory. But it was, in fact, the protest of the Sense Realists which contributed more to the radical reconstruction of the curriculum than anything else. Classical philosophy looked down upon sense experience and looked upon intellect as the only medium for apprehending the truth. But the sense-realists acknowledged the importance of sense experience in education. Under this twofold pressure, Humanism changed itself into Neo-humanism which may be compared to Counter Reformation. As Counter-Reformation attempted to check the progress of Reformation by introducing changes in Catholicism, so Neo-humanism endeavoured to stop the inclusion of Science in the curriculum by introducing modern languages in place of classical languages. Moreover, such social subjects as History, Geography, Civics etc. also found place in the curriculum.

Inclusion of Physical Education

For some time science and Neo-humanities received equal emphasis on the curriculum wherein the tendency to Encyclopaedic Knowledge was clearly visible. As such, it began to accept any subject for which there was also a demand. This outlook was also responsible for the introduction of physical education. Here before the school was considered as a place for mental stimulation only and consequently physical education had little chance of inclusion in it. But Rousseau with his emphasis on Naturalistic interests advocated free bodily movements as an essential part of education. The German educator Frierich Ludwig John influenced by Naturalism-patriotism devised a system of gymnastics for his pupil. He combined patriotic singing and story telling with gymnastics. But John's programme of physical education was extra-curricular, it was organised after regular school hours and was undertaken on voluntary basis. It was another German, Adolph Spies (1810-1858) however, who deserves credit for introducing physical education as a regular part of the school curriculum. He devised graded exercises suited to groups of different age and sex. Later on, Danish and Swedish educationists brought in further improvement in physical education by including the study of Anatomy and Physiology within its scope.

Inclusion of Drawing and Fine Arts

In course of time, the curriculum acceded to another social demand by including Fine Arts in it. As has already been mentioned, Music occupied an important place in the Greek curriculum. But at that time, music stood for something quite different from what we understand by the term Fine Arts nowadays. During the middle ages, even music became formal being confined to chorus singing only. The nationalistic fervour of 19th century, however, received a sort of romantic interest in folk songs. Singing them in schools became a means to develop patriotism among the pupils. Besides this, the essentials of new industries demanded and secured the inclusion of industrial drawing in the school curriculum.

The philosophy for the inclusion of Fine Arts in school came first of all from Rousseau. He emphasised the spontaneous interests of the child and stressed the fact that they found one of their major outlets in Fine Arts. Pestalozzi and Froebel also developed the same idea and gave an added fillip to their inclusion in the curriculum. It is, however, interesting to point out that at first, they were associated with other school subjects as drawing was utilized for teaching, writing and modelling for teaching Geography. But the 20th century secured an independent place for Fine Arts in the curriculum and creation and appreciation of art were to some extent, regarded as inherent in every man. Consequently, the scope of Fine Arts in school began to increase. Dancing and instrumental music were added to vocal music and spontaneity and creativity were urged in painting.

Inclusion of Extra-Curricular Activities

The introduction of extra-curricular activities in the school also deserves special mention. They entered the school in the 19th century as a reaction to the continuous tiresome intellectual stimulation of the class-room, the pupil sought relief in such activities as athletics, drama, school journalism, debating etc. To start with, these activities were carried on outside regular school hours and hence they were dubbed as 'extras'. The idea was to consider them as less important than the so-called curricular activities. Another way of keeping the distinction was to make the former 'non-examination subjects'. The growth of democracy and the movement of education for citizenship led to an increasing realisation of their importance.

But the real and most significant contribution came from Psychology which maintained that from the modern point of view, there was little difference between play and work. 'Play-way' developed in education not as a mere tendency to teach certain subjects or parts of a subject, but as a new attitude to school work. Besides, this education came to be considered as the modification of behaviour affected as a result of organized living in the school community. Consequently, activities outside the class-room were found to be as educative as those inside it. Moreover, the curriculum began to be viewed as activities to be pursued rather than as subjects to be studied. Finally the introduction of 'Projects' in schools assimilated completely the distinction between curricular and extra-curricular activities, forced the schools to take initiative in organizing them and time for the purpose was allotted out of the regular school hours.

The Present Position in India

From ancient times to the advent of the British, there was little change in the curriculum of Indian Schools. The Muslim conquest of India, it cannot be denied, brought a new system of education. But the Hindu system continued on its own lines without being vitally affected by the foreign rule. The Muslim educational system was also dominated by religion. It was a little more secular in its content. It is, however, remarkable that inspite of the fact that the two communities were educated for two different cultures, there was not much difference between the two types of education.

The British introduced their own system of education and it was accepted by the country as a whole. It was decided by Macaulay's Minutes that English and the Western Sciences should be taught in Indian schools. In short. Indian schools were organized on the model of those in Britain. At the time the only change was that Sanskrit and Persian took the place of Latin and Greek. Rapid development of modern Indian languages soon secured the place for vernacular in Indian schools. But the innovations in the British school curriculum resulting from the success of Industrial Revolution did not reach India before the 20th century. To be more precise, the effect of the Industrial Revolution began to be felt in India only after the first world-war. In the meantime, the educated Indians were faced with the problem of unemployment, and thus there developed a demand for vocational subjects in school, science fighting its way successfully entered it. The national movement in the country demanded the improvement of national health, through physical education in schools. The romantic movement in Indian education pioneered by Tagore, emphasised the importance of Fine Arts in schools. Thus, Physical Education and Fine Arts gradually became part of the Indian schools.

With the introduction of some measure of self-government, in the country, the necessity was felt for imparting training in citizenship and this led to the creation of school unions with responsibility to organize the extra-curricular life of the school. Self-government became a regular feature of some schools and even mock assemblies were organised at times with a view to giving knowledge of political institutions to the pupils. After the achievement of independence, however, a greater emphasis is being laid on this aspect of school activity. In short, India has certainly got most of the tendencies which have shaped the curriculum of the progressive countries, but they, it cannot be denied, have not been applied systematically to build up a coherent curriculum fitting in with the sociological conditions in the country.

DIFFERENT TYPES OF CURRICULUM

The following are the different types of curriculum :

1. Traditional or Subject-Centred Curriculum.
2. Activity Curriculum.
3. Experience Curriculum.
4. Un-differentiated or Integrated Curriculum.

Traditional or Subject-Centred Curriculum

Ever since education has aimed at equiping the child with the adult standards, the principle of 'equipment' supplemented with the psychological conception of 'transfer of training' has led to the philosophy of curriculum usually known as 'Traditional Curriculum', that is, conceiving the curriculum in terms of subjects, each one of which is given pre-determined place and allotted a fixed amount of time. The exact and precise extent and scope of each subject which is to be studied in a particular class or in a particular session is carefully and strictly defined. The job is strictly entrusted to and carried out by adults in terms of adult values. Emphasis is laid on learning and acquiring of habits and skills which might not be of any utility to the child in the period of life, he is actually living or passing through, but are supposed to be useful in adult life, for which he is being prepared.

In traditional curriculum, irrespective of considerations of the needs and interests and the psychology of the child, the human knowledge is divided in compartments for the convenience of mastering it. It is properly analysed and classified. The labels attached to such parts of human experience became subjects. This classification is based upon two considerations: *i.e.* nature of the contents and the methods of the teaching. The division is highly logical and pieces of human knowledge are put together in it. There is no place for the view point of the child. The contents are those fixed by the adults for the perpetuation of their standards and values. The method of teaching, more often than not, is rote learning. Neither do contents immediately interest the child nor can methods make learning easy.

Human knowledge is conveniently divisible into three broad fields:

1. Natural sciences including (*a*) the Physical sciences pertaining to the phenomena of the universe, such as Physics, Chemistry, Geology and Astronomy and (*b*) Biological sciences, such as Zoology and Botany.

2. The Social Sciences, which relate to the origin, organization and development of human society, especially to man in association with other men. Such as History, Geography, Civics, Economics, Politics, Sociology etc.

3. Humanities which pertain to that branch of knowledge which humanizes man. They relate to art, literature and human thought, ideals and feelings. All

Philosophy, Literature, Fine Arts, Paining, Drawing, Drama, Music, etc. come under this head. This education restricts itself to the use of words and symbols. It does not present to the child the actualities of life. He is not kept busy in solving some present problem of doing some activity for the achievement of an immediate goal. The criterion being 'Education for Preparation' for future, which is often uncertain, does not leave chances for the child's present. With many defects inherent in such a *conviction* in the highly dynamic modern society in which nobody can fore-tell what is to happen in the near future, in which values are changing and disappearing so fast, the traditional curriculum is nothing but a body of factual information and those essential skills and techniques which man has discovered to pass on to the new generations, through the school, by the process of *explanation* and *repetition*.

The traditional philosophy, thus, regards education as static, something which takes place in the school room during a fixed number of periods everyday. Education accordingly is synonymous with school going. It starts when the child reaches the school and continues as long as he is there and ends when the child leaves it.

Such an education provides ease in the methods of teaching, to the teacher. He is not to worry about the techniques of imparting different kinds of knowledge in different ways. The prescribed book, which limits his course, is required to be learnt by heart by the children. The children are to devour these bitter pills, though with strain and no interest. But knowing the lore, initiative, discrimination, originality, resourcefulness and creative thinking, they settle themselves with ease in the pages of the books.

But logical order in place of psychological consideration of the dynamics of the child mind, domination of books, faulty methods of teaching and prescription of adult standards have done a great harm to true education of the children. The curriculum is narrowly conceived. It prepares the child for the uncertain future at the cost of his present problems. It takes into consideration his literary interests only.

The un-natural division of knowledge into subjects has landed us on such a ground that we see dis-section everywhere. There is no end to that. And as traditional curriculum does not admit knowledge, except literacy, a long list of co-curricular and extra-curricular activities is being added to that. The importance of these activities is being increasingly realized but is not given proper place. And this shows narrowness of the traditional curriculum.

This curriculum is abstract. The child's present needs are neglected for the past human-experience with which the child is to be saddled for being prepared for adult life. The studies become sheer verabalism and are cut off from the life of the child. It does not provide concrete experience to the child which is the fundamental basis of learning.

The method of learning in parts is also psychologically wrong and has led to memorization through drill or recitation of the unrelated information. For teaching different subjects different teachers are employed. This minimises the possibilities of co-ordination of studies. It has increased the burden on the mind of the children for the disconnected mass of information lacking inherent relationship. It is not an easy task for making knowledge a useful means to solve problems of life.

Such curriculum has a specific and fixed programme. The books give a uniform text and a fixed quantitative standard of attainment as the goal. The individual differences are totally ignored and no scope is left for individual attention and development of individual skills, interests and aptitudes. At best, the studies are carried on for a hypothetical average child who does not exist at all. To worsen the situation, the curriculum is framed by politicians or administrators for the utter neglect of those who are concerned with learning and teaching students and teachers. All this has led to uniformity, rigidity and unrealistic nature of the methods of education.

Since education is wrongly considered as synonymous with schooling, the informal agencies of education have no significant place for educative purposes. The effects of home, society, club, play ground and many passive agencies which are powerful media of imparting education to the child are totally neglected. It is paradoxical that the learning is aimed at the preservation and betterment of social standards, yet the society is considered as passive and ineffective for learning. Thus education is supposed to end with the school and is not conceived as a life-long process.

In India, it has done greater harm by laying stress on foreign language, not merely as a subject of study, but as the very medium of instruction. But slowly we are realizing its defects and new schemes are being put to practice. The Basic and Higher Secondary schemes lay stress upon activities and interests of the child besides the cultural heritage of the people.

To sum up, we can say that traditional curriculum is conceived in terms of subjects. It is rigid and static and is constructed by the adults in their own image. It emphasises repetition and memorization. It neglects the importance of other informal agencies of education, and above all, it is not an expression of our cultural and spiritual heritage. Thus, the traditional curriculum is 'narrowly conceived', 'unpsychologically planned and ineffectively executed'. It leads only to intellectual development at the cost of physical, social, moral, emotional, aesthetic and spiritual development. In other words, it is inadequate, unsatisfactory, un-inspiring and un-scientific.

The Activity Curriculum

It is a pity that even at present, educational system in India lays undue emphasis on verbal information. It is universally admitted that whatever has to be learnt, must be learnt by doing. Activity is the cardinal principle of child behaviour. The child is active by nature. He desires to deal with things, to make, to construct, to destroy, to plan, to observe and to enjoy. The formal information regarding things has little value for him. He may cram but does not understand the information memorised by him. Education is not mere craming. To be really educated, one has to assimilate the information so that it may affect his disposition, modify his behaviour and his way of life.

The educationsists and psychologists have realized the need of the child for activity and that is why Montessori method, Dalton plan, Kindergarten and Project method have been used in the teaching of the child. The Naturalists have supported the activity principle. Ross says, "extreme naturalism concentrates in school on the present experience, activities and interests of the child himself, it is these and these alone that may legitimately determine what he is to do in school. Let him have his own proper experience, unhampered and unhindered by adult-interference, direction or even coaxing." A pragmatist also believes in unfettered activities of the child. "Since activity is the essential characteristic of childhood, the child must be active, the experience he undergoes in the school must be firmly based on his natural activities and interests." The framers of Wardha Scheme also took note of activity in framing Basic curiculum. They said, "We have attempted to draft an activity curriculum which implies that our schools must be places of work, experimentation and discovery, not of passive absorption of information imparted at second hand."

For Dewey, activity curriculum is a "continuing stream of child activities, unbroken by systematic subjects and springing from the interests and personally felt needs of the child." Now we have to see what these activities could be? Shall we have only those activities which we nowadays characterise as extra-curricular or co-curricular in the syllabus, or shall we exclude them and give place to literary activities only or shall we have both? Banchara Branford has given a three-fold diversion of human activities as there are three centres of activity—the head, hand and heart of man—a trinity in unity. Accordingly, there are three instruments of culture—science, arts and crafts and language including music and literature of all kinds. Also, man's objects of interest are three—nature, crafts and folk. Hence to keep all the centres of activity engaged, to satisfy human interests and to make use of the instruments of culture, we can introduce in the school (*a*) nature-crafts, study of external nature, (*b*) Handicraft or study of arts and crafts and (*c*) language or folk-craft or study of language in its various forms.

Nunn divides activities in two groups :

1. The activities that safeguard the conditions and maintain the standard of individual and social life; such as the care of health and bodily grace, manners, social organization, morals and religion.

2. The typical creative activities that constitute, so to speak, the solid tissue of civilization, will comprise (*i*) literature, including at least the best literature of the motherland and (*ii*) some forms of art, including music, the most universal of arts. (*iii*) handicrafts, taught with emphasis either on its aesthetic aspects as in the weaving, carving, lettering or on its constructional aspect as in carpentry and needle work, (*iv*) science, including mathematics, the science of numbers, space and time, history and geography should appear in it, in a double guise.

Definitely, Nunn's second type of activities do not comprise simple activities, they become pure subjects of study and include the racial experience in them as Nunn's notion of schools is not merely activity-centred but for him "a nation's schools...are an organ of its life, whose special function is to consolidate its spiritual strength, to maintain its historic continuity, to secure its past achievements to guarantee its value. But since his activities face in line with Branford's division of activities, which make up for past experience for making a good activity curriculum, however by leaving that, the curriculum remains defective.

There are simple activities of kindergarten for very young children. If we narrowly conceive activity-curriculum, we will have the activities related with (*i*) exercises for physical development (*ii*) exercises of daily life, (*iii*) dramatic and constructive plays and various other occupations for muscular, sensory and intellectual development, (*iv*) story telling, observation of nature and discussions arising from handling of things and looking at pictures, (*v*) rhythmic work and singing and (*vi*) work of reading, writing and numbers through various play-activities and projects which engage the child's attention.

These are good amount of activities, but activities for a particular age, that is, childhood. It is difficult to prescribe activities like this for every stage. The only cardinal principle for them is the child's interest, whatever intrests children which varies from stage to stage and from society to soceity, must be included in the activities of the school. That is why, crossing the limit of naturalists, who lay stress on the present needs and interests of the child to circumscribe his activities. Dewey, as a true pragmatist, includes those activities also which prepare him for his future life. Definitely, the child has interest in his future. Thus Dewey, according to natural interests of the child, prescribes activities relating to "the interest in conversation, or communication in enquiry or finding out things in making things or construction and in artistic expression." The 3 R's are to be added to facilitate learning and to serve as tools and not to be ends in themselves.

Thus, the provision for the activity dealing with realities of child's nature and his life facilitates the framing of the activity curriculum. The activity curriculum is (1) 'to furnish the child as sufficiently large amount of personal activities in occupations, expressions, conservation, construction and experimentation so that his individuality—moral and intellectual—shall not be swamped by a disproportionate amount of the experience of others to which books introduce him and (2) so to conduct this more direct experience as to make the child feel the need of resorting to and command of traditional social tools furnish him with motives and make his recourse to them intelligent, in addition to his powers instead of a servile dependency.' And this is possible only when every activity is well thought of before undertaking it and is purposeful. The needs and interests of the child become the medium of the capitalized experience of human race and make activity curriculum cut across the subject barriers and give integrated knowledge. Therefore, instead of subjects, the activity curriculum suggests activities to be performed in the school, the nouns of subjects to be converted into verbs of activities. It must not merely remain a play. The play should, in the words of Sir Percy Nunn, "lead continuously from the irresponsible frolic of childhood to the disciplined labours of mankind."

Mere activity curriculum, if taken in a narrower sense, is defective. We cannot ignore the past experience for mere lies and dislikes of individual children. They can be allowed to play and engage in some activity of their choice till certain age only. After that the social heritage must surely be made to carry. After all the individual is not merely an individual. He is a part of social group, an important humanizing agency. That agency is not to be neglected if individuals are to benefit from it and therefore, its experience and heritage must also supplement activities to make curriculum complete one.

Experience Curriculum

The curriculum that gives rich and varied experiences, knowledge, skills, attitudes and appreciation is called 'experience curriculum.' According to George Santayana "Whatever forces-may govern human life, if they are to be recognised by man, must betray themselves in human experience".

In this context William James opines, "The only function that one experience can perform is to lead to another experience, and the only fulfilment we can speak of in the reaching of a certain experienced end.". Thus experience being both process and end of learning, we cannot ignore it in the curriculum or in the framing of curriculum. The exponent of Wardha Scheme took into due consideration and pointed out, "We have attempted to organise the subject matter into significant and comprehensive units of experience which will, when mastered, enable the child to understand his environment better and react to it more intelligently, because they throw significant light on the problems and conditions of the life around him."

Experience requires direct dealing with the things which result in the modification of the behaviour of the learner in respect of a thing or situation and also to make it serviceable in changed circumstances. But the things and situations to be experienced must have utility for the child. But those things only can be of use which invoke needs and interests of the child or are drawn from his social life. Hence the basis of experience curriculum must be the needs and interests of the child in his environment.

Experience is neither merely 'a knowledge affair', nor a physical thing infected throughout by subjectivity,' nor a thing of the 'past' nor 'committed to particularism' only. It suggests experiments with the present to gain control of the enviroment for future good. It takes the whole situation and all knowledge in an integrated form, into consideration. The mental organism puts together relevant pieces of knowledge obtained from past experiences to be referred in future and to draw inferences. As experience modifies the behaviour of the learner, which leads to the modification of the environment itself, which provided the experience, future good becomes its watch-word and experiment with social and physical environment its means.

Hence let experience be direct, or dealing with the present or modifying the past, it is reflective and takes into consideration the cumulative experience of the past. It cannot ignore the environment with which the experience is held and which is the creation of past generations. "Experience is a process of reflective adjustment of life to changing environment."

Idealism concentrates not so much on the present experience of the individual as on the experience of the human race as a whole. It considers the rounded whole of human knowledge and experience and seeks to epitomize it in the school to bring it to the child. According to James Ross, "It stands on the position that the purpose of the school is to reflect the civilisation itself, the main purpose, therefore, of courses of studies is to epitomize and organize in respective fashion at least, the capitalised experience of the race of which the child is a member."

But experience is at least two fold, being concerned with physical enviroment and fellowmen. Hence we can divide the curriculum broadly in the sciences and the humanities, each one of which can be sub-divided in many courses of studies.

According to psychological analysis we can divide the experience into connation or the active striving experience cognition, or knowing experience and affection or the feeling experience.

Accordingly, the studies must represent what man does and strives to do, what man knows and how does the man feel. Under we can include the major crafts of mankind, specially those which subserve the fundamental needs of food, clothing and shelter; must be the representation of man's major modes of thinking, so language, literature, science, mathematics, history and geography, the traditional intellectual studies may be included; man's main modes of feeling and their expression in arts, music and poetry may be included.

Experience curriculum is centred in learning. It emphasises promoting the all-round growth of the learner.

Contents of Experience Curriculum: Psychologically, human experience is divided into three major parts, namely (*i*) conation or doing and striving experience (*ii*) cognition or knowing experience and (*iii*) affection or feeling experience. Accordingly, the following contents are included in Experience Curriculum):

Human activity	*Human experience*	*Human environment*	*Contents or subjects of study*
Hand	Conation	Aesthetic	Arts, craft and music
Head	Cognition	Literary	Languages and literature
Heart	Affection	Spiritual	Humanities, Religion, Morality, and Philosophy

There should, however, be no hard and fast lines of demarcation. There should rather be complete integration of experiences and contents under the co-operative control of teachers, pupils, parents and others, concerned with the education of children.

Experience and Traditional Curriculum Differentiated

As it has been already discussed, the traditional curriculum laying stress on the subject matter, is meant to serve the needs of the adult life. On the other hand, experience curriculum is a "series of purposeful experiences, growing out of pupil's interest and moving towards an ever-more adequate understanding of an intelligent partcipation in the surrounding culture and group life." Thus, it is clear that these are two extreme types of curriculum.

Hopkins has made an attempt to analyse these two extreme types of curriculum and bring out the salient point of difference between them. His characterization of the type is indeed very useful and profitable. It is, in fact, a masterly analysis of the philosophies, and therefore, I take the liberty of producing it rather extensively. The differences as stated by him are as follows :

Subject Curriculum	*Experience Curriculum*
1. Centred in the subjects.	1. Centred in the learners.
2. Emphasises upon teaching subject matter.	2. Emphasises upon promoting the all-round growth of the learners.
3. Subject matter selected and organized before the teaching situation.	3. Subject matter selected and organised co-operatively by all learners during the learning situation.
4. Controlled by the teacher or some one representing authority, external to the learning situation.	4. Controlled and directed co-operatively by learners *i.e.*, pupils, teachers, parents, supervisors, principals and others related to the learning situations.
5. Emphasis upon teaching facts, imparting	5. Emphasis upon meaning which will function

Subject Curriculum	*Experience Curriculum*
information, acquiring knowledge for its own sake or for possible future use.	immediately in improving the living.
6. Emphasis upon improving method of teaching subject matter of specific subjects.	6. Emphasis upon understanding and improving through process of learning.
7. Emphasis upon teaching specific habits and skills as separate and isolated aspects of learning.	7. Emphasis upon building habits and skills as integrated parts of larger experiences.
8. Emphasis upon uniformity of exposure to learning situation and in so far as possible uniformity of results.	8. Emphasis upon variability in exposures to learning situation and variability in results expected and achieved.
9. Education as conforming to the patterns set by the curriculum and its various associated instruments.	9. Education as aiding each child build creative individuality.
10. Education considered as schooling.	10. Education considered as a continuous, intelligent process of growth.

The Undifferntiated Curriculum

Differentiation means specialization and undifferentiation is the opposite of specialization. "Undifferentiated curriculum therefore, means a curriculum which does not aim at the specialised study of varied subjects."

It is universally admitted that except the learning tools and certain elementary skills, it is not the factual knowledge which is important. Rather the application of knowledge, 'how to use books', 'how to study', 'what to study', is more important.

Selected and organised collectively by all the learners during the learning situation, it is controlled and directed co-operatively by learners, teachers, parents and others concerned with learning, it lays emphasis upon meanings which will function immediately in improving living. It emphasises building habits and skills as integral parts of the learner's experience. There is emphasis upon understanding and improving through the process of learning. It lays stress upon variability in exposure to learning situations and variability in the results expected and achieved. To make a wholesome curriculum, it should not lay more stress upon study of traditional subjects only. Activities must find due place for their own purpose, besides being a tool of the past epitomized experience only. Psychological and physical considerations necessitate that attitude.

"Apart from the minimum essential facts which all must learn, the important thing for the pupils is to leave the school with their curiosity permanently stirred, with the desire to experiment aroused and with a knowledge of how to find out facts, how to think logically, and with a knowledge of how to assess and weigh up evidence and how to live and work with others." This cannot be achieved through piecemeal accumulation of the knowledge. This is the way of dealing with actual problems of life. It is possible through complete knowledge. This can be done only if integration or unification of subjects takes place. The school subjects are integrated with the activities of the society and all the experiences of the child are integrated both horizontally and vertically with all the experiences of the standards and also all the experiences of all the standards or stages.

It was Herbart, who first attempted to secure better integration of the curriculum through correlation. In Basic Education great emphasis is laid upon correlation with the craft and environment, both physical and social and also within the subjects. Correlation facilitates arrangement of subjects. Whenever there is an opportunity, the subjects are inter-related with each other and also with craft or environment. For example while teaching History, topic may emanate from environment, but there may be many opportunities or possibilities for correlating it with Geography, Civics, Literature or Art. In such a case subject barriers and water-tight compartments are neither recognised nor maintained and there are constant cross-references to bring out the implications of the one or the other.

Integration goes a step further. Unlike correlation here subject arrangement becomes quite important. Barriers are frequently crossed and re-crossed. The subjects are so mixed that they appear to be one complete whole of knowledge. But the subjects can be segregated when desired. In fusion this segregation becomes difficult.

The curriculam ranging from subject to experience have been suggested. If we place them on two ends, a scale of various curriculum patterns can be drawn up, which will be like this:

1. Subject curri-culum	(*a*) Correlated curriculum	Broad field curriculum	Units of work curriculum	Experience curriculum
	(*b*) Core-curri-culum	Subject type	Function of social life	
	(*c*) Fused curri-culum	Experience	type	

Undifferentiated curriculum is near to fused curriculum, which aims at re-organizing old subjects around new unifying centres. Some examples of fused subjects are Social Studies, General Science and General Mathematics. But these are to be studied at later primary and junior high school stage. At lower primary stage, complete integration, including that of subjects which is a thing of higher attainment, cannot be aspired. The undifferentiation will be the general rule.

The differentiation or specialization comes slowly as we grow in stages. In the beginning, the whole curriculum must remain undifferentiated and the stress must be laid upon the inculcation of worth while habits, skills and virtues. These habits are not created by the study of different subjects. They are the results of cumulative experience and knowledge provided by the school and environment. Also the child does not learn everything in the school. He comes to the school with some experiences or activities. The very base of these activities lies in the home, the environment from which the child has learnt these attitudes and standards before coming to the school. We cannot neglect that influence particularly when it contributes for the very aim of education, *i.e.* the development of fuller and all-round personality which is possible through the integrated experience. But it is difficult to be provided by the school. The only possible means to bring about this integration is through unification of subjects and activities.

But this arrangement cannot be carried on beyond the primary stage. The psychology of adolescence requires special dealing and deep study of certain branches of knowledge. Also at primary stage, the interest and natural activities of the children are to be taken into consideration. This leads to "some analysis of human experience as a whole, and decides what experiences the child will most profitably undergo in school and this will always involve a certain amount of division of the curriculum into activities that are more or less separate from one another." Thus, the best method is to follow this plan.

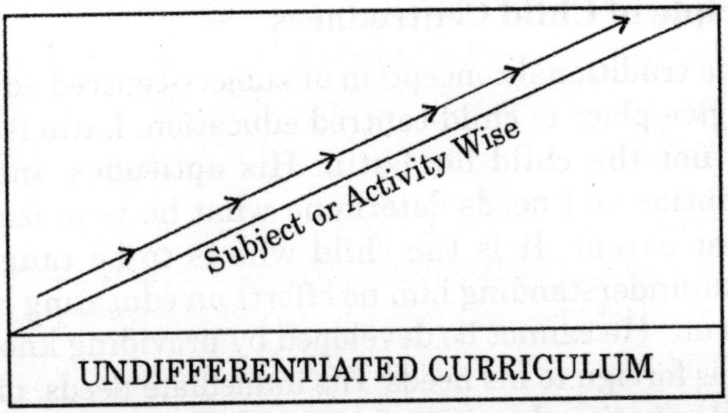

PRINCIPLES OF CURRICULUM CONSTRUCTION

The modern trend in education is diversion from traditional bookish knowledge which is readymade, distasteful mixture, prepared in most cases by the politicians and administrators, neglecting the child for whom it is meant, for the purpose of attainment of certain standards and values. Now we aim at fuller development of the child, body, mind and spirit. We wish to develop his capabilities, potentialities, aptitudes, tastes and interests which are different in children from different walks of life and from different parentage. We wish to draw out of each individual what is the best in him. The regimentation of the students in one type of produce, through the introduction of prescribed courses has to give place to realization of individual differences and development accordingly. Now the call is to make curriculum life-centric.

Education is to be for life and through living. This means that the present life of the child is to be fully developed and through that the child is to be prepared for adult life also. The medium of development is to be living experience of the child with his environment—social and physical—and not the dead and chilly words of the books. For this, we will have to draw certain principles on which the curriculum is to be drawn. They are as follows :

Principle of Child Centredness

The traditional conception of subject-centred education must give place to child-centred education. Latin is for the child, not the child for Latin. His aptitudes, interests, capabilities and needs determine what he is to learn and to what extent. It is the child who is to be taught and without understanding him no efforts on educating him can bear fruit. He cannot be developed by providing knowledge which is foreign to his needs. His immediate needs, physical, mental, emotional, spiritual and social, must be made the basis for imparting knowledge. "Education...regards the child as an individual growing by his own activities, living in his environment and preparing himself for adult life not by imitating the adult but living as fully as possible in the environment of childhood." This opens the matter to question. How to provide environment to the students from different walks of life in the school, particularly in democracies where differences are little recognised. The only way to do so is to provide ample opportunities for activities according to the tastes of the individual in the school and to make curriculum as broad-based as possible. The activities must be made the centres around which the knowledge of the subjects must revolve in variation according to the needs and interests of the child, as is done in Basic Education.

Principle of Activity

This is an another principle, underlying curriculum construction. The child is to be provided with activities for the purpose of learning. The child is active by nature. He wants to make or construct things by himself, to satisfy his instinct of constructiveness and that of self-assertion. That is why, learning by doing is considered as the best method of educating the child. The child's growth, through continuous process of activity, resulting in training of hand, eye and other organs of the body and mind, is facilitated. Hence, in order to stimulate growth at a particular stage of development, activities must be introduced in the curriculum appropriate to the particular stage.

But the activity is not to be introduced for its own sake, only to become frivolous play. It must "lead continuously from their-responsible frolic of childhood to the disciplined labours of manhood." To make education really life-centric, the activity must be purposeful and productive as in Basic Education. John Dewey, both for practical and philosophical considerations, wants to "utilize various forms of occupations typifying social calling." For their intellectual and moral content, the school is to be a miniature social group for active experience. Since "play-ground, shops, workrooms and laboratories, not only direct the natural, active tendencies of youth but they involve inter-course, communication and co-operation."

Principle of Integration

The library, class-room, laboratory, workshop, play-ground and the numerous informal contacts between the teacher and the taught and the community and the child are all educative and help to evolve all-round personality of the child. But they specifically and specially influence the body, mind and heart of the child. This specific work will definitely create lopsidedness in the personality as a whole. Therefore, taking curriculum in terms of totality of experiences, we must aim at its integration to remove this defect. This will bring out integrated personality and at the same time remove false distinction between curricular and co-curricular activities and the life of the child will become the true medium of education.

Principle of Community Centredness

But the child is not to live the life by himself. He is essentially a social being. His capabilities, interests and needs find development in the society and for the society. We cannot neglect his social side merely for the sake of individuality. He is conscious of social rights and liabilities. Without that, social life would be impossible and man will become a beast. Education for life cannot neglect this aspect of the child. He is to be prepared for the present social living and the future adult social leadership.

Principle of Forward Looking

The community centredness leads to the principle of preparation for the future life. We look forward to act in adulthood in future. The foundation for the future of the child has to be laid down. But in the fast-changing scientific age, it is difficult to predict what part is to be played in society, therefore the child must be prepared for the dubious future, otherwise the equipment cannot be ensured. From the child's point of view, of course, we can rest upon the principle of continuity. If life is well-lived at one particular stage, that lays strong foundation for the next stage. Hence the development of the present possibilities in succession is the best method for preparation for the future. If the child has faced squarely the present problems he can surely face them in future. The future emerges out of the present and is in continuation with it.

"What a child learns in the present must help him to adjust himself to conditions of living in this world and must further give him a foundation of knowledge, feeling and willing, which will enable those conditions when they need changing," says W.M. Ryburn. The spokesman of the Board of Education, London said, "Our attitude towards the curriculum has been influenced by a desire to assist children to acquire or develop the habits, skills, interests and sentiments which they will need both for their own living and for that of the people among whom they will live."

Principle of Conservativeness

The preparation for adult life in the community takes us to the principle of conservation of traditions, folk ways, mores, experiences and the heritage of the past. Adulthood stands for the values of the society as does childhood for play. If the child is to be prepared for that life, the heritage, traditions and social values must find place in the curriculum of the school. The society carries the educational enterprise only for its own preservation. Also for the development of the individuality, the child has to have experiences with the conditions in the community, which are already fixed for him. For that also the community's heritage becomes part of the child's education. "All round education is meant to our generation to take up the burden of the previous one and to keep up the life of the community without breach or disaster. The burden of social life is continuous and if at any stage our generation gets completely out of touch with the efforts if its predecessors or in any way gets ashamed of itself or its culture, it is lost." (Book of suggestions for Teachers, Board of Education, London). "It is in fact being increasingly recognised that the various subjects of the curriculum represent certain forms of skill and certain branches of knowledge, which have proved to be of importance to the experience of the race, and which have to be taught to each succeeding generation. From this point of view this the function of the school to preserve and transmit the tradition, knowledge and standards of conduct on which our civilization depends."

But every past experience cannot be carried on. There are dogmas, superstitions, prejudices and unscientific-attitudes. Much becomes obsolete in the context of changed circumstances. Therefore, selective attitude must be blended with the conservative. What does not serve our purpose in the present, must be shattered or modified and the new added. But this must be done cautiously.

Principle of Creativity

This addition too and modification of the past heritage brings us to the principle of creativity. New values emerge in new circumstances and old values beign to leave their hold. In order to prepare the child for life, he must be equipped for ready adjustment to the changing conditions and to evolve new values. This can be done by allowing the child to exercise his creative and constructive powers at present to make him an intelligent creator and modifier of environment and values which he can use in later life to create new things in future according to the needs of the time.

As life is not confined, to one aspect or one period of the whole individual living, all these principles have to be taken into consideration for making curriculum for life-centred education, which aims at all-round development of the personality. The economic, social, cultural, moral, psychological, emotional and aesthetic aspects all make a demand on the individual. For such development, activities and experiences of all sorts must be taken into consideration and provided for. But they must be for the child and not the child for them. The child should never be left without them to handicap or retard his growth. He must make the best use of his leisure also. His urge for activities must be made use of for creative purposes and preparation for the adult life. Also his personality must be integrated by making education child-centred and for the welfare of the child.

Principle of Individual Needs and Interests

The traditional curriculum does not enable the child to be actively free and a worthy member of the society. It does not take into consideration his individual needs and interests. It neglects the child totally which is the main centre of education. Now the circumstances and the conditions have changed. Consequently the new educational system, has also taken a new form. The shift has gone now from subject or teacher to the child in the method and practice of teaching. It is the child for whom education is planned and the child does not exists for the education. The educative process takes into consideration, the age, the interests and the needs of the child. If we do not know the nature of the child and his needs, framing the curriculum is as futile as to prescribe medicine for the patient whose disease a doctor does not know. Thus, the subjects of curriculum must be selected in the light of the knowledge of child nature. If we wish a child to live fully at any stage, we must pay attention to what interests him at that stage. What special attitudes he is likely to have, what is likely to appeal to him, what advantages he will take of the dominant instinctive tendencies of the stage. "Education... regards the child as an individual growing by his own environment and preparing himself for adult life, not by imitating the adults but by living as fully as possible in the environment of childhood," said F. Smith and A. Harrison.

Recent developments in Educational Psychology have made it clear that learning is essentially a need-centred process and a goal seeking activity. It is a cycle process which begins with the stimulation of need in the learner and ends with its satisfaction. In the words of Professor H.R. Hamley, "It is a persistent and continuous process which takes many forms in response to many needs."

These important contributions in respect of the changed concept of learning and better understanding of children have gone a long way in changing, rather revolutionising our concept of the curriculum. Instead of starting with the cultural heritage to be put across the children, so as to be mastered by them or preparing them for a future life, we start with the children as we find them discover their needs, and try to meet them in the best possible manner. These needs are not mental or intellectual needs only, but include physical, social and spiritual needs also. The physical needs mainly mean a mastery over the movements of the body mechanism. This is essential if a child has to find his own way in this world. The social needs of children originate from their gregarious tendencies which are the very foundation of their social life and of their personal relationship with their fellow beings. The physical and social needs do not exhaust the entire store of a child's needs. He has a craving for a particular kind of inner satisfaction which leads to the creation of spiritual needs and these have also to be satisfied. The mental needs lead the child to understand the world around.

As needs and interests go together, we have to take interests also into consideration. Dewey gives four-fold analysis of the natural interests of the child. "The interest in conversation or communication, in enquiry or finding out things, in making things or construction and in artistic expression." These are the natural resources, un-invested capital upon the exercise of which depends the active growth of the child.

The above mentioned needs and interests are personal to every child and their degree of intensity is also different in different cases and at different times. Moreover the learning capacity of each individual is also peculiar to himself and not uniform with others. It follows from these two principles that a curriculum, intended to serve the needs of a community, must be very elastic and flexible. It has to vary from locality to locality, from school to school, from teacher to teacher and even from individual to individual. If it is rigid, mechanical or superimposed from the above, in the form of detailed outlines, it will meet with failure and defeat its own purpose. It has to be elastic so that changes and variations may be made in it, keeping in view the needs of the individual at present and at different stages of his development and the requirements of the environment in which he is placed. Hence, it is not only desirable but should also be possible to have only a general frame work of learning, leaving enough scope thereby, for changes or variations considered necessary to suit individual needs, requirements and circumstances.

This has all the more been made necessary with the emergence of democracy. In democracy generally the education is made free and compulsory by law, as is the case of India. The students are drawn from different walks of life. They have different ways of living, environments, cultural norms, tastes, ideals, aptitudes, capacities and needs. Democracy does not provide different status to different persons in social life. All have to learn together, to reduce disparities and to have lessons in co-operation. Under such circumstances to provide opportunities for the fuller development of the individual personalities and to realize their differences the only way seems to lie in flexibility and broad-based curriculum.

Viewed thus, the concept of the curriculum becomes very broad and fluid. Spontaneity becomes its watch-word and any sort of pre-determination or rigidity is dis-approved, disliked and discarded. Besides, it emphasises on the attitudes more than acquiring knowledge or skill and even that in the spirit of freedom combined with maximum of self-direction and self-determination.

It has been suggested above that the curriculum should be child-centred and that it must be based on the present needs, requirements and circumstances of the child. This is the first and most important principle of curriculum construction. But it is not enough by itself. The curriculum should not only be based on psychology of the child, it must have social relevance also. This is so because in thinking and in planning for children, we must keep two facts in mind. Of these two facts, the first is that each child is an individual and must be treated as such. Secondly, he will always have to live with other individuals, and therefore, it is just desirable that, as far as possible, his needs and desires must harmonise with the needs and desires of those amongst whom he has to live.

To sum up, the curriculum must have individual relevance. When education was considered identical with the imposition of knowledge upon the child, the question of individual relevance did not arise. The child was regarded as a passive agent in education. He was to be prepared for his future life and moulded and disciplined as the teacher though+ fit. The curriculum could, thus, be settled in advance, for the pupils and the arrangement of the curriculum was, therefore, logical rather than psychological. The area of knowledge to be acquired and the logical steps to be taken for the purpose were determined in advance without any reference to the pupils. But Educational psychology has proved that teaching may not necessarily result in learning, because learning cannot be successful without interest, spontaneity and free initiative on the part of the learner. Hence the curriculum must be child-centred. It should be based on the present needs of the child. In fact, every activity undertaken in the school should suit the age, intellectual ability and the level of attainment of the pupils. Moreover, it should be meaningful to the pupils, and as far as possible, should be voluntarily selected by them. Every activity in it must have connection with one or more felt needs of the pupils.

The latest trend in education is not to approach the curriculum in terms of activities. According to this curriculum, the nouns of subjects will be coverted into verbs of activities. Hence the activity curriculum is to develop a spirit of scientific enquiry and problem-solving attitude so that children may be able to form independent judgment. The Wardha Education Committee says, "We have attempted to draft an activity curriculum which implies that our schools must be places of work, experimentation and discovery not of passive absorption of information imparted at second hand." We can base activity-curriculum upon physical activities, environmental activities, constructive activities, creative activities, imaginative activities, community activities and tool subjects. Here, the needs of the child will be integrated with different activities in the curriculum. It should, however, be realised that the activities of life are complicated enough to require the services of accumulated experiences of the human race for their successful completion and understanding. But, the knowledge of that experience is to be given through activities and the difficulty which arises in this type of curriculum is that every subject cannot be taught through activity.

Inspired by the philosophy of Herbart, Ziller suggested concentrated curriculum. This plan suggests the making of a particular subject as the core or the pivot of study, the other subjects being studied in relation to it. The Basic-curriculum is based on this principle. According to this principle the curriculum is pychologised, socialised and also integrated. In the Basic-curriculum, the handicraft is the pivot around which the teaching of other subjects like Mathematics, History, Geography, Nature Study etc. should revolve. Inspite of its so many advantages, it also suffers from certain drawbacks. It lays stress upon the craft in place of the child, it fails to provide for individual differences, it emphasises impracticable self-supporting aspect and provides for the choice of special optional too early.

BASIC CURRICULUM

The framers of curriculum for Basic Education had in mind the creation of a new co-operative-society and helping of the individual to adjust actively and intelligently to the new and changed circumstances. They psychologically socialized and also integrated the curriculum for this purpose, and prescribed (*i*) Basic-Craft (*ii*) Mother-Tongue (*iii*) Mathematics (*iv*) Social-Studies (*v*) General Science (*vi*) Arts and Music as subjects of study. Thus, they gave it a definite orientation, laid stress upon practical aspects of education and tried to develop national consciousness. In all fields of study emphasis has been placed on developing social and co-operative attitude so that a child may become a fit citizen of the new society which will be based upon co-operation and non-violence. It has gone to the extent of subordination of cultural values to the basic needs of the poverty-stricken Indians. Thus, it has the essential features of scientific education. True, education should be organised, co-ordinated and integrated around dominant interests. And in India, "the dominant interest is two-fold; the promotion of livelihood including the standard of living in the comprehensive sense of the term and the inculcation of civic-responsibility." By developing national consciousness, the curriculum has created interest in the culture of the people but has kept in abeyance narrow nationalism and aggressive imperialism.

Advantages of Basic Curriculum

The advantages of such a curriculum are many and varied :

It respects the freedom of the child : As the curriculum is not purely academic, theoretical and bookish and provides for the direct experience of the children through activity, it does not impose adult standards upon the minds of the children. It provides for the interests and needs of the children and is psychologically best suited to their nature and capacities.

It provides for the all-round growth : Unlike the traditional Education, it does not emphasise mental development only. It trains the hand, heart and head of the child simultaneously. It unites theoretical and practical experiences. The child achieves "the literacy of the whole personality."

It helps to achieve social unity : The society is torn up in different groups. By keeping the child engaged in productive work, the social distinctions of caste, colour, creed, wealth or occupation are removed. Basic Education emphasizes the dignity of labour, develops ethical and moral character and brings about human unity in the true sense. There is free sharing of interests and purposes and society becomes democratic.

It helps to imporve vocational competency : The Basic craft if carried on intelligently and in the right spirit will increase the productive capacity of the learners. It will teach proper utilisation of leisure besides providing a means of subsistence on a post school career. The skilled and trained student of a Basic School can be economically self-sufficient and socially self-reliant.

It brings the school and the community together: As school programme provides community service, it provides chances to the students to realise the problems of the community. Also by stimulating interests and satisfying needs related to the community and environment, it converts the school into a factory for the manufacture of the parts which constitute the machinery of community living. Thus the school becomes a miniature society.

Disadvantages of Basic-Curriculum

There are many drawbacks of this scheme which have already been discussed. A few are given below:

The curriculum centres upon craft in place of the child : Craft-centred curriculum leaves many gaps in the child's knowledge as correlation is not possible for each topic. It often becomes forced and artificial. Also the emphasis upon vocational aspect is too early and it neglects the child's immediate needs and interests.

The curriculum does not have provision for religious education : Admitted that a secular state like India cannot preach any religion, but miseries and sufferings of the world necessitate spiritual progress in this materialistic era. A desire for the inculcation of absolute values ought to be created in the pupils through common fundamentals of all the religions.

The self-supporting aspect is impracticable : India needs earning while learning, but it is not possible to the extent of complete self-sufficiency. Craft has great educational possibilities and can be used well for this purpose, but to expect economic emancipation from it is too high an ideal.

Choice of special options is too early : Basic curriculum provides many options in the choice of crafts from which a child has to choose one. But at this stage, it is premature to expect a child to decide the matter for ever. Early childhood must be concerned more with general development than with specialization.

It fails to provide for individual differences of the pupils : Basic education prescribes a few adult-chosen subjects without caring for the individual nature, needs, interests or capabilities of the children. There is no provision for their individual differences and so equality of opportunity is not achieved and the blunders of traditional education continue to harm the individuality of the child. But, it is due to inefficient teachers. The theory of Basic Education takes into consideration and also provides chances for equal opportunities for individual development.

WHICH IS THE BEST CURRICULUM?

Now, the question arises, which is the best curriculum? It is a very complicated question and is beyond the capacity of the individual to decide as to which is the best one. From the study of the above, we have have come to know that every curriculum suffers from certain defects. The other problem of the curriculum, with which we are confronted, is that one type of curriculum has laid too much emphasis upon one aspect only. For example, the child-centred curriculum lays too much stress on the education related to the child-life. It is desirable, no doubt, but it has neglected the society and its heritage. The same argument applies everywhere. Therefore, by taking the good points from all the above mentioned curricula, a synthetic curriculum should be prepared which the teacher like a doctor may apply to the educational system for his patient.

To attain this ideal, the curriculum should be made flexible, spontaneous, broad-based, child-centred, community-centred, activity and also experience-centred. The shortcomings of experience-curriculum are absent in child-centred curriculum. But we cannot neglect the community and its heritage. Thus the best suggested curriculum would be the *broad-based curriculum, a fusion of both—the subject type and the experience* type.

We can conclude in the words of Ryburn, "Apart from the essential minimum of facts which all must learn, the important thing is for pupils to leave school with their curiosity permanently stirred, with the desire to experiment aroused, and with a knowledge of how to find out facts, how to use books, how to study, how to think logically, how to assess and weigh up evidence and how to live and work with others. Hence in framing a curriculum we need not have every subject under the sun included in it. We can include representative subjects. We can aim at opening up paths of future intellectual adventure, rather than seeking to give pupils a large amount of factual knowledge in every subject they take."

5

Methods of Teaching

We have already discussed, the aims and objectives of education and the curriculum which aims at achieving those aims and objectives. The curriculum is to be given to the pupils and for this purpose some methods of teaching are required. In this chapter, we propose to discuss various methods of teachings.

TEXTBOOK METHOD

Textbook method may be defined as "that teaching procedure in which the mastery of the textbook is the immediate objective". This is not an improper or unworthy objective, as some people may think it to be. It means that this is the procedure which "revolves around the textbook just as another procedure might revolve around the problem or the project."[1] However, within the limits of the textbook method, we may find good as well as bad teaching. Since the textbook is very widely used, it is highly desirable on the part of the teacher to utilize it to the best advantage of his pupils.

Textbook is a very useful means of getting concise and up-to-date information. An oral lesson on the other hand, may become lengthy, complicated and unintelligible. In a textbook, the subject matter is logically and systematically arranged for the students. As such, it gives the minimum essentials and enables them to work out problems and projects and also pursue further discussion.

The textbook procedure may, however, become very undesirable if the teacher bases all of his teaching upon a single textbook. The procedure, generally followed in schools is that the teacher or one of the students, reads the textbook in the class. Difficult words and sentences are explained by the teacher and other flaws in reading and pronunciation are removed. This may be a suitable procedure in language teaching. But this is highly objectionable in case of Social Studies. If this is the textbook method of teaching Social Studies, it should be discarded forthwith. Only a judicious use of a Social Studies textbook should be made, both by the teacher and the student. Textbook is not an end in itself. It is only one of the means. In this sense we may say that in fact, textbook method is no method of teaching Social Studies. A textbook is only an effective aid and must be taken as such. One textbook should never be completely depended upon. Other textbooks, references and resources should also be consulted to supplement the subject matter given in one particular textbook. The teacher should also tell his students how to make the best use of a textbook. He should give a demonstration himself, along with his comments and then ask the students to follow that manner.

Advantages of the Textbook

1. Meets the needs of the students : A textbook is written from the students point of view, recognizing their limitations. It, therefore, meets their requirements by the use of simple language, headings, sub-heading, questions, assignments, maps, charts, pictures and other illustrative material.

2. Helps in developing study skills : A textbook provides a common basis on which the process of reading, analysing, outlining and summarising can be mastered. It, thus, furnishes a common laboratory in which study skills can be developed. The student forms the habit of studying the textbook independently at home and understanding its content.

3. Gives an accurate account of the subject : A textbook gives a reasonably correct account of the subject field or area in an organised manner. Its treatment is logical and systematic. It is, therefore, very useful for the pupils.

4. Suggests application of the material : A textbook also suggests application of the subject matter, through assignments, drills, questions, projects and other activities.

5. Reflects and establishes standards : A textbook indicates what the teacher is required to teach and what the pupils are supposed to learn. Thus, by its teaching and learning aids, it greatly affects methods and reflects and establishes the standards of scholarship. It furnishes a definite basis for specific assignments, problems and projects. So the teacher can easily establish class as well as individual standards.

6. Expands and limits its scope and size according to needs : A textbook can expand and delimit its scope, size and content according to the changing needs of education. Thus, it may sometimes lead and sometimes follow the educational process.

7. Can serve as basis of other methods : Almost all other methods can be used with the textbooks as a basis of study. Thus, assignment procedure or telling and discussion method or even problem, project and unit methods can be used effectively with the help of a textbook.

8. Presents different and opposing points of view on historical and current events : A textbook presents history and current affairs in such a way as to help pupils to develop an appreciation of different points of view.

9. Presents content relating to human relationship: A social studies textbook gives an accurate account of our environment, the values and principles which guide our actions and the processes through which we hope to improve ourselves. It, thus, helps in improving the physical and mental well-being of our pupils.

Limitations of the Textbook

1. Memorisation : Pupils generally memorise textbook word for word and reproduce the same in black and white at the time of examination. They accept blindly what is given in the textbook and feel that it contains all the needed information and knowledge. This attitude is very dangerous. However, an enriched scholarship on the part of the teacher can be a suitable guarantee against this danger.

2. Possibility of errors : As the whole field of the subject matter in a textbook is to be condensed and encompassed by an author to meet the requirements of students, there is a possibility of errors of detail of interpretation. The defect can also be removed if the teacher is competent enough to correct and counteract prejudiced interpretations.

3. Contains only minimum essential : A textbook contains only a summary treatment of the subject-matter. It does not give lively details and thus leaves a lot to be done by the teacher, without whose planning and direction the students cannot derive full advantage of the textbook.

4. Complete domination of the textbook : A textbook, because of its definite and convenient subject-matter may dominate the entire procedure of teaching. The students and teachers may fall into the rut of covering a certain number of pages and thus drift into the habit of routine procedure. They may accept anything that they see in print. This danger can also be overcome by the utilization of other aids besides the textbook.

Conclusion

Thus, we may conclude that too much reliance and emphasis upon the textbook should not be placed because the textbook method is not a complete method in itself. In order to reap its best advantage, teacher should make a liberal use of the lecture method and other devices and also the generous utilization of supplementary references, maps, charts, pictures and other aids and material. In case of classes where a single textbook is used, the pupils should be encouraged to make use of a variety of supplementary material, according to their interests and abilities. Assignments should be given to meet individual differences and to facilitate learning. Each such assignment should be challenging so as to motivate the pupil for self-activity in learning and self-study.

It should, however, be clearly noted that textbooks are not the panacea for all ills. Effectiveness depends upon the ways in which the teacher uses them. On the other hand, they represent the best course of information and suggest activities organised for the specific purposes of a Social Studies programme.

LECTURE METHOD

The most common and believed to be quite easy and effective teacher-directed method of teaching is lecture method. All lectureres in colleges and universities use this method invariably. Some teachers in India also use this method for teaching senior secondary classes, as they find it very convenient. However, many of the teachers in schools as well as colleges really do not know how to use the lecture method effectively. They also do not know that it is not very useful method for schools.

For effective use of the lecture method, it is desirable that the lecturer or the teacher keeps the following points in mind :

There are three phases or steps in delivering a lecture:

1. Introduction of the Lecture
2. Development Phase
3. Consolidation Phase

Introduction of the Lecture

The teacher must select the topic and plan properly what contents he would like to include in his lecture. Then he should put them in a systematic or logical order and decide how he would present them and when – in the beginning, in the middle or in the end. He should start the lecture in such way that the students may easily and instantly get attracted towards it; they may be interested in listening to it with rapt attention. He should introduce the topic with some interesting related questions or with the mention of some recent news, catchy story or anecdote or description of an event or the like.

Development Phase

In this phase, the teacher should present the subject-matter related to the topic of his lecture in a lively manner with effective voice and use one or more teaching aids and illustrations like picture, map, chart, model etc. systematically. He should develop his lesson gradually and very effectively in the manner as had already been planned by him. He should ensure that the students' interest is sustained throughout the lecture and they are indeed able to gather the necessary information. He should ask some questions in the course of his lecture.

Consolidation Phase

The teacher should summarize the main points of his lecture towards the end. He should recapitulate or recall the main points briefly so that the students can recall and remember them. This can be done by asking some questions to know how much of the lecture the students have been able to understand and remember the subject matter. If the teacher finishes his lecture abruptly or suddenly without asking recapitulation questions, then the students might not be able to understand clearly the main points and their inter-relationship.

A good or effective lecture should have these features:

1. Lecture should contain new information and it should be delivered in a lively manner.

2. The lecturer or the teacher should speak in a well-modulated and clear voice.

3. The teacher or the lecturer should ask a few questions to the students in between the lecture and try to elicit their knowledge, information, experiences and/or views. He should appreciate them and properly assimilate or integrate them in his lecture.

4. The teacher should try to show some interesting and relevant picture, map, diagram, model or real object, or use any of the teaching aids like filmstrip, tape recorder, VCR, DVD etc. so that the listeners' attention is drawn towards his lecture points.

5. The lecture should neither be too long nor it should be of a very high level or in a difficult, incomprehensive or terse language.

6. The teacher should use humour also once or twice (not more often) to create a pleasant environment, to break the boredom and keep the listeners' attention glued to his lecture.

7. The teacher should not lecture in a threatening or commanding voice. He should not be provoked, angry and offensive if any student in the lecture room asks him a question. He should reply the students' question/s in a polite, amiable and gentle manner.

8. It is a good idea if the synopsis or a very brief summary of the lecture in points is given by the lecturer to the students a day or a few days in advance before the lecture so that the students may come to the class to listen to the lecture having read that synopsis. This definitely helps them better in understanding the lecture.

Advantages of Lecture Method

If used properly with care, Lecture Method shall have definite advantages, some of which may be stated as under :

1. Spoken word more effective than a printed one: It is a fact that a spoken word is always more effective than a printed one. The teacher can indicate by his tone, gesture and facial expression the exact sense or a meaning which he wishes to convey. He can dramatise a scene, a story or a message he wishes to convey. Thus, his lecture can have that colour and vividness which a printed book cannot.

2. A lecture can be immediately repeated and modified : Whenever the teacher feels that his idea not being followed or appreciated by his pupils, he can at once repeat it or expand and modify his statement. A sensible teacher would never like to "talk over the head" of his pupils.

3. It gives pupils good training and experience in learning by hearing : In democratic countries we have to train children in schools for the adult life so that as democratic citizens they may participate fully and effectively in the affairs of national and international importance. And as we all know lectures and talks play an important part in one's adult life these days whether we lead or follow others. For this children are to be prepared from the school stage. Thus, occasional talks and interesting lectures should be arranged for all types of school children.

4. It saves time and energy of the pupils : Sometimes facts of Social Studies, because of their complicated nature, are not clear to students as they read their textbooks. In textbooks, details are seldom given and sometimes interpretations may also be wrong. The students may, thus, be lost in the maze of facts. They may spend uselessly, a lot of their valuable time and energy in going through other sources for the clarification of such complicated points. In that case a well-presented talk by the teacher is most helpful.

5. It is a good means of stimulating students : Since lecture demands a lot of preparation on the part of the teacher, its advantages are transferred to the class as a whole. Teacher's own preparation, his enthusiasm and his interest do stimulate good students who may, therefore, like to pursue projects, problems and other such activities in order to gain more and more knowledge.

When to use this Method?

This method may, however, be used with advantage only on suitable occasions for :

1. **Stimulating students :** In the beginning of a new topic or unit we can stimulate our pupils by presenting the outstanding aspects of the events or movements or the achievements of significant persons in very simple and easy words. This will arouse interest among the pupils and they will like to know more about that topic.

2. **Clarifying concepts :** If the students are not helped in time, they may form wrong notions after memorizing certain facts from the books without understanding their meaning and importance. The teacher, through an informal talk, should correct such wrong notions and clarify the pupils' doubts.

3. **Supplementing the knowledge of the pupils :** Whatever amount of study the student may have done, there is always need for further addition of the subject matter by the teacher, as a result of his own reading and experience. This can be done through a talk or lecture on the topic under study.

4. **Summing up the findings of the pupils :** After independent group or individual work, the students may disagree on several points. It may also not be possible for them to outline and summarize the main points of the topic or chapter or unit studied by them. It is then for the teacher to pick up the loose ends and unite them into a presentable whole for the convenience and advantage of his pupils.

5. **Preparing the students to undertake an assignment, a project or an activity :** Before any

assignment or activity or project on group level is undertaken by the pupils, it is always advisable to give them an informal talk. This will save them from unnecessary wastage of time and energy in searching relevant material and guide them to achieve the maximum in the shortest possible time and with the minimum labour.

Limitations of Lecture Method

1. Not a natural way of learning : Lecture Method is not usually considered to be a natural way for the pupils to learn. It places them in the position of passive listeners. They may, thus during the course of the talk, wander off to some more pleasant thoughts and may not attend to the talk at all.

2. Cannot be used effectively by all types of teachers : Many teachers do not know how to lecture in an effective way. They cannot prepare and deliver well-connected and relevant talks on the topic given in the textbook. This method will not succeed when used by such teachers.

3. It means a heavy teaching load on the teachers: A teacher who is required to teach in the school right from the first period upto the last without break, is not expected to lecture in each period. He will neither have the capacity to prepare so many simple and interesting lectures each day, nor it will be physically possible for him to speak continuously for four or five hours a day.

4. Its extensive use is harmful : If used extensively, the lecture method tends to substitute the teacher for the textbook. Thus, only occasional and informal talks are desirable for realising definite purposes in view.

5. It may become monotonous and dull : There are only exceptional teachers who can stimulate interest through their talks at all grade levels. A successful teacher is he who uses a variety of methods and not only one or two of them to avoid dullness and to give effectiveness to his lesson. If only the lecture method is used, the lessons may become dull and dry.

Conclusion

We may conclude by saying that teaching through an informal talk or lecture is "A method and not the method". It should not be used too frequently and too hopefully. It should always be accompanied by illustrations, comparisons, charts, pictures, diagrams and other aids. A talk should always be carefully planned, outlined and mastered before hand. It should be remembered that lecturing is an art. Its successful performance depends upon the teacher's extent and depth of knowledge and upon his awareness of human factors of interest and motivation. A lecture is primarily meant to reinforce key ideas and facts and to place them in a context of thought. It is to present a philosophical whole out of a number of related fragments of information that can be obtained piecemeal by other means, but not put together sensibly without the mature judgement and wisdom of a good teacher. It is, therefore, obvious that lecture method itself is not bad. The real culprit is the bad lecture or the unsuitable topic. After all, people flock by thousands to listen to lectures or talks which are interesting, fascinating, inspiring, informative and exciting. The same type of talks should be presented in the classroom to ensure success.

The teacher may utilize this method profitably for (*i*) giving background of a topic, (*ii*) giving an overview of a large unit, (*iii*) creating interest in the pupils, (*iv*) explaining and correcting some faulty ideas or introducing an intelligent assignment.

LECTURE-CUM-DISCUSSION STRATEGY

Most of the lecturers in colleges and teachers in schools just deliver their lecture in the class and go away. They do not hold discussion on the main points of the lecture, mainly due to shortage of time. But it is desirable to give at least about 10 minutes, just after the lecture, for discussion among students so that their own experiences, comments, views, difficulties in understanding any point of the lecture may come to the fore and the lecturer may know them and reply to them or clarify them. His reply or clarification should be very brief; it must not assume the form of another mini lecture forced upon the students again. As many as possible number of students, at least 3-4, should be given the chance to speak out within the time available and they should be encouraged to participate in the discussion.

This strategy builds an active verbal interaction between the teacher and the pupils and among the pupils themselves. Judged from the psychological as well as sociological points of view, this is indeed a very effective strategy of teaching provided the teacher knows that without proper preparation and mastery in human dynamics this strategy can fizzle out.

Usually, the students sitting on the front benches and those who are very bright or those who are lecturer's favourites dominate in the discussion. The lecturer should encourage other students also to express their views and experiences. This strategy of lecture-cum-discussion needs longer time. Hence it is advisable to combine two periods of the class to hold a proper lecture-cum-discussion.

DISCUSSION METHOD

The present age is an age of discussion. We come to define conclusions and decisions after thorough discussion. This remark may be applicable to discussion on political level. But it is equally applicable to education. Discussion has now come to challenge the authoritarian methods through which education was imparted in old days. In those days the teacher's authority was accepted in all matters. The pupils had little say in the instructional programme. But now the entire literary and non-literary activities, to be carried on, in and outside the classroom, are first discussed in a socialized atmosphere by the teacher and his pupils and then given a practical shape. Discussion may assume the form of a conference, a symposium or a seminar. Herein lies the importance of discussion as a procedure of teaching. But it should be remembered that discussion is not only difficult but also dangerous. Once a subject is put to discussion, we cannot withdraw it, nor we can clothe it again with mystery. The main purpose of discussion is to educate young children in the process of 'group thinking' and 'collective decision'.

Essential Parts or Constituents of a Discussion

The essential parts of a discussion are : A leader, *A* group, A problem and A content.

The leader : The leader, no doubt, is the teacher himself. In organising a discussion, a lot of study, preparation, selection and planning will be done by the teacher while acting as the leader. But the teacher must not dominate the entire scene. Such an attitude will block rather than facilitate the 'meeting of minds'. The teacher should watch carefully while discussion is going on and act as a prompt guide when the pupils are face to face with difficulties.

The group : The group is clearly the students in a Social Studies class. The group is generally composed of all types of temperament and all varieties of minds. There are slow as well as stubborn pupils in the class. The teacher's duty is to encourage every student to participate in the discussion. Even the humblest member of the group should be heard and his contribution appreciated.

The problem : The problem or topic for discussion must be one which the students should feel their own. The problem should be made as precise and exact as possible. The selection of the problem should be made by the teacher with the cooperation of his pupils. It must be real and functional and within the capacity and comprehension of the pupils.

The content : The content is the body of knowledge, the needed material of study. It should also include maps, charts, pictures, diagrams and other audio-visual aids. Facts, of course, cannot be discussed. These may, however, be proved true or false. But propositions, which are "statements about values", can be discussed and their truth established. It is about these statements that difference of opinion arises and discussion takes place.

Evaluation : At the end of the discussion each participant should evaluate whether discussion about that particular problem or topic has added to his knowledge and information, changed his ideas, attitudes and prejudice and increased the range of his interest. A successful discussion must bring in the necessary change and make the participant a more active citizen than before.

It should be remembered that classroom discussion is not an occasion for practising the art of public speaking or skill in debating. "The debater always tries to win an argument. He knows no compromise. Discussion, on the other hand, is a sharing and weighing of all sides, which may be as many as there are conflicting interests of values." The participants in a discussion are inter-related in "a process of competitive cooperation." *Agreement* is the declared purpose of a discussion. It is always organised and undertaken in a disciplined atmosphere. Discussion is an important means of exchanging ideas with others and "often results in pooling opinions and joint action." A good discussion, in fact, is well-planned and well-mannered conversation. As such, every participant in a discussion, must be courteous, clear, good-natured, tolerant and sincere.

Advantages of Discussion Method

Collective decision making : A classroom discussion is an organised process of collective decision-making. It seeks agreement. But if it is not reached, it has the value of clarifying the nature of disagreement.

Gives knowledge : In discussion there is no rote-learning. Definite factual knowledge must be possessed by the participant in discussion, otherwise he will not be able to participate. Then during the course of the discussion very many arguments will be given and listened to, which will definitely add to the information and knowledge, already possessed.

Inculcates tolerance : There must be difference of ideas and understanding. But this difference need not result in disaster. Different people may believe in the same thing differently for different reasons. Participants in a discussion must have the patience to listen to divergent opinion and tolerate arguments contrary to their own.

Conclusion

It should, however, be noted that discussion method is not the only method of teaching Social Studies. It is, of course, one of the methods. But it is successful only with senior students and under the guidance of a capable and hard-working teacher.

PROBLEM SOLVING METHOD

The main purpose of our schools these days is to train pupils to be useful members of our society. This can be possible only when school life is interlinked with social life outside. For the achievement of this aim we create real life situations in the school and the children are equipped to meet these problems, to the best of their ability and capacity. Knowledge, thus, gained becomes useful and purposeful and the child acts as an active participant in the entire process.

Therefore, problem solving is a method in which the felt difficulty to act in an educational situation is realized and then an attempt is made in a conscious, planned and purposeful way to find its solution.

Meanings of Problem Solving Method

According to Good's Dictionary of Education, "A manner of dealing with that which is problematic, a method involving clear definition of problem confronted, formation of hypothetical solution (hunch or suggestion) deliberate test of hypothesis until evidence warrants its acceptance."

According to Risk, "Problem solving may be defined as planned attack upon a difficulty or perplexity for the purpose of finding a satisfactory solution." "Problem solving method", according to Yokam and Simpson, "is a method in which a person uses his ability to solve the problems which confront him, enables a man to exercise control over his activities and his environment. Without it he is at the mercy of nature and cannot make intelligent social progress." According to Ross, "Problem solving is an educational device whereby the teacher and the pupils attempt in a conscious, planned purposeful effort to arrive at an explanation or solution to some educationally significant difficulty."

Outstanding Characteristics of Good Problems

1. It should be a real problem rather than an artificial one.

2. It should be an educationally significant problem, one productive of important and worth while learnings.

3. The solution should be possible, *i.e.,* it should not be too deep for the particular group of students, and specific information needed for solving the problem should be available.

4. The problem should be related to the sub unit, the unit and the course.

6. The children must possess some background of the problem which they are going to solve.

General Principles of Problem-Solving

1. The pupils must feel the problem as their own : The problem must include interest plus *values* to arouse the curiosity of children for finding its solution. The children must feel it worth-while to make efforts for its solution.

2. The problem must be stated definitely : After the pupils have come to feel the problem as their own, the teacher must next-see that it is stated in definite terms. If it is defined clearly, the pupils will be able to keep it in mind while working on the references.

3. Selecting material for problem-solving : The means of solving the problem must not be vague to the pupils, otherwise most of the value of the procedure will be lost. Therefore judicious selection of the material must be made as it may be too vast and complicated in case of many subjects like Social Studies for secondary school students.

4. Solutions must be definite and clear : Many means should be adopted to arrive at definite conclusions. One of the pupils should be asked to summarise the conclusion before the whole class. Then let the other pupils evaluate and criticise it until it is accepted by all. This definiteness of the conclusion or solution must be emphasised. The teacher, then should help the pupils to apply the newly learned principle or skill to some immediate problem situation. The manner of application will depend upon the type of the problem, being solved. Thus problems, become useful and educational and the method pertaining to their solution also serves a useful purpose, if the problems are according to the base of reality, understanding and effect.

Sources of the Problems

1. **Subjects :** Mathematics, science, history, geography, civics, health education provide numerous opportunities for problem solving.

2. School life furnishes many practical problems like, collection of funds for Red-Cross.

3. The students can suggest a problem.

4. The teacher can put a problem before the students, but it should be accepted by the students as their own problem.

Steps in Problem Solving

The following steps should be followed to solve a problem. These steps should not be followed rigidly. They may be adopted according to the needs of the pupils.

1. Raising the Problem : The problem may be stated first and then interest aroused in it. Usually, raising the problem requires considerable questioning and discussion covering the situation out of which the problem will arise. No rigid rule can be followed. The teacher must see that the problem gets before the children in such a way as to arouse their interest and challenge them to study it.

2. Interpreting the Problem : The teacher may explain the problem in detail or the pupils may interpret it through discussion. The age and intelligence of the students should be kept in mind at this stage.

3. Gathering and evaluating Data : After pupils have grasped the meaning of the problem they must then be stimulated together and evaluate data for its solution. The teacher should indicate sources of collecting data. As material and data are collected then it is necessary to evaluate it. Superficial material must be eliminated and only the pertinent data included.

4. Formulating tentative Solutions : All inferences bearing on the data at hand must be considered tentatively. This phase of problem solving demands an unusual amount of guidance and patience on the part of the teacher. He must suggest solutions and inferences in a judicious manner, without injuring the feelings of the students.

5. Verifying the Results : When the class has accepted the conclusion which is most likely to be the best, one step must be taken to prove its correctness. This may be done in a variety of ways :

(*a*) by applying the hypothesis to new situations

(*b*) by experimenting further with it, and

(*c*) by gathering new data through study and investigation.

Role of the Teacher

1. The teacher should create problem situations.

2. The teacher should give assistance in defining, organising, collecting the data and interpreting the data by the students.

3. The teacher should have confidence in them.

Advantages of the Problem Method

1. It conforms to life : Every one is confronted with problems all through life. Training in problem solving in the school, will help the boys to form certain attitudes and skills, so essential for adult life. It, therefore, constitutes a realistic method for presenting the type of experience that will face the pupils throughout their career.

2. Develops the power of critical judgment : Children because of self activity, become interested in their study programme and develop a power of critical judgment. This is of vital importance in a democracy where the success of a government depends upon the judgment of the people.

3. It makes for pupils' activity : The pupils are stimulated to struggle for solutions of certain problems. They are then no longer passive members of a class but active participants.

4. Knowledge easily assimilated : Knowledge is gained as a result of purposeful activity, connected with pupil's everyday life. So it is easily assimilated.

5. Develops the traits of open mindedness and tolerance : The pupils find that there are so many facets of a problem and they listen to different points of view. So they become tolerant in outlook and open-minded in their attitude.

6. It tends to develop initiative and responsibility: The pupils begin to feel that the process is not a task which is assigned but an inevitable requirement of the situation. They, therefore, get a fine chance to think, to judge and evaluate, to compare and select what is the best. In this way it tends to develop their initiative and responsibility.

Limitations of the Problem Method

1. Requires too much reference material : Some problems require too much reference material for their correct solution. All this material may not be available to students. Suitable books are also not available in the school library.

2. Takes too much time : Preparation and initiation of the problem solving procedure may take a considerable portion of the teacher's time. Too much time of the class, may also be consumed by this procedure. So it is not possible to make a continuous use of this method. The teacher has to cover the assigned syllabus in his subject in each term, which may not be possible if he takes to teaching by this method.

3. Tends to become monotonous : If used too frequently, it may become monotonous. It should, therefore, be combined with other procedures.

4. Does not always achieve satisfactory results : Sometimes satisfactory results may not be achieved due to certain factors. In that case the pupils may become dissatisfied and discouraged.

Conclusion

We may conclude by saying that problem solving method can be used profitably on certain occasions at all stages by resourceful and intelligent teachers. A problem can be very simple like a simple question and complicated like a research topic for research scholars; so students must be encouraged from the beginning to think and try how to solve problem successfully which face them at all stages of their life as students and individuals.

With all the above limitations problem solving method develops the ability to criticise suggestions in an open minded and unbiased manner. The ability to plan is developed among the students in this method. They learn what is relevant and what is not from group discussions, because so many sub-problems and unexpected difficulties arise from the discussion of the data collected. All these abilities integrate into the one large ability to think independently.

PROJECT METHOD

The Project Method is a modern contribution to educational theory and practice. It is a result of John Dewey's philosophy of education and is a natural extension of the problem method. But the credit for initiating this method goes to Professor William H. Kilpatrick, who has defined it as "a whole-hearted purposeful activity, proceeding in a social environment." Dr. J.A. Stevenson who perfected it as a method of teaching says, "A project is a problematic act carried to completion in its natural setting." Ballard gives another definition when he says, "A project is a bit of real life that has been imported into the school." In Burton's words, "The problem is a project which results in doing. The motor element is not what makes the activity a project, but the problem-solving of a practical natur accompanying the activity."

According to C.V. Good, "A project is a significant unit of activity, having educational value and aimed at one or more definite goals of understanding. It involves investigation and solution of problems and frequently the use and manipulation of physical materials. It is planned and carried to completion by the pupils and the teacher in a natural lifelike manner".

If we analyse these definitions, we shall come to know that project method lays great stress on the actual action or activity on the part of pupils. Nothing is imposed upon them from without—not even from the teacher, who takes upon himself the duties of an adviser and a guide only. It is a reaction against dull, monotonous, purposeless and lifeless classroom teaching. In this method, the curriculum, content and techniques of teaching are considered from the child's points of view. Thus *'learning by living'* is a better description of the Project Method than *'learning by doing'*.

Philosophy behind Project Method

The basis of Project Method is the Philosophy of Experimentalism which is the outgrowth of the Pragmatism of William James and the Instrumentalism of John Dewey.

It does not impose task from outside, so the object is not to make the pupils a store-house of knowledge. This method has a philosophy of its own. In America, Russia and Europe, this method is used for teaching and the formal teaching is given up. This method encourages a maximum amount of purposeful activity on the part of the children. This activity might be either an intellectual problem or a mechanical manipulation and construction or it may be concerned with physical performances or with appreciation, or with combination of any or all of these elements. This idea of the project method, *i.e.* making boys learn by doing is not a new idea. In the past also, teachers put it into practice although they did not give it a name. Thorn, a philosopher had said long ago, "We should not play life, or study it, but earnestly live it. Youths best learn to live by trying the experiment of living. We should link what is called knowledge with the larger complex called *life*." Boys should not be kept aloof from the activities of life.

Basic Principles or Features of the Project Method

This method is based on the following principles :

The principle of purpose : The method impresses upon pupils the why of doing things in the school. So they put their life and soul in the work. They do not take interest in an activity which is aimless or which is not purposeful.

The principle of activity : A child is active by nature. So opportunities should be provided to the child to be active and to do things for himself. The project method gives ample opportunities to pupils to think and plan things independently and then carry out the project in cooperation with others.

The principle of experience : The child gains knowledge through experience which, in turn, comes through some purposeful activity. The Project Method enables the child to work in groups. He, thus, learns to cooperate with others and to share his interests and purposes. He gets valuable social experiences in cooperation, character building, practical democracy and citizenship.

The principle of reality : Human life is itself a big project. If education is a preparation for life, we must create real life situations in the school. In Project Method the pupils are provided with opportunities to exercise their powers in real life situations. Therefore, they feel genuinely interested in such activities.

The principle of freedom : The desire for any activity should be spontaneous and not forced by the teacher. It should grow out of pupil's own needs and purposes. If the children are to gain real experiences, there should be no imposition and restriction. They should be left to themselves in an atmosphere of freedom—freedom to choose the activity according to their capacities and powers and freedom to gain useful purpose as a result of that activity.

The principle of utility : The knowledge gained through activity must be useful and practical. Experience obtained through project ensures utility because they are carried out under natural education. It gives useful training.

Planning of the Project Method

The project method is learning by living. In other words, we can say that for educating the child, real life situations are to be presented before the student. The problem and situations *i.e.* projects are presented in daily life situations as life is a big project, but problem lies with the selection the appropriate problem and presenting it to the students appropriately. The guiding steps for carrying out the project are given below.

Providing the situation : A Project is never to be forced upon the pupils. The teacher's job is to provide such a situation, according to the interest and attitude of the pupils, which may give them a spontaneous urge to carry it out. Situations may be provided by conversation on different topics, discussions on pictures, buildings or cities, by telling stories or taking out children on excursions and educational trips.

Choosing a project : After the situation has been provided, the next step is the choice of a good project. Only such a project should be selected as may satisfy some real need of the pupils and is for the good of all of them. The pupils must feel that the project is their own. In the words of Dr. Kilpatric, "The part of the pupils and the part of the teacher in most of school work, depends largely on who does the purposing. It is practically the whole thing". The project must be chosen according to the capacities of the pupils and according to the expense to be involved.

Planning : After a suitable choice has been made, the next step is to prepare a plan for the execution of the project. The entire planning is to be done by the pupils, under the guidance of the teacher, after a good deal of discussion. Each child should be encouraged to participate in the discussion and offer his suggestions. The entire plan should be put in black and white by the pupils in their project book, before working on that plan.

Executing : When the plan is ready, the teacher should encourage the pupils to put it into practice. He should ask the pupils to assign duties and distribute work among themselves, according to their individual interest and capacity. Each child must be given some duty to do for the successful completion of the project. Then they should be asked to work in cooperation with one another till the project is completed.

Judging or evaluating : After the completion of the project, the students should be asked to review their work. They should note down their mistakes, if any, and see whether they have proceeded according to the plan or not. It is a sort of self criticism which is a very important form of training and should never be neglected.

Recording : All the pupils should maintain a project-book in which they should put down a complete record of all the activities connected with the project. This record will include the choice of the project, its planning, discussions held, duties assigned, references and books consulted, information gathered, difficulties felt, experiences gained, guidance sought etc. Important points for future reference and guidance are also to be noted down.

Chief Characteristics of a Good and Successful Project

Usefulness : The project must be individually and socially valuable and must have a practical aim.

Maximum number of activities : It should provide a number of activities *of* various types. These should be quite suitable to pupils' undertaking the project and should be able to draw the best from them.

Availability of resources : The material connected with the project should be readily available in the school or in the neighbourhood of the school. The pupils should be able to handle it without difficulty.

Economy : The project should not be expensive. It should give the best of results in the shortest possible time and with the least possible expense.

Best experience : It should provide experiences of a very high standard, including social contacts and character training. It must fulfil some educational purpose.

Merits of the Project Method

Based on the laws of learning : The method is in accordance with the psychological laws of learning, namely the law of readiness, the law of exercise and the law of effect. The law of readiness requires the child's mind to be ready for acquiring knowledge. The planning and selection of the project prepares the child's mind for the work, he is about to do. The law of exercise requires the child to practise what he has learnt. As we have already seen the method is not only based on learning by doing but also on learning by living. The actual doing of things gives effective knowledge. The law of effect requires that learning should be accompanied by happiness and satisfaction. By actually doing and achieving things in the project, the child gets pleasure and satisfaction. All this makes the study of social studies interesting and effective.

The method is economical : As the work is of the children's own choice and interest, it goes through very speedily. It gives the best of results in the shortest possible time and with the least wastage of money and energy.

Training for democratic way of life : In the project method, the pupils work in cooperation with one another for a common purpose. Thus they acquire foresight, power of judgement, independence of thought and action, initiative, responsibility, resourcefulness, tolerance, self respect etc. All these are useful social habits which lead to real training for citizenship and a democratic way of life.

Dignity of labour : Since the pupils are required to do all types of work with their own hand, including manual work, it upholds the dignity of labour.

Correlation : All the subjects are correlated. There is no isolation of learning in water-tight compartments. Thus, knowledge is gained as a whole in its natural setting.

Imparts education according to real conditions of life : The projects are related to everyday needs and experiences of the child. Various subjects are taught to the extent, they are applicable in practical life. So knowledge gained is real, practical and useful, leading to the formation of proper habits and attitudes.

No cramming and memory work : Learning is effective because it does not come as the finished thought-product of the teacher. It comes as a by-product of useful activity. Children learn by doing things themselves. There is, thus, the problem solving attitude and exercise of thinking and reasoning power of the child.

Individual interests and skills are easily aroused: The examples of project activities given above indicate that their range is very broad. Scarcely any pupil would fail to find a challenge somewhere for himself.

Incidental learning : A lot of incidental learning takes place as the project is pursued by the pupils. In order to attain fair accuracy and success in the project, the pupils seek answers and solutions to many questions and problems which are not covered in a textbook.

Limitations of the Project Method

It is expensive : This method requires a lot of material for its successful completion. It may not be easily available locally. So ordinary schools may not afford to adopt this method because they are not in a position to spend much on projects. It not only requires a lot of money and material but also a lot of time, which we can seldom snatch out of our busy school programme.

Knowledge comes in a haphazard and scrappy manner : The project method disturbs the logical arrangement of subject matter which is so essential in particular subjects like social studies. So there is no systematisation. Loose ends of knowledge are bound to be left here and there, if work in different subjects is done according to this plan. Certain portions of the subjects cannot come into the project at all. So this method is also to be taken up only occasionally.

Too much strain on the teacher : The Project Method expects too much from the teacher. Every teacher cannot be efficient in all subjects. He is not expected to be so intelligent and resourceful as to suggest suitable projects and impart knowledge through them in a correlated manner. Moreover suitable text books, written on project method are also not available. This adds to the difficulties of the teacher.

It disorganises the school work : It is not possible to follow any fixed time table if the school is to be run on project method line. As there cannot be any fixed curriculum, the prescribed syllabus in various subjects is seldom finished in time. It is possible only if usual procedure of teaching is followed.

Balanced learning for all pupils is not possible : Some children are inclined to take all the responsibility upon themselves. Being more developed and capable, they want to do all the work, keeping others in the background. It thus provides ample opportunities to shirkers to merely look on and do very little. All the pupils are not expected to engage themselves in activities with equal seriousness and zeal. Moreover, this method is more suited to the pupils in lower grades than those in higher grades.

Conclusion

It should, however, be noted that most of the disadvantages of project method would disappear, when modern concepts are accepted. Pupil's growth and development are much more important in the educational process than the memorisation of too many obscure facts, which are all forgotten too soon. In the project procedure, pupil cooperation in planning and execution is almost secured. Moreover at the successful conclusion of the project, both the individual and the group enjoy an immeasurable satisfaction and pleasure. This method can, therefore, give excellent results if utilized in accordance with class desires and teachers' aptitude and interest.

Home projects may also be given to individual students or groups of students, living in the neighbourhood. One day in the week may be set apart for projects. The teacher may complete the first two steps and the last step in the class. Execution may be done at home.

PROBLEM-PROJECT METHOD

Many writers do not make any distinction between the problem and the project. They point out that "problems involve projects and projects involve problems." Both the processes are fundamentally alike in providing individual interest, thoughtful planning, logical development and complete fulfilment. It may, however, be helpful to regard *projects* as belonging primarily to the junior basic and lower middle schools and the *problems* as belonging primarily to the secondary and high schools.

"Even more important than this general practical distinction is a recognition of the fact that the project requires the completion of the problem by some physical act. The project ends in something beyond mental perception and satisfaction."

The fundamental value of these methods, however, is not to be found making a clear cut differentiation between them, but in the wise utilization of the method that is chosen on a particular occasion. "Both methods are equally useful in providing motivation in indicating a definite procedure, in allowing for individual tastes and interest."

Conclusion

We may conclude by saying that Project Method is not an educational panacea so as to neglect the use of other teaching devices. The projects are rich in possibilities for teaching when combined with direct learning, with systematic study, with demonstration and experiments and with discussion of the development of subject-matter. It may be used as a supplement to class-room teaching. For half the day projects may be carried on, and for remaining half, there may be class-teachins in essential subjects. This system is possible in primary and lower-middle classes in our schools.

PLAY-WAY METHOD

"Just as a poet cannot restrain himself from writing a poem, a musician from singing, a dancer from dancing and an actor from acting, so too the child cannot restrain himself from playing." Play is a natural tendency of the child. In play the child experiences the pleasure of doing a thing for its own sake. Thus, when pleasure is introduced in an activity, it is said to be done in the 'play-way'. An activity is done and learnt in the 'play-way', when that activity is according to a person's ability and inclination, fulfils his need and gives him happiness and pleasure.

The term *play-way* was first used as a method of teaching English by Caldwell Cook at the Perse Grammar School. It was the outcome of his experiences of teaching English Grammar, Composition and Literature. While teaching Shakspearean plays to his students, he felt that class-room lessons were dull, uninteresting and distasteful. He employed a method by means of which his students began to take a keen-interest in the subject. He asked them to select parts according to their tastes and abilities and dramatise those plays in the literature periods. The students organised an open-air theatre in the school compound, divided up the parts amongst themselves and memorised them with great eagerness. Thus, learning became associated with spontaneity, freedom and pleasure through practical activities. The meaningless sentences and words became meaningful and significant. In this way Caldwell Cook came to the conclusion that "good work is more often the result of spontaneous effort and free interest than of compulsion and forced application. Effectiveness of learning lies not in reading and listening, but in action, performance and experience." Thus school education can be made tangible and practical if it is imparted on play-way lines.

Underlying Principles of Play-way Method

The play-way method is based on the following principles :

1. Learning through doing : Learning should take place through doing in an atmosphere of freedom.

2. Knowledge related to life : The knowledge gained through various subjects, should be related to everyday life. It should not be abstract and bookish.

3. Methods according to needs and interest of pupils : Methods of teaching must not be rigid and formal. These should be natural and suited to the needs and interests of the pupils.

4. Sympathetic attitude of the teacher : The teacher should not behave like an absolute monarch who is always to impose his will on others. He should, rather, be quite sympathetic, humane and kind.

5. Opportunities for self-expression : Natural expression of the pupils should not be curbed by authoritarianism. On the other hand, ample opportunities should be provided for self-expression and self-activity.

6. Self-discipline : Play-way is the basis of all progressive methods in education. It should be applied as an important medium for teaching self-discipline to the students.

Application of Play Principle in Modern Methods of Teaching

In the words of Mr. Griffith, "Play is the child's characteristic mode of behaviour and any system of education which hampers this natural direction for the expanding of energy, endangers the mental and physical health of the child." According to Smith and Harrison, "Play is an all-absorbing activity in which initiative, fore-thought, control and skill can be exercised in full measure." The introduction of the element of play gives meaning and purpose to the child's activity. That is why play-way principle is now, more or less, applied in all the progressive methods of education as also in other school activities. It is applied in :

Kindergarten Method : This method of teaching is based on *learning through action*. The very introduction of gifts and balls means the provision of playing toys for children. Play-songs and movements are the main characteristics of this method.

Montessori Method : In this method muscular and sensory training is given to children through the didactic apparatus, which is specially designed for them. The child is free to handle this apparatus which consists of bars, stairs, cubes, frames and prisms etc. And these are all playing toys for children, designed after the play-way principle.

Project Method : In this method activity is combined with a purpose in view. The children keep themselves busy in the performance of their assigned duties. In this method, the three important features of play namely, freedom, responsibility and interest are provided an important place.

Dalton Plan : In this method, complete freedom is given to children to do their school work according to their interest and capacity. They are at liberty to move from one room to another according to their wish. So there is the joy of learning and the pleasure of doing things of one's own interest and choice. Thus the play-way principles are inherent in this method.

Heuristic Method : In this method the child is made to discover things himself. So there is a spirit of joy and a curiosity to learn. The child takes keen interest in his work and is always mentally active.

Basic Education : In the Basic system of Education also, play-way is considered to be one of the most important means of learning. Craft which is the core of entire educational procedure, is *good enough to play with.*

Co-curricular Activities : In schools these days, co-curricular activities, like boy-scouts, girl-guides, N.C.C., A.C.C., school excursions, community service, celebrations of fairs and festivals and outdoor life etc. are all important efforts in the direction of applying play-way spirit to the school work.

Utilisation of Play-way in the Teaching of Different School Subjects

Languages : Play-way spirit can be utilised in various ways, *e.g.* story-telling, recitation and singing of poems, dramatisation, word-building, spelling-games, class-meetings, debates, declamations and discussions etc.

Arithmetic : Knowledge can be imparted in play-way spirit through various games and projects like running a shop, managing a post office, opening a co-operative store, managing the school farm, running the school kitchen etc.

Social Studies : This subject can also be taught in play-way spirit through dramatics, pageants, tableaus, stamp-collecting, drawing of maps, cartoons, graphs, charts and pictures, globe-making, time-lines, models, picture-albums, historical and cultural excurisons and tours etc.

Nature Study : Play-spirit can be utilised by planning and laying out of gardens, growing of plants and flowers, arranging nature-walks and rambles, collecting specimens of leaves, flowers, plants, feathers etc. and keeping them in the nature-museum.

General Science : Individual and group experiments, collection of specimens of metals, manufactured articles, minerals and other things for class museum, preparation of charts, models and graphs, cuttings from news-papers, scientific Journals and magazines, introduction of scientific hobbies like soap-making, photography and chalk-making, preparation of sauces, squashes and jams etc. Thus we find that play-way is an important contribution to modern teaching procedures which has helped a lot in removing class-room monotony and dullness.

Advantages of the Play-way

Provides motivation : It is based on the natural urge of children. So there is no dullness and boredom. Children are motivated to under-take to learn and do the work in hand.

Caters to the needs of the whole child : By providing physical, intellectual, aesthetic education in a natural surrounding, play-way caters to the needs of the whole child and not to a part of him.

Training in self-discipline : Play-way gives opportunities for self-advancement through self-education. Children experiment and discover facts for themselves. There is the spirit of adventure, initiative and enthusiasm for doing things. This is all a good training in self-discipline.

Provides incentive to original creative work : In play children plan out new and original ways of doing the things. They make use of their thinking and reasoning power and thus receive valuable intellectual training. Play-way is, thus, a best means of self-expression which is a pre-requisite of the rich personality.

HEURISTIC METHOD

The Heuristic Method, as the name implies, is a method by which the pupil discovers things himself. The word *'heuristic'* has been derived from the Greek word *'heurisce'* which means *'I find out'*. Therefore the spirit of the Heuristic method lies in the fact that pupils are made to find out truths for themselves. Pupils are told as little as possible and induced to discover as much as possible.

> According to W.M. Ryburn, "This method as the name implies, is a method by which the pupil discovers things for himself. The pupil is put in the position of a pioneer, and he finds his way along the path of knowledge as did those who first discovered the facts, principles and laws which are now known to all."

This method was first used by Professor Armstrong for the teaching of science. Its success then led it to be adopted in the teaching of nearly all school subjects. In the Heuristic method, the pupils are placed in the position of origional discoverers as far as possible. They find out facts for themselves and receive as little as possible of dogmatic instruction by the teacher.

Aims and Objectives

The main aim of the Heuristic Method is to develop a scientific and critical attitude in the children. Nothing is to be accepted without being proved and established by their own efforts. The fact or truth should be the outcome of one's own personal experience, as far as possible. Hence the main aim is not so much to teach how knowledge of facts may be obtained, how it can be systematised and how it may be used. According to an eminent educationist, the object of the Heuristic method is "to make pupils more exact, more truthful and dexterous; to lay the solid foundation for future self-education and to encourage the growth of a spirit of enquiry and research." The pupils are faced with a certain problem. They try to gather information about that problem from books, journals and other sources, discuss the matter with fellow-pupils and teachers, put questions and listen to answers and in this way, arrive at the solution of the problem. There is no spoon feeding on the part of the teacher; the pupils learn through their own efforts. They are not passive listeners but active participants in the teaching-learning process.

Its Technique and Procedure

In teaching by Heuristic method, the inductive process is largely used. Pupils are led to acquire information by their own efforts from various sources. The principle which is the foundation of the individual work method, is the heuristic principle.

The Heuristic method uses the fact that a pupil's own experience is the basis of real learning. It is an activity method, in which the pupil is mentally active all the time. The pupil is, thus, placed in the position of an inventor, a discoverer or a research scholar. It however, does not mean that every student is turned into a research scholar or an inventor. It simply means that every student must get some insight into scientific and critical approach of doing things. Students should come to know how to tackle their work in all subjects in a scientific spirit and with a scientific attitude. They should form the habit of weighing evidence and also of exercising caution in accepting statements even if they are in books or newspapers. This method, thus, throws the whole weight of the teaching process on the process of the growth of mind rather than on the storing of ill-digested knowledge.

In adopting the heuristic plan, the entire class is given the same problem to tackle. Each pupil is made to feel responsible for finding out something with his own efforts. He is given freedom of movement from room to room, from room to laboratory, from class-room to art or craft-room in order to gather the necessary information. Free questioning and discussions are allowed. At times, the teacher may also put questions to stimulate pupils and to keep them on the right track.

Role of the Teacher

1. The teacher must be an expert. He must have ample knowledge, information, learning himself all the time. He should keep his store of knowledge up-to-date.

2. He should guide the students' activities and to meet their enquiries.

3. He must have good study habits.

4. He should be sympathetic to the children.

5. The teacher should give minimum help to the students. He should not disclose the facts of the knowledge in advance.

6. The teacher should maintain the atmosphere of freedom in the class-room.

7. The teacher should plan and devise problems which are in accordance with their age, aptitude, interest and ability.

8. The teacher must be curious and observer. He must have the spirit of scientific investigation.

Use of Heuristic Method in different subjects

Prof. Armstrong used it as a method of teaching science. But it is a method of teaching which can be used in any subject. The scientific method not necessarily confined to the subject of science. Examples of following Heuristic method can be found in most of the subjects; for example :

In Language : Pupils may collect a number of examples of a rule in grammar and then state the rules for themselves.

In Science : The pupils will perform the experiment and find out the results for themselves.

In History : The students may examine the sources and then compile an account of a historical event.

In Geography : The students may observe the phenomena of days and nights. Their duration at different times in the season and formulate general principles.

In this way, "whenever we are able to put the pupil into the position of a discoverer, who, by the way in which he uses the tools and information available, is able to reach a conclusion of his own, then we are teaching according to the Heuristic method." W. M. Ryburn.

Principles of Heuristic Method

Heuristic method is based on the sound footing of Psychology. The main principles of this method are being given below:

Principle of discovery : Spencer says, "children should be told as little as possible and induced to discover as much as possible." This thought is fully used in Heuristic method.

The principle of learning by doing : Prof. Dewey says, "The mind is not a piece of blotting paper that absorbs and retains automatically. It is rather a living organism that has to search for its food, that selects and rejects according to its present conditions and needs and that retains only what it digests and transmutes into parts of energy of its own being." Heuristic method also gives all these opportunities to the child to get knowledge which is fully based on the learning by doing by the pupils.

Principle of freedom : There are no obstacles in the way of the students. They are fully free to do experiments. The students are free to think, to discover and to do.

The principle of logical thinking : Inductive and deductive methods are used in this method. Inductive and deductive methods are fully based on logical thinking.

The principle of purposefulness : In using this method students have definite purpose before them. They solve definite problems. They discover definite rules and laws. Therefore, they have definite purpose before them. Ryburn also says that "Teaching by Heuristic method throws the whole weight of the teaching process on to the process of growth of the mind rather than on the storing of the knowledge." Hence Heuristic method is purposeful.

Principle of individual work : In this method every student works according to his own rate, way and ability. "He solves the problems according to bis own mental capacity. The amount of work done is also judged on the basis of an individual's capacity." Hence it is based on the principle of individual work.

Advantages of Heuristic Method

Develops scientific attitude : By encouraging personal observation and experiments and by arousing a spirit of enquiry and adventure, this method develops a scientific attitude of mind.

Learning by doing : Knowledge is not transmitted as a readymade object. It is self-acquired. It is gained through experience. So it is easily assimilated and remembered. It is all learning by doing.

Forms habits of hard work : Both, the teachers and pupils, have to gather information from various sources. They have to study many books, consult various references, weigh evidences and reach definite conclusions. All this implies hard-work and industry.

Encourages self-activity and self-confidence : The pupils learn through self-activity. They also learn to depend upon themselves. Discovery of facts for oneself gives a sense of pleasure that cannot be measured. It is a great incentive for further work.

Makes the learning permanent : Learning through this method is more or less permanent. Pupils generally retain facts much longer if they have discovered and learnt them through self-efforts.

Prepares the pupils for life : This method provides for the mental growth of the pupils and real development is possible only through the use of mental powers. The students learn how to handle sources, how to form judgments and how to arrive at definite conclusions. All this is preparation for later life.

Can be used in almost all school subjects : This method can be used with advantages in almost all subjects in the curriculum. In languages, when pupils collect a number of examples of a rule in grammar and then state the rule themselves, they use the heuristic method. In science when experiments are done by the pupils themselves in real sense of the word *'experiment'*, they use this method. In history, it is used, when original documents are compared and then an account of a historical event is compiled. Similarly in mathematics, civics, geography and other subjects numerous ways and means can be devised to use the heuristic method.

Limitations of Heuristic Method

Not suitable for beginners and immature pupils : This method is not suitable for young students in primary classes whose knowledge is quite shallow. Heurism requires pupils to be placed in the position of original discoverers. But discovery is possible only with a great deal of knowledge of facts and previous achievements in that direction. So this method can not be worked out successfully with young and immature children.

Slow progress : If we adopt heuristic method for class-room teaching, very slow progress will be made. A single period of 35 or 40 minutes duration is too short a time to discover a fact. If there are gaps between periods for the same subject, there shall be no continuity in thought and action which is essential for discovery or finding out facts. Then there are many facts which cannot possibly be discovered by pupils. These must be told by the teacher.

A strain on already over-burdened teacher : The success of this method depends upon the efficiency and hard work of the teacher. It is not an easy job to guide students to find out facts for themselves. It requires special training, experience, enthusiasm and initiative. But our teachers in schools who are already overburdened with work, because of heavy curriculum, cannot stimulate pupils to think properly and proceed methodically.

Lays more emphasis on the process than on the product : As we have already noted, in the heuristic method it is the process of thinking, finding and discovering which is more important than the result. But some teachers may make the mistake of putting more stress on obtaining correct answers or solutions from their pupils and ignore the real heuristic attitude.

Conclusion

We may, thus, conclude by saying that in spite of all its limitations, the heuristic method can yield better and more lasting results, if used properly and if heuristic attitude is carefully maintained.

DALTON PLAN

One of the most radical methods for providing individual attention, is known as the Dalton Laboratory Plan. In 1920. This Plan was first introduced and tried by Miss Helen Parkhurst in a Dalton High School at Dalton in America. So the scheme has been named after the school and City 'Dalton' as Dalton Plan. It was the outcome of modern psychological development in education which attaches a great importance to the individual child, his nature, needs and interests. It was devised as a reaction against collective class-room teaching.

Dalton Plan was devised as a reaction against collective classroom teaching. The scheme aims at no change of curriculum but only in the teaching procedure.

According to Miss Parkhurst, Dalton Plan is an economic and simple reorganization of school, whereby students are permitted a greater degree of freedom to work and the teacher and the students work more effectively.

The Dalton Plan, in fact, is not a new method of teaching. It is only a new organisation of school work, which helps children to learn more effectively than the traditional system. It does not require any change in the curriculum nor it depends upon any particular method of teaching. It simply approaches the problems of teaching from individual pupil's point of view. Thus it provides equal opportunities of progress to the bright and the slow pupils alike and may be used profitably in middle and high classes.

Principles of Dalton Plan

The principle of individual work : According to this plan each child works at his own rate and speed. There is no time restriction nor there is any restriction from the teacher. Children may divide their time according to their needs and devote more time to the subjects in which they are weak.

The principle of freedom : Every child is free to work as he thinks fit. He is free to move freely from one room to another and consult any one he likes.

The principle of self-effort : Every child has to face and solve problems himself. There is no spoon-feeding. Self-effort and self-activity teach self-reliance, give confidence and train for sharing responsibility.

The principle of cooperation and group-life : Miss Parkhurst has put it herself by saying, "There must be mingling of individuals on self-set errands, development by exchange of opinion, not a life of text books but a stimulating life of eager human soul, seeking the solutions to real problems through the interactions of group life on a large scale."

Working or Salient Features of the Plan

Assignments or contracts : In the Dalton Plan, the syllabus in each subject is drawn up in outline for the whole year. This is further divided into monthly units. Such monthly units of work are called *'assignments'*. In such assignments complete directions and references for study are made. Books, maps and other aids, to be consulted, are suggested. In other words complete guidance is provided as to what work is to be done and how it is to be undetaken and accomplished. Before undertaking the monthly assignment, each pupil has to sign a promise (or *contract*) to complete the work in time. Each subject has its own separate assignments. The pupils may begin with whichever subject they please and work at it as long as they like. But they must complete it to the entire satisfaction of the teachers concerned within time. A new assignment is given only on the successful accomplishment of the previous one.

Subject teachers : There are no class teachers. There are only subject teachers, specialists in their own subjects. They prepare assignments in their respective subjects, supervise the work of each child, solve his difficulties, offer suggestions for improvement and encourage him to complete his assignment in time.

Subject rooms : There are no class-rooms like the ordinary schools. There are only subject-rooms which are called *subject laboratories*. These subject laboratories are under the charge of subject teachers concerned. Each laboratory contains books, magazines, pictures, models, charts, apparatus, appliances and other material relating to that subject. The students need not have any text book. They are free to move from one subject-room to another and consult any book according to their needs. The subject teacher is there in each laboratory to help those who come to him for advice and guidance.

Records : Pupil's progress in each subject is regularly recorded by means of graphs or diagrams. These represent the units of work, covered by each pupil in specified time. There are three types of records of which two are kept by the pupils, showing their progress in parts or as a whole and the third, by the subject teacher, hung in his subject-room. The teacher's record enables the teacher to check up the work of each individual child and guide him accordingly.

Conferences : Under the Dalton plan, the children are left to themselves from morning till recess. During this period they move freely from one subject-room to another, preparing their assignments. In the afternoon session group discussions and oral lessons are held. These are called *conferences*. Instead of daily class teaching, the subject teacher holds class conferences in order to remove common difficulties, give some further oral instructions and discuss other items of interest and importance. He also holds a conference when he wants to give an appreciation lesson in poetry or in history or when he likes to introduce something new or difficult to the class.

Advantages of the Dalton Plan

Individualised instruction : This plan provides an excellent technique of individualising instruction and thus it enables each pupil to proceed at his own pace and speed according to his interest. There are no jerks and shocks. The brighter pupils have not to wait for the slower and the slow ones need not feel neglected. Each child thus gets personal and individual attention which removes one of the greatest defects in all the class-room teaching.

Continuity of work : Under the Dalton plan each pupil works at his own speed. He gets the next assignment after completing the previous one. So the question of failure and subsequent frustration does not arise. Moreover his work does not suffer if due to illness or otherwise he has to be absent from the school for some time. He can start the work where he has left it and can make up his defficiency. Thus the continuity of work is assumed.

Promotes self-reliance and confidence : There is no spoon-feeding for the child. He does not get ready-made knowledge. He has to discover it through his own efforts, under the teacher's guidance. He has to study books, consult references and seek information for himself. He faces difficulties and problems and learns how to solve them. This self-effort promotes self-reliance and confidence and equips him better for later life.

Develops initiative and resourcefulness : The responsibility of completing the assignment is thrown on the shoulders of the pupils. This sense of responsibility stimulates him to work hard. It arouses his interest and proves as a constant reminder for accomplishing the task in hand. He devotes himself, heart and soul to the work. This whole hearted devotion to work develops initiative and resourcefulness and ultimately leads to success.

Problem of discipline is simplified : The child works according to his interest and speed in an atmosphere of freedom. So there is no question of fatigued boredom or mischief. There is no compulsion or external imposition. Thus there are no truants or mischief-makers and so there is no problem of discipline.

Problem of evaluation is solved : The record system of the plan, enables the teacher to assess the progress of each individual pupil. So there is no need of frequent tests and formal examinations. It also does away with the system of awarding of marks, leading to unhealthy competition.

Limitations of the Dalton Plan

Not suitable for average and weak pupils : The plan is excellent for cleaver and conscientious workers. But it is not suitable for average and weak pupils who are in the habit of postponing work. They are not expected to make much progress if left to their own efforts.

Oral work is discouraged : In the teaching of subjects like physical training, music and languages, oral work plays a very important part because we require 'inspirational teaching'. These subjects are meant to be taught collectively, for which there is no provision in the Dalton plan.

Little development of social virtues : The plan fails to provide liberal group activities. It is purely intellectual which develops individualistic tendencies in children. So social virtues like cooperation, tolerance, fellow-feeling etc. cannot be instilled and developed in the pupils.

Suitable teachers not available : The plan involves a lot of hard work and responsibility on the part of the teacher. He is to prepare assignments, give directions, help pupils individually, check their work, watch their progress, keep records, issue books and receive them back and also keep his subject laboratory up-to-date. The average teacher finds it difficult to do all this work efficiently. And teachers who can really do it, are very rare.

Suitable books and equipment not available : Preparation of assignment is not an easy job. It requires a large number of suitable text and reference books and other equipment. But such books, especially in Indian vernaculars, are not available. Maps, charts, models, diagrams, appliances and a variety of other material are also needed. It is neither available in a suitable form nor an ordinary Indian school can afford to purchase it.

Difficulty of a suitable building : The plan cannot be adopted in the existing school buildings without radical changes and alterations. It requires buildings which have to be specially designed for the purpose. In our country most of the schools are over-crowded and lack sufficient buildings. So work on Dalton plan is well-nigh impossible.

Conclusion

In spite of the above limitations and short-comings, the Dalton plan does carry some important advantages. It may, therefore, be adopted for use in middle and high classes in a modified form. School time table should be so arranged that there is certainly some scope for self-study and individual work. Some well-graded assignment may also be given for independent work to students along with formal class-room teaching. Graph-system of keeping records is very useful. It may also be introduced in our schools. It is very economical in checking up the progress of the pupil.

MONTESSORI METHOD

Maria Montessori was born in 1870 in Itlay. She was the first women in Italy who was awarded the Degree of Doctor in Medicine in 1896. She worked as a Professor of Anthropology from 1900 to 1907 in the University of Rome.

She came into the contact of mentally deficient children at this place. She took keen interest in the study of such children and in their education. She discovered the following points.

1. The mental deficiency results from the dullness of the senses.

2. Sense training was the best method to achieve good results in their education.

3. If the same method of sense training is employed to educate normal children much better results could be achieved.

Establishment of Children House

She was appointed the Director of Rome Association to supervise some schools. Children between the age of 3 to 7 were attending such schools which were named as "Children Houses". Only those children were attending these schools whose parents were not staying at home in the day time. Here she developed a new method of educating children through sense training.

In 1922 she was appointed as Inspectress of Schools. These schools were meant for infants. She also started giving training to nursery school teachers. Teachers from other countries of Europe including England started taking training.

Due to Mussolini's dictatorship she was compelled to leave Italy, because she believed in freedom instead of dictatorship. She also visited India in 1939 and remained here upto 1951. She propagated her new method in India also. She returned to Holland in 1951 and died in 1952.

Thus Dr. Maria Montessori had so many qualities in her life times as a scientist, an anthropologist, an educationist and a doctor. She was a catholic, a democractic and a scientist—all rolled into one. In this pattern, it is not difficult to integrate her philosophy, her psychology and her methodology. As a catholic, she could be neither pragmatist nor naturalist. As a democrat, she upheld individual liberty and sought the full and free development of children. As a scientist she aimed to teach children through realities by providing concrete material and observing learning situations for pupils.

According to Good's Dictionary of Education, Montessori Method is defined as below :

"A method of Primary and Pre-primary instruction, developed by Maria Montessori, an Italian Psychiatrist and former pupil of Seguin and Itard based on the faculty of Psychology, and emphasizing free physical activity, individual instruction, early development of reading and writing skills, and extensive sensory and motor training; introduced originally in Italy, the method spread to England and to the United States but has been generally abandoned here in favour of Froebelian methods."

Principles Underlying Montessori Method

Education as a developmental process : The child is a potential being. Education should develop the child fully. The purpose of this scheme is only unfolding and developing what already exists in him. The aim of education is unfolding of individuality. The child has a body which grows and a soul which develops. The teacher is 'Director' because he or she has to direct the child.

Perfect freedom : Full freedom should be given to the child. Freedom is always the exercise of one's own will. It requires self-sufficiency on the part of the child. This freedom leads to discipline and self-control which is necessary for growth and development.

Psychological education and individuality : Individual attention should be paid for the proper development of the child. For all round development of the child's physical, mental, emotional and social aspect are to be kept in mind. The internal incentives are more important than the external incentives. Therefore, she does not advocate the prize or rewards as external incentives for learning.

Sense training : Montessori asserts that senses are the gate way of knowledge. Hence her approach to the mind is through senses. Sound sensory training is necessary for acquiring knowledge. Sensations of colours, sound, weight, touch, temperature etc. provide good exercises in thinking. The sense of tough is the fundamental and therefore her method is sometimes called as education by touch. Hence sense training is of primary importance according to this system of education.

Self education : It does not believe in teaching, but it believes in learning. Self-education is the best education because the child is not disturbed here. The teacher should not interfere the child in the process of self-education. For this purpose, *i.e.* self-education Montessori has devised the didactic apparatus.

Motor efficiency : A sound mind is found in a sound body. Muscular activities are the only way of getting motor efficiency. Therefore, Montessori also aims at motor efficiency along with sensory training.

Procedure and Plan of Montessory Method

1. Atmosphere of full freedom should be provided to the students.

2. Furniture and equipment is specially meant for children, suitable in size.

3. There is didactic sensorial apparatus to provide for various types of exercises, motor, sensory and intellectual.

Provision of children house : The 'Children House' is a many roomed school with a well laid-out garden. Shelters are provided in the garden for children to take rest and for taking food and enjoying open air.

Main room of building is joined with small rooms. These rooms are lunch room, rest room, manual work room, laboratory and a bath room. These rooms are equipped according to the spirit and needs of the method.

Activities of Montessori Method

Three types of activities are provided in this method. They are :

1. Exercises in practical life.
2. Exercises in sensory training.
3. Didactic exercises for teaching language and arithmetic.

Exercises in Practical Life

Accordings to Dr. Montessori these exercises are called "Exercises in Practical Life", because "in the Children House real every day life is carried on in which all house work is entrusted to little ones, who execute with devotion and accuracy their domestic duties becoming singularly calm and dignified."

1. They sweep their room dust and clean the furniture.
2. They learn to blow their noses quietly, wash their hands etc.
3. They also learn dressing and redressing.
4. All the furniture in child house is of such size and so constructed that the pupils can handle them easily.
5. Low black boards, small musical instruments and small pieces of carpets in different colours are available in the house.
6. Lunch room is also decorated. It is well equipped. There are low tables, chairs, and drawers, plates, tumblers etc. very well arranged in small cup-boards. The children lay their tables themselves and lunch together.

7. There is also the Paedometer, *i.e.*, instrument to measure height. There is the weighing machine to measure the weights themselves.
8. Formal gymnastic exercises to develop in the child co-ordinated movements are provided.
9. Practice in hand work is also provided through exercises in clay modelling, making of tiles and bricks with the help of simple moulds. Children are also taught to walk in straight lines and balance themselves properly.

Exercises in Sensory Training

Exercises in sensory training are imparted through the finely graded didactic apparatus, various types of apparatus is provided for the perception of size, form, weight, touch, hearing and colour etc.

1. For the perception of size : There are series of wooden cyclinders varying in height only, in diameter only or in both demensions at once, blocks varying regularly in size and rods of regularly graded length.

2. For the perception of form : There are geometrical insets in metal, wood (prism, pyramid, sphere, cyclinder, cone etc.) a chest of drawers containing plane insets, a series of cards on which are pasted geometrical forms in paper etc.

3. For the perception in colour : There are pink cubes, brown prisms, green and alternately red and blue rods and coloured tablets, etc.

4. For discrimination in weight : There are tablets of wood similar in size but differing in weight.

5. For discrimination in touch : There are rectangular tables with rough and smooth surfaces, a highly polished surface and a sand paper surface and so on.

6. For discriminating in sounds : There are a collection of closed cylindrical boxes, wooden boards on which are painted the lines used in music, a double series of music bells and small discs for the notes etc.

The procedure adopted is as follows :

(*i*) Associating the sensory material with the name *e.g.* This is brown. This is heavy.

(*ii*) Recognition of the object *e.g.* give me the brown; give me the heavy.

(*iii*) Recalling the name, *i.e.* what is this ?

In this way Montessori method emphasize too much on sensory training.

Didactic Exercises for Teaching 3 R's

After sense training, children are taught reading, writing and arithmetic. Writing comes before reading in Montessori method. This depends on "Transfer of training", could be converted and reduced to a mechanism by means of repeated exercises, not in work itself but in that which prepares it. Her principle is to attend to the subject and not the subject matter in this respect. She is concerned with the movements which the child makes and not the matter, which is written.

On this basis writing depends on three principles :

Recognition of forms of letters : Letters of the alphabet are cut in sand paper and pasted on card-board. Children are asked to pass their fingers over these letters. The roughness of the sand-paper trains for accuracy of movements. The same is practised later on, with closed eyes.

Learning of phonetic sounds : Sounds are also associated with the forms of the letter. In this, the ground for the teaching of reading is prepared.

Control of the pen : The children are given opportunity to place the metal frame on a piece of paper and draw a line round it with a coloured chalk. In this outline, then, the child is required to place the metal inset and then draw an outline of the inset with a chalk of different colours. Thus two figures are produced in different colours upon the paper. The figure obained is thus filled up with another piece of chalk pencil. The children are asked not to move their pencil outside the outline. In this way the children are taught to control over the pen.

Teaching of Reading

To Montessori "Reading is the interpretation of an idea from written signs and not merely barking at print". Slips of paper cards are used. Words and phrases are written in bold letters on them. The child is given a card with the name of a familiar object written on it. The child translates the writing into sounds slowly. The child repeats it quickly later on. The child arranges the cards according to the objects after learning the pronunciation of the words. Sentences are also written on the slips of the paper. The child selects the slips. He reads the slips. He does the action contained in it later on.

Teaching of Arithmetic

For teaching number and four simple rules of arithmetic 'a long star' is used. It is a set of ten rods varying in length from 1 to 10 decimetres, the intermediate rod diminishing in length by decimeters. The rods are divided into decimeter parts, the spaces on the rods being painted alternately red and blue. First of all the child is asked to arrange the rods in order of sizes. Then he is required to count the red and blue division. He is required to name the rod one, all the four fundamentals of arithmetic are taught like this.

Other Activities

Activities like care of plants and animals are also provided to the children. In this way they are taught to bear responsibilities. They also learn that plants and animals are mostly dependent upon their care, feeding and watering. Building with blocks and sticks and clay moulding are also included in these activities. Through these activities children learn patience and mercy.

Limitations of Montessori Method

Lack of suitable teachers : The success of this method depends on the availability of the trained teachers on the lines as suggested by Madam Montessori. Such teachers are not easily available in our country. The teachers are also not expert in child psychology which is necessary for them.

Neglects the training of imagination : All educators agree on the point that imagination of children is to be used and developed. But there is no place for fairy tales in this method. These fairy tales develop the imagination of the childrn. According to Montessori "the imagination of modern men is based upon the positive researches of science". So fairy tales are not allowed in this method.

It is very expensive : Such schools cannot be established in India because of financial limitations. The apparatus costs too much and an ordinary school cannot afford to meet the expenses. The apparatus is a formal one and cannot be even improvised by reducing the cost.

The idea of auto-education has been carried too far : The idea of self-education or auto-education is good in general but its specific working with the help of the didactic apparatus is not free from defects. Self-education is reduced to a mechanical manipulation of the didactic apparatus. Life is full of so many situations which can give the facility of self-education.

Neglect of emotional and moral development : Montessori says, "Just as in the early development of mankind practical activities must have figured more largely than the literacy, so the early education of the child should be more realistic than humanistic." She, therefore, stressed on the development of the physical personality of child and neglected the psychological aspects of temperament, character and emotions.

It neglects the social factor : Montessori neglects the group activities. Therefore, there is no scope for social development. The whole system involves individual growth through individual learning. There are very limited activities of social value except the activity in the dining hall.

Senses cannot be trained in isolation : Modern Psychology has given us the greatest of all truths that an individual reacts as a whole. Senses cannot be trained in isolation. Only the training of senses is not sufficient for child development. But in Montessori method sense training is primary for the child's education. Faculty psychology used senses training. But faculty psychology is no more accepted these days.

The theory of formal training exploded : The idea of sense training in Montessori method is similar to the old theory of formal discipline theory. She believes in transfer of training. It is very much doubtful whether results of sensory training in specific spheres may be transferred to other sensory spheres.

Inadequacy of self-expression : The child is supposed to follow mechanically. There is no scope of self-expression in this method.

The educative value of play is limited : Play does not find any place in Montessori method. Whatever play is involved, that also is a sort of work. The child is too much tied with the activities of reading, writing and arithmetic.

Advantages of Montessori Method

Scientific concept of education : Curtis says, "Montessori was a catholic, a democratic and a scientist. As a catholic she was neither pragmatist nor naturalist. As a democrat she held up individual liberty and sought to foster the full and free development of children. As a scientist she aimed at educating the child by providing concrete material and by organising learning situations for pupils." She gave us experimentation, observation and other scientific methods in education.

Reverence for small children : To Madam Montessori "The child was God. Her school was the temple and diety of the temple was essence of childhood." She further says, "To-day there stands forth one urgent need—the reform of methods in education and instruction, and he who struggles towards this end is struggling for the recognition of man." This shows that Montessori gave much importance to the child.

Individual teaching : The child is the 'unit of teaching.' Individualism is the key note of Montessori Method. Her method is a reaction against collective teaching.

Emphasis on sensory training : Madam Montessori greatly emphasized sensory training in her scheme of education. No one can deny that senses are the gateways to knowledge.

Emphasis on complete freedom : This method advocates complete freedom for children. Children develop the qualities of self-reliance and self-discipline. Freud once remarked admiringly that children trained in the Montessori spirit were bound to make poor customers for psycho-analysis later in life.

Learning by doing : Her idea of providing practical life is very significant. They learn practically through the process of doing practically. The exercises provided at the time of taking meals, dressing and undressing, washing and clothing are all useful. They provide practical exercises to the child. The teachers are simply to guide and to bring the system and order in children movement.

Method of teaching, writing and reading is unique : Montessori has emphasized that writing should come after reading. She has also laid stress on motor efficiency. The fact that intellect will follow action cannot be disputed.

Special role of the teacher : In this method teachers are directors. They are, in other words, as friend, philosopher and guide. The main duty of the teacher is to provide the required environment and material at the right moment and thus help in the auto development of the child.

Emphasis on self-discipline : Madam Montessori has laid emphasis on self-discipline. She believes that discipline should come from self-control and self-directed activity of the child. Forced discipline is not at all desirable in her scheme of education.

Conclusion

To conclude, we can say that Montessori method has its own merits and demerits. It is sure that this method, though, is being used in India, but the real shape of this method is rarely seen anywhere in the country. Moreover this method is meant only for infants and early childhood stages. It is not giving its due to the secondary and higher education which is one of the most imporant features of education of the country.

KINDERGARTEN METHOD

Friedrich Wilhelm August Froebel was the creator of Kindergarten method.

Life Sketch of Froebel

Froebel (1782-1852) was the son of a pastor in Thuringian in Germany. His mother died when he was only of nine months. Therefore, he was neglected in his youth and the memories of his life made him, in later life, more eager in promoting the happiness of children. He grew moody and subjective. He came into the contact of nature.

Education : He was not interested in school education. The teaching was abstract but he did well in arithmetic. His early education was without any purpose. "The young Froebel was a dreamy, poetic, highly sensitive lad, in love with nature and inquisitive about natural phenomena, religious minded and hungry for companionship and friendship."

His education was by no means obtained in the lecture rooms and laboratories only. He carried on private study in German literature in anthropology. He joined many professions like manager, accountant and an architect. But he could not find happiness in it.

Froebel as a teacher : As an architect he felt that he really wanted to work with people to build not houses but men. At twenty-three he was pursuaded to become a teacher in the Pestolozzian Institute at Frankfurt and thus *recovered* his life calling.

Influence of Pestolozzi : In this institute he learnt in detail the methods and principles of Pestolozzi. He found that curriculum is a patch work with many gaps. This contact with Pestolozzi prepared him for his educational research. He found the following defects in the system of Pestolozzi:

1. The schools lacked organization.
2. There was no unity in the whole work.
3. The subjects of study lacked integration.
4. In the early education of children, co-operation of mothers was not forthcoming.

Through his experiences he found that singing, movement and speech are three correlative forms of expression. He was influenced by the practical work in drawing and practical occupations.

First publication : In 1826 he published his famous book ' The Education of Man'. In this book he elaborates that a true method of education consists in considering the mind of the child as a living whole in which all the parts work together to produce harmonious unity.

1. Education of Man.
2. Pedagogies of Kindergarten.
3. Education by Development.
4. Mother Play and Nursery Songs.

Meaning and Basis of Kindergarten

Kindergarten is a German word which means, the children's garden, *i.e.* a place where children grow up as trees and flowers. Froebel considered the school as a garden and the teacher as a gardener, who is to look after the little human plants and water them to grow to beauty and perfection.

He based his system of education on his idealistic philosophy and opened the first kingdergarten, an institution for the children of the age of 4 to 6 at Blackenberg in 1837.

Principles Underlying Kindergarten Method

The principle of unity : Froebel believed in the principle of inter-connectivity. He believed in the idea of unity in diversity. He told that there is an eternal law, the law of unity in all things. This eternal unity was called as God by him who is source of all things which are linked together.

The whole universe is inter-connected in three-fold.

1. *Unity of substance* : The substance determine the existence of all things.

2. *Unity of origin* : God is the origin of all things.

3. *Unity of purpose* : There is a common purpose all things striving towards perfection, *i.e.* God.

The principle of continuity or development : Froebel believes that life is characterised by continuity; it is ever evolving and developing. All parts of the universe are growing from within through the force of their own being. Thus dynamic growth from within is a manifestation of striving towards the same eternal unity.

The principle of self-activity : It is self-activity that leads to real growth and development. It can give joy, freedom, contentment and peace to the world. Self-activity is innate to us. Forced activity is artificial and unnatural. An acute observer can know what the child is or what he is to become. "All this lies in the child and can be attained through development from within". Play activities have been utilized to direct and develop the whole child, the intellectual, emotional, physical and moral.

The principle of crystallography and symbolism : Froebel believes that there is a connecting force which connects the things. He describes this force as :

"It is different from all other forms, yet contains all of them, it is formless yet the most perfect form. Neither point nor line, neither plane nor side can be discerned on it yet it is all pointed and all sided, contains all the points and all, etc. of all the earthly structure and forms."

This is the principle of crystallography and symbolism which underlines in the choice of his gifts to be presented to the children to play with.

Froebel's Principles of Education

1. According to Froebel the aim of education is not to make the mind master of 3R's. He writes "The essential business of school is not so much to communicate a variety and multiplicity of facts as to give prominence to the ever living unity that is in all things." Again he writes : "Human education requires the knowledge and appreciation of the intimate unity of the three, the school and we ourselves are lost in the fallacies of bottomless self-provoking diversity."

So the aim of education is to enable the child to realize unity in diversity.

2. He believes that the school is to be a social laboratory where the children get training in primary virtues such as, co-operation, sympathy, fellow feeling and responsibility. In other words the school is a miniature society of its own.

3. Play is the base of education according to Froebel. The child expresses himself best in play and at the same time learns much which otherwise would have greatly taxed his memory.

4. The occupations in kindergarten have changed the face of modern method of teaching. Learning by doing, dramatics, work experience, self-expression are fully hidden in this scheme of education. Inclusion of manual work is a great influence on the mind of the teacher.

5. It is based on the principle of proceed from concrete to abstract. The provision of gift in the first place of the scheme is based on it. It provides sensory training to the child.

6. His emphasis on the nature study and gardening has fulfilled a long felt need of children for observation and love of the world in which they live.

7. The child should be educated in free atmosphere. Freedom means obedience to self-imposed law.

8. He devised songs, gestures and construction as the chief means for stimulating the imagination of the child.

Thus the function of education can be summed up as "Education should lead and guide to clearness, concerning himself and in himself to pace with nature, and to unity with God. it should lift him to knowledge of himself, to mankind, to a knowledge of God and of nature and the pure and holy life."

The sum and substance of the education aim according to Froebel is the realization of the law of unity through the development of one's mind in accordance with its own inner law, being self-active in a free and social atmosphere.

Procedure and Plan of the Method

Freedom is core of this method. Play and joy will be typical of such an atmosphere. There are no books in it. Storing of knowledge is not required in it. Expression is the key of this method. The learning process is activity-centred. It is imparted in three ways :

1. Through songs.

2. Through movements.
3. Through construction.

All these activities will be well connected as a unit. Play will be pivot of the whole process. Every thing is experienced through songs by them. Children express themselves in creative activities like paper construction or use of card-board or wooden blocks.

Thus concrete means are adopted to stimulate mental activity on the part of children. They are trained intellectually, physically and emotionally.

Teacher's role : The teacher's job is to select songs, device plays and games to show pictures and to arrange activities, *i.e.* construction.

Songs, Gestures and Games

Songs : Every song has three parts :

1. A motto for the guidance of mother or teacher.
2. A verse accompanied by music.
3. A picture illustrating the song.

Example :

"Let us have a drill today,
  March along grand array,
And who ever steps the best,
  Shall be captain over the rest,
And lead us on our way."

Along with these songs the children play. All these songs are given in his famous book "Mother and Nursery Songs."

Characteristics of Songs

1. The child is able to use his senses, limbs and muscles.
2. Nursery games are provided in each song.
3. All sorts of needs of the child are fulfilled through these songs.

Gifts and Occupations

To provide activities, Froebel devised suitable material known as gifts. The gifts suggest some form of activity and occupations are the activities suggested by the gifts. These gifts have been carefully graded. The order of gifts is devised in such a way that it leads the child from the activities and thought of one stage to another.

First gift. The first gift consists of six coloured balls contained in a box. The balls are of different colours. The child is to roll them about in play. The occupation consists in rolling them. These balls give an idea of colour, material, motion and direction.

The rhymes are like this :

Oh, see the pretty ball,
    So round so soft and small,
The ball is round and rolls each way,
    The ball is nice for baby's play."

Second gift. It contains a sphere, a cube and a cylinder contained in a box. When the child plays, he notices the difference between the stability of the cube and the mobility of the sphere. The cylinder is both, movable and stable and thus harmonises the qualities of both.

Third gift. This gift is called, "The first building box". The child can make a number of constructions out of these *e.g.* benches, steps, bridges.

Fourth gift. It is a large cube divided into oblong prisms in each of which the length is twice the breadth and breadth is twice the thickness. The child can construct different kinds of building patterns when combined with the third gift. The cube song is sung with it.

Cube song :

"As cube I stand here in my place,
    As surface now, I show my face,

Yet always am the same,
  I like this pretty game.

Now without delay,
  Divide me in your play,

Making fleetly,
  But yet neatly,

Two quite equal parts."

Fifth gift : It consists of a large cube divided into 27 small cubes, three of which are again divided diagonally into halves and three into quarters. Many beautiful forms and patterns can be built by combining the third, foruth and fifth gift. The child can be taught form and number through the third gift.

Sixth gift. It is useful in teaching numbers. It helps the child in constructing more designs. It is a large cube divided into eighteen whole and nine small oblong blocks.

Seventh gift. It is prepared of a set of squares and triangular tablets of very fine wood in two colours. It can provide training in geometrical form and mosaic work. The gifts are altogether twenty in number but the first seven are only called by this name now. Several of the remaining gifts provide material for many occupations, such as paper cutting, threading of reels, mat making, basket making, modelling and drawing etc..

The Teacher's Job

1. The teacher should not remain passive after presenting gifts.

2. The teacher gives demonstration of the gifts.

3. Only such things and plays to be introduced which can be used very effectively for education.

Second Stage

Boyhood is the second stage of development. At this stage the boyhood is at work.

Curriculum : Curriculum for this stage is as under:

1. *Manual Work:* Froebel emphasises manual work at this stage. He says:

(*a*) "Scholastic education of our times leads children to indolence and laziness and a vast amount of man power remains undeveloped and is lost."

(*b*) "Manual work is a necessary condition of the realization of pupil's personality, though it comes to himself."

Froebel gives importance to manual work because it provides a concrete form of represssion of ideas. He attaches spiritual importance to manual work.

2. *Other subjects :* According to Froebel the main purpose of education is all round development. He has divided the curriculum as below :

(*a*) Religion and religious instruction.

(*b*) Natural science and mathematics.

(*c*) Language.

(*d*) Art and objects of Art.

3. *Nature study :* Nature study would create a sense of wonder and admiration in the minds of the children for the works of God. Nature study would result in religious uplift and spiritual insight. Therefore the child must have knowledge about all the important facts of Nature.

Merits of the Scheme

1. It emphasises on pre-school or nursery education.
2. It contributes to idea of child-centred education.
3. Freedom of expression in this system is provided.
4. He broadened the concept of school as an essential social institution. The school is miniature society according to this system.
5. Playway technique is quite natural in it.

6. It gives the importance of the Psychological principle of 'Learning by doing.'

7. The seeds of work experience of Kothari Commission are found in it.

8. It is based on experience curriculum.

9. It gives importance to sensory training through different gifts.

10. It believes in the maxim—proceed from concrete to the abstract.

11. It includes nature study and gardening.

We can say, "Froebel Kindergarten has greatly influenced the educational procedures. His contribution to educational reform, in the sense of child centredness, play, self-expression, manual work, freedom, social participation, development of individuality and a host of others have got full recognition today."

Activity principle, the play spirit and learning by doing form the core of this scheme of education.

Limitations of Kindergarten

1. The underlying philosophy of idealism is very difficult to understand.

2. He expects too much from the child.

3. In the Kindergarten too much stress has been laid on the development from within. The importance of the environment has not been recognised fully.

4. Some of the songs and pictures suggested by Froebel are old and out-of-date. The gifts are of a formal nature and the presentation is quite arbitrary.

5. There is correlation in the subjects in Kindergarten whereas it stresses on inter-connectedness and the Law of Unity.

6. Too much of socialization is there, but a little emphasis is laid on individual development.

7. It is more applicable to younger children than on elder children.

8. It is difficult to find expert teachers in this scheme.

9. It is not possible to accept his excessive emphasis on play in education, as it is likely to detract the child from serious learning.

But, inspite of these limitations, the kindergarten is unique in its methodology and is significant in its contributions. We can end with Boyd words: "Mothers and teachers may be content to be ignorant of the obscure philosophy behind the kindergarten and its methods, but they can never cease to admire the insight and resource of the great inventor of educational plays and games."

Comparison between Kindergarten and Montessori Methods

Kindergarten	*Montessori*
1. *Based on Philosophy* : The principles of education are based on the Philosophy of Froebel. He was a philosopher first, but educator later. His Philosophy is necessary for understanding his method.	1. *Based on scientific attitude* : She was a Doctor and a scientist. Therefore, her method is based on scientific foundations. Its principles are clear cut.
2. *Scope of imagination development* : Story telling, songs and story explanation play etc. are the basis of development of imagination in this method.	2. *No scope of imagination development* : There is no place for such things like fairy tales, plays and songs which develop the imagination of the child.
3. *More scope for social development* : According to Froebel the school is a	3. *Very less scope of social development* : There is not much stress on the

(*Contd.*)

Kindergarten	Montessori
miniature society. Children work in groups. They are taught together. They play together.	development of the individual child and less on social development.
4. *Class-room teaching* : A fixed time-table is follwed. There is important programme of class-room teaching in it.	4. *Individual teaching* : It is quite individual. There is no set time-table. Students are free to learn according to their interest and taste.
5. *Sense training through gifts* : (*a*) There are seven gifts in kindergarten. These gifts are to be presented in a specific order. Each child is provided with an occupation with the gift.	5. *Sense training through didactic apparatus* : (*a*) There are Sensory apparatus for the development of senses which is entirely different from that of kindergarten.
(*b*) Sense training is a part of the other training in this method.	(*b*) Sense training is the primary or basic purpose of this method.
6. *Emphasis on playway* : Play and play activities are greatly emphasised in Froebelian system. All the lessons are accompanied by songs, movements and gestures.	6. *Self corrective apparatus* : No such importance to play is given in Montessori method. There is the self-corrective apparatus and the pupils work freely with it.
7. *The teacher as gardener* : The teacher in the Kindergarten system is like a gardener who looks after the young human plants. He supervises their activities and guides their songs and movements and there is class teaching.	7. *The teacher as Directoress:* In Montessori method the teacher is only a spectator. The didactic apparatus itself is self-corrective and the pupils perform the activities left to themselves. It is on this account that the teacher is called "directress" in the Montessori method. There is free discipline and no commands or

(*Contd.*)

Kindergarten	*Montessori*
	orders are given by the teacher.
8. *Importance to manual activities* : Froebel attaches great importance to manual activities like, gardening, paper cutting, and bead threading etc. Nature study forms an integral part of the curriculum. No exercises for practical life as serving and dining, washing and dressing one-self are given.	8. *Importance to practical activities of daily life* : In Montessori syllabus more importance is attached to the training for practical activities of daily life. They are imparted as a sort of training for citizenship and to be self-sufficient and independent. Dusting, sweeping, cleaning etc. is done by the students themselves.
9. *No place to 3 R's* : The Kindergarten ignores the teaching of 3 R's in its scheme of education.	9. *Special place to 3 R's* : Three R's *i.e.* reading, writing, arithmetic find a very important place in Montessori method and a detailed system of teaching has been devised.
10. *It is not costly* : The Froebel's method can be easily applied to and practised in any type of infant school. The formal gifts may not be made use of, no elaborate material is needed to equip a school to be run on Kindergarten lines. Therefore the apparatus is dispensable.	10. *It is very costly* : A Montessori school requires an elaborate apparatus which is very costly and the school cannot work according to the method advocated unless the apparatus is there. The teacher also requires special training in this method. Hence the apparatus is indispensable in this method.

(*Contd.*)

Similarity between Kindergarten and Montessori Methods

1. Both have invented a method of educating infants. They have given revolutionary change in the concept of the pre-school age.

2. Both of them lay stress on the development of the child from within. They believe that inner nature of the child should be developed.

3. Congenial atmosphere has been stressed by both of them. In this congenial atmosphere the inner growth of the child will take place.

4. Reverence and affection for the child have been greatly emphasized by them. The child's personality should be recognised and even worshipped.

5. Stress on sense training has been given by the two educationists.

Conclusion

The importance of Kindergarten and Montessri Methods has been universaly admitted and most of the Pre-Primary Schools use these Methods in their Pre-Primary Schools which may be named as Nursery, Pre-Nursery, Montessori or Kindergarten Schools.

6

Teaching Devices

We have already discussed various Methods of Teaching in Chapter 5. To make Methods of Teaching interesting and effective, efficient teachers use different Teaching Devices and Audio-visual Aids. In this chapter we propose to discuss various Teaching Devices.

EXPOSITION

"To expose means to open, to exhibit, to display, to disclose, to subject to light."

Purpose

1. Exposition is to enable the children to take an intelligent interest in the proceedings of the lesson.
2. It helps to grasp the purpose of what is being done.
3. It helps the students in developing their intelligence and insight.
4. Its main purpose is to enable the children to grasp the sense or meanings of the subject matter presented in a more comprehensible form.
5. It develops mental activity.

The following points should be kept in mind while using exposition :

1. During exposition children should be encouraged to ask questions to clear their doubts if they have any.
2. The teacher should test the success of the method of exposition in recapitulation.

3. Language used in exposition should be familiar and suitable to the level of the students.

4. Logical sequence should be kept in the exposition. This will develop the student's power of systematic thinking.

5. Rate of exposition should be decided according to the capacity and power of the teacher and students.

6. Use of black-board should be made whenever it is necessary.

7. Sufficient repetition should be done, but it should be in a new form every time.

8. Proper stress should be laid on important points.

EXPLANATION

"Explanation means to make things plain, manifest and intelligible." To explain means "to make plain, manifest, or intelligible; to clear off obscurity; to expound; to lay open the meaning of; to elucidate." According to Panton "Explanation forms a kind of bridge between telling and revealing knowledge to the learners, and it involves a number of techniques as well as narration and description. Throughout the process the teacher must keep in close touch with the minds of his pupils suggesting lines of thought, questioning them, answering their questions, setting them on practical work, examining the result obtained, discussing significant problems etc."

Difference between Exposition and Explanation

1. Exposition aims merely at placing facts clearly before the learner. While explanation aims at showing facts in their proper relationship to other facts in a system.

2. There should be a logical sequence in it.

3. Personal mannerism of speech and behaviour such as repeated 'you see', 'I mean to say' and chalk tossing and ruler wagging are the enemies to the success of oral teaching and should be dettached firmly by the teacher.

4. Black-board should be used to explain important and difficult points.

5. Explanation should come at proper time. No time should elapse between when it is due and when it is tendered.

6. Proper stress should be laid on important points.

7. The aim must always be kept in view.

Limitations of Oral Explanation

1. Oral explanation may take too much time—specially with a talkative teacher.

2. Poorly planned and poorly done, oral explanation wastes time, is ineffective and lacks interest.

3. Teacher's talk invites passivity on the part of the students. When it becomes a pouring in process, it is poorly adopted to adolescent interest in activities.

4. Ineffective explanation fails to hold the interest and attention of the students, and is likely to increase difficulties with discipline.

5. Even good explanation gives no assurance that the students have learnt.

6. Explanation does not provide the opportunity to explore things through learning by doing.

NARRATION

"Narration is an art in itself which aims at presenting to the pupils through the medium of speech clear, vivid, interesting, ordered sequence of events in such a way that pupil's mind reconstructs these happenings and they live in imagination through the experiences recounted either as spectators or possibly as participators."

A good narration well done makes a strong appeal to children's interest. A teacher who has developed considerable ability in narration can do much towards vitalizing school work for children. Experience in narration should develop among children the spirit of cooperation and other qualities so necessary in socialized living. Good narration should result in the development of desirable language habits among children. Narration should linger with children after they leave school.

The chief form of narration is story telling. It gives the teacher rich dividends if he is a good story teller.

The teacher should keep in mind, while using Narration as a device:

1. Narration should be made interesting.

2. Purpose of narration or story telling should be clear in the minds of the students and teachers.

3. Narration or the story should be utilized to inspire the students. Opportunities may be provided to play the story.

4. Narration should be well prepared and the sequence should be kept.

5. The teacher himself should be interested in narration. It should be given in direct speech and not in indirect speech.

6. Narration loses its charm if it is read from a book, magazine or newspaper. It should be told vividly and in a natural tone and manner.

7. Actions should be used where ever they are needed.

8. Narration should be suited to the students.

9. Narration is a gift, but it can also be acquired by the teacher.

DESCRIPTION

"Description is a portrayal in words of a person, object, things or events. It involves a good use of speech and language." According to dictionary meaning "to describe" is "to set forth, define, depict, or portray in words" and description is defined as *"the act of representing a thing by words; account of the properties or appearance of something."*

Purpose of Description

1. The purpose of description is to give a definite mental picture of the same to the pupils.

2. Through description we can give an account of the properties or appearance of something.

Points to Keep in Mind to make Description Effective

1. Description should be simple. Suitable langauge should be chosen for it.

2. It should be clear and vivid.

3. The teacher must have a clear image of the object he wants to describe.

4. Avoid too much details and over-elaboration.

5. Description should be illustrated through models, diagrams or pictures.

6. Description should be continuous. It may be repeated if it is felt so.

ILLUSTRATIONS

According to Good's Dictionary of Education illustration means any material or apparatus that is used by an instructor to clarify points in teaching; concrete objects or material used in teaching, to facilitate understanding and to aid in building standards and in developing judgment and appreciation. For example, articles of clothing, watches, charts, pictures, posters, labels, animals, food etc.'

To illustrate a thing means to explain it, to make it intelligible and to throw light upon it. To illustrate a thing means to make clear, intelligible or apprehensible, to elucidate, explain, or exemplify as by means of figures, comparisons and examples.

Uses of Illustrations

1. Illustrations make an appeal to the senses and the imagination of the learners.

2. They make the idea clear and help the children to acquire correct knowledge.

3. They stimulate interest and excite curiosity. They are helpful in description.

4. Easy and familiar things are used to explain difficult ideas.

5. Abstract ideas are put in concrete form.

6. Illustrations are ready means to fix attention of the children on the topic.

7. They help in developing observation and perceptual dexterity.

8. Illustrations lessen the intellectual tensions, knowledge load is lightened.

Hence, they give vividness and definiteness to children's ideas, strengthen the retention of knowledge learnt and help to recall the facts readily. These illustrations facilitate the learning process and are an effective means to elucidate what is presented to the children.

Types of Illustrations

1. Non-verbal, natural objects or concrete illustrations: for example Models, Real objects, pictorial or photographic representation, black-board sketches, diagrams, paintings, graphs, maps and charts.

2. Verbal illustrations : Analogies, comparisons, similes, word pictures, etc.

The relative importance of these two types of illustrations depends upon the nature of the subject and the level of pupil's development. Lower the classes, the more useful will be concrete illustrations. As the child grows and his intellectual level rises we can use pictures, diagrams, sketches and graphs etc. Verbal illustrations should be used among the children with a higher level of intelligence. They should be used with children at the high stage.

These illustrations are a means to an end and not an end in themselves. These are good servants but bad masters. The following points should be kept in mind while using illustrations:

1. Simple illustrations are more effective. Therefore highly finished illustrations should be avoided.

2. Try to develop illustrations in the presence of the class and should be worked out during the lesson. For example a map in geography should be prepared in the class.

3. Too many illustrations spoil their value. These should be kept in limit. Only relevant illustrations should be used.

4. They should be properly handled and exhibited.

5. Illustrations should be exact and accurate.

6. Varied types of visual aids should be used.

Suggestions for Verbal Illustrations

1. Use those verbal illustrations which are common to the students' experiences.

2. Use an illustration the meaning of which is obvious.

3. Use illustration that actually illumines the idea.

4. Unusual language should be avoided.

5. Use those illustrations which are appoximately accurate.

Caution

The success of the lesson depends upon the right use of illustrations and not on more number of illustrations. "Wisely selected, timely presented, intelligently used, they are an unparalleled asset. Clumsily handled they may spoil the whole show and prove to be the worst liability. Be cautious and careful."

QUESTIONING

Questions are needed particularly in the preparation of unit plans, study guides and work sheets. The teacher is required to formulate questions that will stimulate the child's curiosity and arouse his desire to learn. Questioning is one of the techniques of teaching which all teachers will do well to study.

An efficient teacher said,

> "I keep six honest serving men;
> They taught me all I know,
> Their names are 'What', 'Why' and 'When';
> And 'How' and 'Where' and 'Who'.

Purposes

The following are the purposes of questioning :

1. They help the teacher to test the previous knowledge of the students.

2. The teacher is able to keep the students alert and attentive. He is able to stimulate interest and effort.

3. The questions help the teacher to know whether the children are understanding the knowledge presented or not. Are they following the steps of the lesson or not?

4. Questions guide, encourage thought and thus stimulate mental activity.

5. They help the teacher as a device of fixing the knowledge in the minds of the students.

Prof. Frank A. Butler emphasises the following purposes of questions :

1. To change view points.
2. To bring out cause and effect relationship.
3. To develop new ideas.
4. To promote understanding.
5. To apply information.
6. To stimulate thinking.
7. To develop appreciation.
8. To discover the status of group and individual learning.
9. To create mind set.
10. To test the objectives taught.
11. Questions may also be used for drill purposes.

According to Yokam and Simpson, "Questioning can reveal to the teacher the mental processes of the pupil, they are range and breadth of his knowledge. Questioning may reveal lack of assimilation by the child of even the basic information necessary in thinking about a subject or inconsistencies in his thinking about it, and indicate to the teacher what remains to be done in order that the child may think more adequately." "By questioning the teacher may find that pupils are poor readers, careless in interpretation of questions, lacking in vocabulary, unable to locate information, inferior in organizing ideas independently, weak in comparison, evaluation and judgement."

In the end we can sum up in the words of Ryburn: "A question may have any number of purposes; to stimulate pupil's mental self activity; to motivate the pupil to think; to encourage pupils to participate in the lesson; to focus pupils' attention on the key points of the lesson; to relate the various parts of the lesson to the principal aim of the lesson, unit, and course; to ensure pupil mastery of the basic knowledge and understanding; to evaluate pupil's learning and achievement."

Classification of Questions

Gatto's classification :

1. Memory questions. "Where is Bombay?"
2. Organization. "How did people in colonial days travel?"
3. Causal reasoning questions.
4. Evaluative questions. "Is it a true story?"
5. Inference questions. "Would you like to go to America?"
6. Comparison. "Which was the greater man Nehru or Gandhi?"
7. Analysis. "What makes this flower beautiful?"
8. Interpretation. "What does census mean?"

Classification according to discussion :

1. Detailed questions. It requires single statement. "What happened on 15th August 1947?"
2. Topical questions. It requires a discussion of a topic. "What were the causes of American revolution?"

An Error Classification :

1. Leading question. It gives clue of the answer. "Nehru was better known for his works than for his administration, was he not?"
2. Pumping question. The teacher fires many questions in one question.

Example : "Who was Columbus? What did he do? When did he do it? Why?"

3. Double questions. The teacher puts two questions in one question. "Who was Nehru and why was he famous?"

4. Direct question. "Was George Washington well known for his military genius?"

5. The alternative questions. "What or who was the cause of the Thirty Years' War?"

Classification according to teaching function :

1. Natural questions.
2. Formal questions.

Type of Formal question there are two types of formal questions:

1. Testing questions
2. Teaching on developing questions

Testing Questions

Testing questions are of two types :

1. Preliminary questions.
2. Recapitulatory questions.

Preliminary Questions: These questions are asked in the beginning of lesson

Uses :

1. They are used to test the P.K. of the students.
2. The teacher is able to know what to start and where to start.
3. These questions bring the knowledge of the students in force-front for the new knowledge.

Precautions :

1. These questions should be a few in number.
2. Questions must be relevant to the topic in hand.
3. They should help in brief revision of the previous knowledge.

Recapitulatory questions : These questions generally come at the end of the lesson.

Uses

1. They make the teacher sure that the students have properly learnt the subject matter.
2. They fix the knowledge in the minds of the students.
3. They help the teacher to measure the success of his lesson.

Precautions

1. Children should be allowed to think for a while.
2. Writing on the black-board should be rubbed off.
3. The questions may be detailed questions or topical questions.

Teaching or developing questions

These questions are the back-bone of the lesson. They are used :

1. To develop a particular line of thought.
2. To formulate new generalizations particularly in inductive type of lesson.
3. To build knowledge step by step.

Precautions

1. Such questions should be asked carefully.
2. While narrating a story, questions should not be asked.
3. Patience is required on the part of the teacher.
4. Questions for the sake of questions should not be asked.
5. These questions should lead the students to discover new facts and to solve new problems.

Characteristics of Good Questions

A good teacher should be familiar with the characteristics of good questions. These are:

1. Questions should be concisely stated.
2. Questions should require thought.
3. Questions should not be ambiguous.
4. Questions should be adapted to the age and ability of the students.
5. Questions should avoid 'yes' or 'no' response.
6. The form of the question should not suggest the answer.
7. Questions should involve single idea.
8. Questions should reflect a definite purpose.
9. Questions should conform to the immediate objectives of the teacher.
10. Problem or thought questions are particularly valuable in teaching because they are stimulating to the child's power of thinking.

Techniques of Questioning

By the technique of questioning we mean the ways in which the questioning is carried on. The teacher may use good questions for a good purpose, but if he handles the questioning ineffectively, the procedure may be poor.

There are no hard and fast rules to be followed, but there are procedures that experience has shown to be ineffective. The following criteria are based upon the experiences of good teachers; if judiciously followed, they should enable the teacher to carry on his class work effectively :

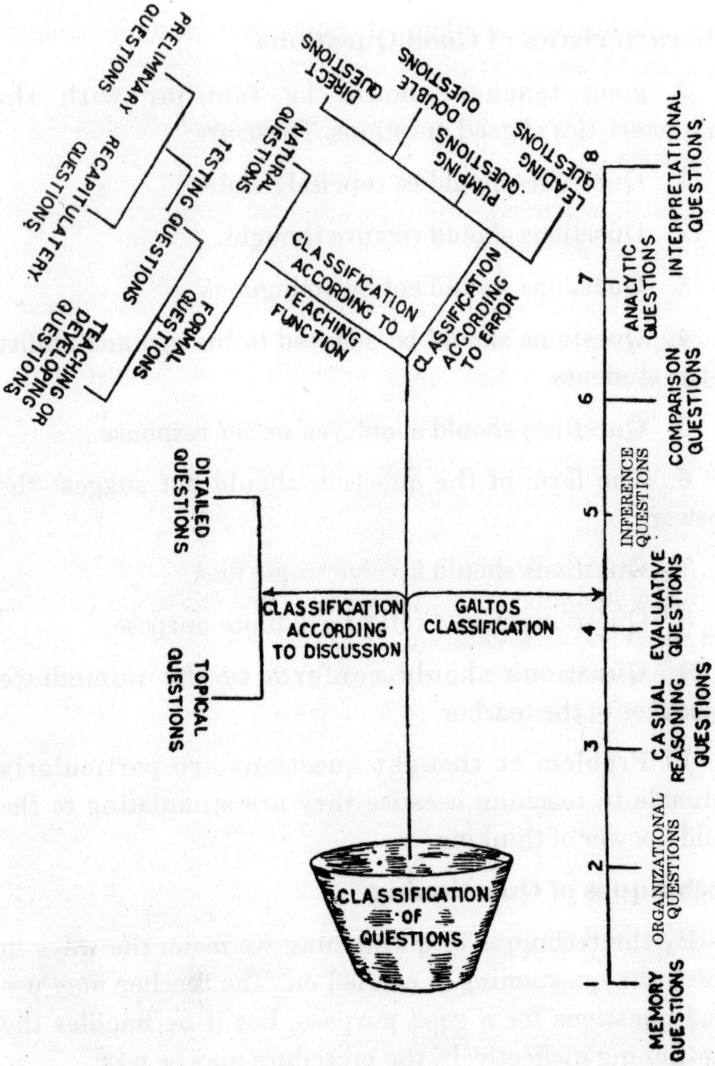

1. Questions should be asked in a natural, interested and conversational tone of voice.

2. Questions should ordinarily be addressed to the group before any particular students is called upon.

3. Questions should be distributed among members of the class to keep every-one interested and alert.

4. The pace of the questioning should be adapted to the objectives.

5. The distribution of questions should be adapted to individual differences.

6. Students who are not paying attention may be asked questions as a means of drawing attention to the work at hand.

7. The teacher should be sufficiently familiar with the work of the course so that he can proceed with the questioning independent of the text book or the lesson plan.

8. Questions should be asked to preserve the unity of the phase of work being undertaken or keep the questions flowing in a developmental stream. Each question should be in proper sequence to ensure that the aims are being achieved.

9. Avoid purposeless questioning.

10. Avoid predetermined distribution of questions to the class in terms of row, alphabet or marks. Every student at times should think that he will be called on to respond.

11. Use words within the vocabulary range of the pupils.

12. Refrain from tricky, misleading or 'catch' questions.

13. Avoid questions which can be answered by a simple 'yes' or 'no'. Such questions do not evoke deep thought in the pupils.

14. Do not, in most cases, repeat the question or the answer; otherwise the students will not be motivated to

constant attention, during the entire questioning process, since they know the teacher will repeat what they missed during their span of inattention.

15. Allow sufficient time for the whole class to think out the answer. It is useful for slower students.

On the whole skilful questioning is not a quickly learned art. It often takes a teacher many years of class-room experience, professional reading and self-evaluation to develop into a proficient questioner. All the while the teacher must make a constant and persistent effort to improve his questioning ability and technique.

Students' Responses to Teacher Questions or Dealing with Answers

Quite as important as the asking of questions is the manner in which the teacher accepts the answers of the pupils. A teacher requires the same care in dealing with pupils' answers, as in questioning them. The students' answers can be classified as below :

1. Right and correct answers.
2. Correct but incomplete answers.
3. Partially correct and partially wrong.
4. Wrong but intelligent answers.
5. Ridiculously wrong answers.
6. Mischievous answers.

Correct answers do not require any special skill to deal with. Other types of answers require sympathetic and careful treatment. The following can be reasons of wrong and incomplete answers :

1. Difficult language by the teacher.
2. Defective explanation of the material presented.
3. Inattention on the part of the pupils.

4. Lapses of memory.

5. Complexity and toughness of the subject matter.

The teacher should observe the following technique to receive the answers of the pupils :

1. No answer, not even totally incorrect one should be flicked off by the teacher. Rather, he should ask the pupil further questions in an attempt to help the pupil to discover for himself why his original response was wrong.

2. No wrong answer should be allowed to slip by, else the pupils will learn wrong facts and concepts.

3. Other members of the class should be encouraged and even asked to correct a pupil's totally or partially incorrect response.

4. Correct answers should be praised to the degree of their worth.

5. Student's responses should be enunciated in a loud, clear voice and expressed grammatically.

6. Responses should not be shouted aloud by the whole class, but rather made by only one student. Collective answers should be discouraged.

7. Answers should always be accepted in complete sentences. Incomplete answers are not to be passed over.

8. Answers should be concise, relevant, exact and accurate in working and content.

9. Children should be given sufficient time to think of the answer.

Student's Questions

Students should be encouraged to ask questions on those points which are not clear to them. This gives them an opportunity to remove their difficulties. Pupil's questions reflect pupils' mental activity.

The teacher should treat all sincere questions with equal interest and consideration, regardless of their source. He should discourage irrelevant questions. If the class as a whole will profit by a discussion of particular questions and they cover points significantly related to the objectives, then they will merit much more than equally important questions that are of interest to only one or two individuals. Questioning the teacher's opinion should not be viewed by the teacher as impertinence, but as a genuine effort on the part of the student to arrive at the truth in his own mind. This is especially important for a democratic country like India.

Techniques which the Teacher should use in responding to Students' Questions

1. Do not immediately answer a pupil's question. Ask another pupil to answer the question. This creates a child-centred class-room situation.

2. Students should be encouraged to ask questions politely.

3. Pupils should be required to frame their questions in good language.

4. Indiscriminate student questions should not be permitted. Educationally insignificant questions should be dismissed by the teacher.

5. Students should be encouraged to ask questions that go deeper than mere factual level.

6. Students who ask questions primarily in an attempt to show off their intelligence should be privately counselled by the teacher.

7. If a teacher is unable to answer a pupil's question, he should say so forth rightly.

ASSIGNMENT

According to Good's Dictionary of Education assignment means, "(1) The act of allotting to classes or individuals specific mental or physical tasks; (2) the work that has been allotted to the pupil or class."

The nature and meaning of the term 'assigment' as described by older view has little place in the modern educational theory and practice.

The modern educationist would like to define the term as applied "to that part of the instructional activity devoted to the clear recognition and acceptance by the pupil of the next unit of learning to take place and of the processes by which this learning may be achieved most effectively." This new meaning of assignment implies four important factors in the process of teaching and learning *viz.* (*i*) laying out a task to be done; (*ii*) fitting to the task a suitable procedure for accomplishment; (*iii*) teacher's guidance but pupil's will to accept the task and do it accordingly, and (*iv*) assumption that the effective learning takes place as a result of pupil's self-imposed activity.

Thus, in the new schools the assignment may be taken as a planning and organising period when both the teacher and the pupils put forth their respective suggestions and proposals for the next work to be done. It becomes a cooperative project in which the teacher is a sympathetic director or guide and pupils are willing workers. Not necessarily that children should always succeed in their efforts; the teacher is there to help, give suggestions and provide direction; he must so manage that they will undertake the work cheerfully and persist in their efforts to solve the problems, collect the material, prepare the reports and do the practice etc., that are necessary for carrying on the activity.

Importance of Assignment

The assignment as a technique of successful teaching has received some attention from the writers, though its importance, until very recent times, has not been fully realised. The significance of assignment is based on the fact that the desire to learn is more important than are methods of teaching. It is pupil's attitude towards learning that matters and not the well-organised courses of instruction. These reasons specify the educational importance of assignment. Teachers ali over have started realising that pupil's interest in learning has to be directed and this can best be done with the help of assignment. In the words of *Douglas and Hubert* : "The assignment represents one of the most important phases of teaching." They have further suggested that the assignment should be recognised "as an aspect of teaching instead of just a preparatory step to teaching." *Prof. Yoakam and Simpson* have rightly observed, "The assignment gives them that guidance (in their activities) in an expert way, prevents failure, provides for the arousal of interest, and makes success reasonably sure. Independent study is not possible without good assignment. That is why the teachers are coming to realize that time and thought spent on planning and making the assignment are likely to affect profoundly the study habits of children and to result in economy in both learning and teaching. If good assignments are made, children can and will study independently with success; but if poor assignments are made, children will fail to profit by the time spent in independent or supervised study."

Purpose of Assignment

The assignment being centrally important in the technique of teaching, may be said to fulfil the following chief purposes :

1. It provides the teacher opportunity to give direction to the learner's activity.

2. It provides the stimulus to which the subsequent activity is the response.

3. It is the determining factor in directing the development of effective habits of study.

In short, the assignment motivates study, stimulates thinking, encourages initiative, clears up misunderstandings, develops insight and understanding.

Characteristics of a Good Assignment

The chief characteristics of a good assignment are :

1. A good assignment relates new unit to previous knowledge to give the impression of *continuity of learning*.

2. It is definite in outlining the work to be done.

3. It is clear and well-defined to the extent of reducing to minimum the loss of pupils' energies in meaningless or fruitless activity.

4. A good assignment clearly indicates the sources of reference to be used during the act of learning.

5. It is interesting and stimulates interest.

6. It guides learning by anticipating difficulties that are likely to arise during the execution of the work in hand. It also suggests ways and means to overcome them.

7. In a good assignment the essential points are emphasised and attention is drawn to them.

8. A good assignment is not just like one-way traffic. It is cooperative and develops with the joint efforts of both the students and the teacher. In this way it emphasises the *'we'* spirit.

9. It stimulates thought and develops insight and understanding for carrying out work.

10. The assignment should be concise but sufficiently detailed to enable each student to understand the task assigned.

11. Motivation is a definite function of a good assignment. For that reason it should arouse interest in the advance work.

12. By making use of the element of suspense, assignment can be made more attractive and more useful than otherwise.

13. The assignment should be motivated chiefly by the hope of worthwhile achievements rather than scholastic reward or the fear of punishment.

Suggestions for Making the Assignments

It is generally believed, and for good reasons, that assignment should be prepared in written form. But it is more useful if the task, to be done, is discussed by the teacher in the class orally, in order to pin-point the essential features of the work. It is also desirable that the teacher should indicate the relevant portions to be studied to guard the students against wasting their time in irrelevant and unnecessary engagements.

"In making the assignment, the teacher must avoid acting like a commander in charge of troops. He must rather regard the assignment period as a time for co-operative thinking and for suggestion." This means there should be *'we'* feeling rather than *'I'* feeling. The teacher should give the impression that he is helping the students, whereas the students should be made to indulge in maximum individual independent work.

Time factor : When to make the assignment, is a widely debated issue. In fact, it is not a matter of hard and fast rules. The only thing for consideration is that the assignment should not be made in a hurried moment. From practical point of view, assignment may be made just in the beginning of the lesson or it may be made at the close of the period. In the former case, the main advantage is that the assignment will attract better attention and will be prepared less hurriedly.

In the later case, the chief advantage is that the assignment will enable the teacher to adapt the assignment to the progress that was made during the period. In making the assignment at the outset of the period of work, the teacher cannot be sure that it will be completed as planned.

Steps in Making Assignments

The teacher must avoid acting like a commander incharge of the troops. He should take co-operation and suggestions from the students. Anyhow he should follow these steps while making assignments :

1. Reference to a previous experience.
2. Discussion.
3. Proposal of a new activity.
4. Discussion leading to the acceptance of the activity.
5. Explanations and clearing up of difficulties.
6. Outlining the materials to be used.
7. Distributing the tasks to be done.
8. Overseeing the beginning of the work, if possible.

The assignment should be recorded either on the black-board or in children's exercise books or in the form of cyclostyled or typed sheets. In this way, it is likely to be forgotten and the child may use the material as a guide in his studies.

Length of the Assignment

The length of the assignment varies with the age and maturity of the children. The following division, though tentative, may be quite convenient.

Primary School	:	Fifteen to twenty minutes duration.
Middle Grades	:	Thirty minutes to an hour and a half duration.
High or Higher		
Secondary school	:	About two hours duration.

Assignment Materials

Assignment materials, the chief among which are the text-books, special reference books, maps, charts, pictures, guide sheets, work books, etc. involve special skill in their handling. Teacher's familiarity with such materials and his skill in their use will create interest in the task in hand and will help both the teacher and pupils in successful completion of the assignment. The choice of printed as well as audio-visual materials should be made strictly according to the needs of the children. This will promote independent study and it "goes a long way towards creating interest, defining work to be done, preventing failure and ensuring progress."

Techniques of Giving Assignments

Techniques to be followed in giving assignments are given below:

1. It should involve the students in its solution and formulation.
2. It should be meaningful for the students.
3. It should further the major aim of the present or future lesson.
4. It should result in educationally significant learnings.
5. It should reinforce past learning.
6. It should be motivated.
7. It should be stated in terms of a problem or problems which will involve the student's creative as well as the assimilative powers.

Evaluation of the Assignment

The progress of independent work, done by the pupils, must be evaluated, because without evaluation the assignment will have no value. Though it is a difficult task to do so in the absence of some experimental procedure, yet a resourceful teacher can make the evaluation by using a good check-list, which he may prepare of his own, based on the criteria laid down above or he may use the check-lists prepared by some writer of repute. Such check-lists have been given by Carr and Wagge in *The Lesson Assignment,* by Yoakam in *The Improvement of the Assignment* and by Bossing in *Teaching in Secondary Schools.* In evaluating the assignment, maximum accuracy with the minimum of detail should be the ideal.

If pupils definitely show some progress in their study-periods and exhibit more interest in the subject, we can attribute a part of it to the effectiveness of the assignment.

Some teachers may feel that it is an extra burden on them, but it has to be done for successful teaching and for realizing the immediate objective of instruction in view.

HOME WORK

According to Good's Dictionary of Education 'Home work' means : "School assignments to be completed out of regular school hours at the residence of the pupil." *Ford* says, "Home study or home work is that which is undertaken outside the normal school day. It is usually done in the student's home." In the words of *Adams*, "It is a step towards self education, enabling the child to use his own resources and work unsupervised." Home-work is a kind of independent work which pupils are expected to do at home, away from the atmosphere of the class and in the midst of home surroundings, to supplement instruction received at school. The child is expected to carry out this work with the assistance of the class-room instruction or sometimes with the help of his parents, elders or private tutors. As a practical teaching device, home-work is a step towards self-education, to steal a phrase from Adams. It is a means of enabling the child to use his own resources and work unsupervised.

The Two-fold Controversy

Contrasting views regarding allotment of home-work have come down from teachers, educators and parents.

Arguments Against Home Work: Those who opine unfavourably say that no home-work should be given to the students. It often seems to parents that home-work is bound to become a cause of friction between home and school in the sense that "the school makes unreasonable demands on the child's powers and time, and is guilty of carelessness in organising such work." They feel that home-work snatches away the easy moments of the child and begets worry, fatigue and distaste and hence, is bound to become a source of weakness.

1. Many teachers use home work as a means of punishing the child.

2. It encourages habit of copying among students.

3. Heavy load of home task may effect the health of the students.

4. Large amount of home work may create distaste for the school.

5. Home work may compel the child to evade home duties, which have an educative value too.

6. Irregularity in attendance, playing truancy from the school and bad habits of copying from others are sometimes the products of home work.

7. It may lead the child towards the *hatred* of the subject and the teacher concerned.

Actually it is not home work that is objectionable, but its nature and amount which invites criticism. Whatever may be the case home work has the advantages too.

Arguments in Favour of Home Work

There are others who believe that home-work is necessary to supplement the five or six hours work at school. They agree that "home work affords a valuable opportunity for the pupil to develop the power of independent and unaided work," and thus gain confidence that he knows what he is taught. Even certain parents especially mothers also feel that some amount of home-work is fundamentally necessary to enable the child to engage himself in useful activity at home. Otherwise, he is necessarily to become a 'devil's workshop' in the spare moments when he is even free from home responsibilities. Home-work spread over the prescribed syllabus is an efficient means of fixing up the subject-matter taught in the class. In fact, home-work "properly understood, skilfully planned, intelligently assigned and sympathetically checked, is indispensable."

P.C. Wren favours it, he says, "An average guardian also feels that some work should be given to the student which he should do at home."

Strange suggests the following purposes of home work :

1. Home work is useful to stimulate voluntary effort, initiative, independence, responsibility and self direction;

2. To encourage a carry-over of worth while school activities into permanent interests;

3. To enrich the school experience through related home activities;

4. To enforce school learning by provoking the necessary practice, integration and application;

5. To consciously relate school learnings to real life;

6. It may also prove as a link for teacher-parent co-operation.

7. It may establish habits of working hard and that too regularly.

8. It utilizes the leisure time of the children which, otherwise would have been wasted.

Dispassionate View: A dispassionate examination of the two-fold controversy would lead us to understand that it is not the home-work that is objectionable, but its nature and amount that stands critical examination. Homework has to be given if success in teaching and learning is our aim. The true objection may be directed against unproportionate, unintelligent and unsympathetic assigning and checking of the same. It is not in one subject that child is expected to do the home-work; he has to satisfy the demands of all the courses of study. Over-burdening the child is simply sinful. The whole charm of concentrated study loses its significance and the child being away from the playground, is likely to develop school mania. Thus, home-work should be carefully manipulated.

"Home-work, no doubt, is important. For many reasons it is desirable to assign. It leads to the formation of independent effort and self-study, the acceleration of the advance of pupils in their work, and the opportunity of securing more effective co-operation on the part of the parents in the education of their children."

Suggested Conditions for Assigning Home-work

Follwoing Conditions must be Observed while Assigning Homework:

1. Home-work should be devoted to the topic covered in the class or to practice in activities already understood.

2. Home-work should form an integral part of the course of study which is being followed at school. Apart from academic work, it may involve informal activities like hobbies connected with various school subjects.

3. Home-work should bring into play, to some extent, individual likes and dislikes. It should satisfy the needs of the particular age-group of children for whom it is meant. For this reason home-work should also be graded, its nature and amount be determined according to the individual's interests, capabilities and convenience.

4. Home-work should be so assigned as not to give the impression of punishment. The pupils should feel that it is meant for their self-improvement.

5. There is no harm if the parents help their wards in successfully completing the home-work. But as far as the work lies within the ability of the pupil, it ought to be done without the help of parents or friends.

6. Home-work should be definite and limited in scope and should be adjusted to the time at the disposal of the pupils. Preferably it should not exceed half-an-hour for lower class children, one hour for children of about thirteen years age, and two hours for boys and girls of above thirteen years.

7. Home-work should not be hastily assigned and carelessly planned. Asking the pupils to "learn the meanings of a few words" or to "read the next paragraph" or to "solve a few arithmetic sums" or to "read from your books whatever you have learnt today in the class," etc. does not speak of certain forthought given to the problem of home-work.

8. Mere assigning of the home-work is not all that is desirable. It should not be sympathetically checked and encouragingly corrected. In the absence of regular checking, the pupils are likely to cheat their parents as well as teachers, thus defeating the very purpose and utility of the task.

9. Prof. Cole is of the opinion that "since the parent knows better than the teacher whether the work is too much or too little for the pupil, the parent ought to be consulted from time to time about home-lessons and a half done lesson ought to be accepted when the exercise book bears a parent's initials."

10. The teacher should not be very rigid in getting the children do the whole of the alloted work. The slow learner should be given the advantage of some reduction in the amount of work; for more intelligent and very quick workers, he should invite the performance of additional voluntary tasks. The pupils who do extra work should be commended in the class to encourage the rest of the pupils to improve their habits of independent work.

11. Peculiar home conditions which are likely to interrupt the work of some students should be discussed with them. They should be advised to arrange their work at a time least likely to be interrupted by domestic duties, or by visitors, or by the affairs of the other members of the family.

12. Home-work should also encourage library reading. Library facilities should be made available to the students for the maximum possible time.

Suggested Type of Home-Work

The current trends in educational practice provide numerous opportunities through home-work which can be best utilised for the development of not only academic side of the pupils but also various hobbies according to the tastes and interests of the pupils. So, instead of becoming a means of spending some dull and dreary hours on the printed pages of the texts, home-work can be rendered an affective tool for developing many-sided personality of the child. A few types of home-work are suggested below:

1. Academic type, such as assigning some exercises in school subjects like mathematics, languages, social studies, science etc. These exercises are based on the principles, rules and generalisations learnt in the class. These exercises are mostly meant for giving practice in the work or subject-matter already done in the class.

2. Cultural and practical type, involving the use of hobbies and other activities in which the pupils are likely to take interest. This type of home-work is meant to break the monotony and boredom of the academic engagements of the pupils. Making models, charts, maps and a few drawings, collecting pictures and preparing scrapbooks, planning out some play and asking the interested students to learn their assigned role, memorising certain lines in respect of debates and declamations, are some such exercises.

3. Advance preparation for the new lesson can be very helpful both to the teacher and to the pupils. The teacher should guide the pupils through well-prepared assignments for the advance work. It should not be taxing. In languages the pupils may be required to find out difficult words, phrases and sentence-patterns; they may just go through the new lesson in History or Geography or even science and so on.

Factors Affecting Home Work

Home work depends on the teacher, the curriculum, parents and the pupil himself.

1. *Teachers* should not emphasise text-books home work. Collateral reading should be given so that the students may use public libraries.

2. *Curriculum.* The nature of the curriculum will also decide the home work.

3. *Parents'* influence on the quality of pupil's home work is considerable. Lack of parental co-operation can do much to vitiate and even sometimes paralyze a youth's efforts at

home work. The teacher should constantly work closely with the parents so that the child is put in a learning atmosphere at home.

4. The pupil's personal attitude towards home study is a significant factor affecting its quality.

Suggestions for Making Home Work Effective

1. Home work should be graded. Its nature and amount must be determined by the individual's capacity.

2. Home work should not be considered as a sort of punishment. Home conditions of the child should be kept in mind.

3. Home time-table should be prepared. All the subjects must get due share of home work allotted.

(*a*) One hour work for age group 11-13.

(*b*) Two to three hours work for age group 14-16.

4. Home work should be duly checked and corrected.

5. It should be assigned after careful thought and planning.

Home work should be selective, attractive, useful and recreative too as far as possible. "Intelligently planned, selectively assigned and carefully checked home work may make the best of the teaching process."

7

Audio-Visual Aids

We have already discussed various Teaching Devices which a good teacher uses to make his lesson interesting, intelligible and effective. He also uses some Audio-Visual Aids for this purpose. We propose to discuss these Audio-Visual Aids in this Chapter.

AUDIO-VISUAL AIDS

There was a time when greater part of learning was thought to be a communication by the word of the mouth. Language was, and it still remains, the most effective tool in learning and teaching. The recent years have seen many new trends in the media of teaching and learning. "In addition to the language tools certain mass media are now gaining acceptance under the general heading of Audio-Visual Aids." More and more teachers have started recognising the over-whelming utility of Audio-Visual education. It is now recognised that Audio-Visual devices are in accordance with the natural learning activities of human beings. They render the teaching learning process interesting, yet they do not simply amuse the pupils as if they were "cheap tricks to kid the pupils into learning." So, they are not to be regarded as ends in themselves but only *means to an end,* the end being creative teaching and purposeful learning. In short, Audio-Visual devices "are means that can be employed to teach pupils what words mean and to aid them in critical thinking, which is the basis of the higher forms of learning. Such, then become, devices or procedures that help to make learning more meaningful, more interesting, and effective."

VISUAL AIDS

Visual-Aids work through the eye-gate. *A visual-device is any instructional device that can be seen but not heard.* Whatever is seen by the child easily leaves its imprint on his mind and thus aids learning. In visual devices we may include such common place aids as chalk-board, bulletin board, flannel board, posters, cartoons, drawing and sketches, use of colours and school museum, pictures, flash cards, films, etc. Most of these aids can be successfully improvised or easily procured by a resourceful teacher for his use in the class-room. In the following pages we shall describe these aids.

THE CHALK-BOARD OR BLACK-BOARD

Meaning

A chalk-board or a black-board is a medium upon which words or illustrations can be written or drawn in chalk. The chalk-board is one of the most common of all the audio-visual materials.

According to Good's Dictionary of Education, chalk-board means, "a smooth surface for writing or drawing with chalk or crayon; generally, made from slate, glass, plastic, porcelain, metal or wood or composition board painted with a dull finish usually coloured black, pastel green, or yellow and written upon with chalk or crayon of sharply contrasting colours."

Importance

The chalk-board or more commonly named as black-board is the never-failing friend of a teacher's equipment for visual instruction. This is probably the most widely used visual aid. The importance of this visual aid lies in the fact that in spite of newer and better devices in vogue, the chalkboard remains irreplaceable as well as indispensable for teachers, one and all. The importance of the chalkboard has been pointed out by saying that today it is "as much a part of teaching institution as the desks, chairs, registers, and other important materials. It is the cheapest and most valuable teaching device and continues to be *sine qua non* of our educational system." It is not only the most universally available medium of visual instruction, but also "one of the most valuable devices for making instruction concrete and understandable." Prof. Struck observes : "It should be regarded as a medium to be used by both teacher and pupils. For the teacher, it is a means of making instruction effective; for the pupil, a means of self-expression and sense participation."

Need and Use of Chalk Board

As essential tool of instruction, it is used :

(*a*) to explain and illustrate certain difficult points in a lesson;

(*b*) to make confusing verbalism clear with the help of sketches, diagrams, outline etc.

(*c*) to provide motivation in the class and to enlist pupils' attention to pertinent aspects of instruction.

(*d*) to give convenience to the teacher in the presentation of his lesson. The teacher can use it to list items, the important points of his lessons or to draw illustrations for the class and having explained them, he can rub off the chalkboard writing to leave it as fresh as ever for further use.

(*e*) to help the pupils in notes-taking. By writing the information on the board, the teacher will ensure accuracy and clarity.

(*f*) to provide group instruction. Its size, location and economical use makes it an indispensable teaching device.

(*g*) to work out group projects. Group projects in various school subjects *viz.* Social Studies, Art, Nature Study, Science, Arithmetic etc. can be planned, illustrated and executed through the medium of chalkboard.

(*h*) to make out how far the pupils have understood the main points of the lesson. The pupils can be called upon to use the chalkboard to show their grasp.

Advantages of Chalk Board

(*a*) It fosters pupil's participation in the lesson, especially during those times when they can write or draw on it.

(*b*) It provides a good medium for pupil practice, particularly it is beneficial when witnessed by the whole class under the guidance of the teacher.

(*c*) It enables the teacher or the pupil to write down concise principles, key words, out-lines and summaries of the lessons.

(*d*) It is inexpensive.

(*e*) It can be used again and again to explain a point.

(*f*) It is handy for making a diagram or for writing something.

Types of Chalk-boards

1. **Fixed black-board :** Fixed in the wall facing the class-room.

2. **Black-board on Easel :** It is portable as well as adjustable.

3. **Roller black-board :** Such a board is made of thick canvas wrapped on a roller. The teacher keeps on rolling the baord and continues writing.

4. **Graphical board :** It has graphical lines and is used for teaching mathematics, science and statistics.

5. **Magna board :** A sheet of soft steel is mounted on such a backing, as a black-board and painted whatever colour is needed. Small magnets are used to hold suitable objects fixed where-ever they are put on the vertical surface. Pictures, charts etc. can be fixed easily on it.

Any how, due consideration should be given to the size, colour and quality of a chalk-board. It should be painted with a good black paint and should not shine.

Suggestions for Proper Use of Chalk Board

The following points may be kept in mind while using the chalk-board :

1. As Summer puts it, "The clue to all black-board work is boldness and simplicity." It is not good to crowd the chalk-board.

2. The teacher should present the material in brief, concise and simple statements.

3. All words and illustrations should be large enough to be seen by the entire class.

4. All words should be legible and illustrations clear.

5. Graphs, charts and diagrams should be employed where ever they are needed.

6. It is good to plan the chalk-board layout ahead of time and not in your lesson plan.

7. Difficult illustration can be put before the class begins.

8. The teacher should collect and use everything needed for the chalk-board use—chalk, ruler, eraser and other necessary materials.

9. Use coloured chalk for emphasis, beauty and aesthetic appeal.

10. The teacher should stand by the side of Chalk Board to enable the pupils to have full view of the board and a side view of the teacher. He should avoid turning his back to the class. This way the chances of indiscipline are decreased and the attention of the class is focussed on the material of the chalk-board.

11. The teacher should ensure that his writing is seen by every pupil in the class.

12. Important points may be underlined and explained with the help of a pointer.

13. The chalk used should be of good quality. The chalkboard surface should be even and smooth.

14. When not in use, keep the chalk-board clean.

15. The teacher should prepare the complicated illustrations before the class meets.

16. Divide the chalk-board into convenient parts and explain different lesson units in each part.

17. The pointer should be used when discussing a point or a word which is written on the black-board.

18. The chalk-board should be cleaned with a wet sponge so that its surface remain clear.

19. Due consideration should be given to the size, colour and surface quality of the chalkboard. The chalkboard surface should not give out glare.

To conclude, the chalk-board is an indispensable teaching device and is useful for planning, crystallizing main points and for summarizing and reviewing results.

THE BULLETIN BOARD

Closely associated with the chalk-board is another visual aid known as the bulletin board. According to Good's Dictionary of Education, a bulletin board is, "a board to which can be fastened pictures or other materials that are intended for display."

Bulletin boards provide the cheapest and multipurpose nucleus for visual education.

The bulletin board is a kind of display board which can be adopted to every teaching process—tutorial, lecture assignment or group work. These boards are generally made of wool with thick flannel cloth on it and a wooden frame running around with glass set inside. The bulletin board display can be an integral participant in the life of the classroom. It provides a natural outlet for pupil's artistic and creative tastes. It enriches the textual atmosphere of the class-room. It provides suitable place for displaying current news items from the newspapers and magazines. School news connected with students' outstanding achievements in studies, co-curricular activities, sports, hobbies etc. can also be displayed on such boards. Some important school announcements can also be conveniently displayed on the bulletin boards.

Suggestions for Proper Use of Bulletin Board

The following guidelines should be kept in mind while using the bulletin-board as a device :

1. The bulletin board should be placed at the most frequently visited place. It should be placed where it can easily be seen by all the students.

2. The teacher should capitalize on all bulletin board space in the class-room.

3. Various articles for display on the bulletin board should be arranged in an attractive and artistic manner. Use coloured tape for divisions and underlinings.

4. Reference to the bulletin board displays should be made during the instruction periods. This will draw the children towards the boards.

5. Do not overcrowed the board.

6. The bulletin board is primarily a mirror of students' activities. Encourage them to actively take part in bulletin-board activity. A Students' Committee under the guidance of a teacher should be constituted to keep feeding the board. The material should be frequently changed and carefully edited every time.

7. Make the bulletin board tell a story.

Where there is a bulletin board on display, such eye catching sign boards as "Stop, Look, Read and Think", "Tomorrow's News Today," etc. should be put.

Content of the Bulletin Board

The bulletin board is a place for bulletins, news items, announcements, multifarious items and visual displays that are of absorbing interest to the students.

Purpose of Bulletin Board

1. They motivate and arouse curiosity in the pupils.

2. To display graphic and pictorial material, possibly related to the curriculum, attractively and invitingly.

3. To introduce or summarise a unit of work or to analyse a topic graphically.

4. To display work done by the pupils.

5. To provide basic means of general communication.

Uses

1. Motivational : Poses problems, asks questions, excite curiosity.

2. Developmental : Keeps track of what students are doing.

3. Cumulative : They put graphic cumulation.

4. Miscellaneous : News events, students' events are displayed.

Arrangements of the Bulletin Board

1. Choose and illustrate the head line which should be easy to read from any spot. Use either script or block letters.

2. Arrange and illustrate contents, use illustrative materials, *i.e.* photographs, drawings, charts etc. Match the arrangement and materials against the background. Use arrows, colours, highlight the main theme by a catchy device. Use colours, because they have functional aspects. Use warm and cool colours together.

3. (*a*) The bulletin board should be attractive and aesthetically pleasing.

(*b*) The materials displayed should be changed frequently, probably every week.

(*c*) Each class-room should have its own bulletin board and each department should be responsible for one or more bulletin boards in the corridors.

(*d*) Bulletin board material should be organized and built around the central theme; present a problem solving situation.

(*e*) Relate what is on the bulletin board to the pupil's past learnings and experiences so that learning is facilitated.

In short, make the bulletin board as an interesting affair and as useful a device as possible.

THE FLANNEL BOARD

The flannel board is a stationary or portable surface covered with a rough flannel-like cloth, usually in black, dark blue or grey colour. It can be used for displaying various objects such as pictures, magazine or newspaper, cut outs, graphs, drawings, text book material and illustrations. An outstanding feature of the flannel board is that the objects to be placed on the board have 'flannel like' backing and so adhere to it without using any tape. This enables the teacher to develop an idea step by step in a very dramatic and impressive manner.

In teaching, the flannel board serves a function similar to that of a chalk-board. The boards may be designed in any size depending upon the needs of the teacher, as regards the amount of material to be covered and the time allotted for the presentation. Again, the use of the flannel board depends upon the learning situation. The specific techniques to be employed in the use of the board is determined by the nature of the material to be covered in the class-room. The possibilities of using the flannel board in teaching are quite sufficient in every subject in the curriculum. It is a useful device for teaching arithmetic, science, social studies, languages, fine art, music, industrial and home economics. Kindergarten-primary teachers are now using the flannel board to supplement story-telling and to help children grasp the rudiments of readings. Stories, poems, essays etc. in teaching languages can be effectively illustrated through the F.B.

Purpose

1. To save time during the class presentation.
2. To encourage visual presentation of ideas, concepts and colours.
3. To show movements and arrangements.
4. To show cumulative process.

Suggestions for Proper Use of Flannel Board

1. All the objects on the flannel board should be unified into a single concept or impact.
2. The board should not be cluttered with too many objects.
3. Objects should be arranged in an interesting and attractive manner.
4. Lettered signs should be large enough for the entire class to be sen easily.

POSTERS

Meaning

Good's Dictionary of Education defines poster as "A placard, usually pictorial or decorative, utilising an emotional appeal to convey a message aimed at reinforcing an attitude or urging a course of action."

A poster is a pictorial device designed to attract attention and communicate a story, a fact, an idea or an image rapidly and clearly. "Posters either advertise and sell an idea or convey a message to educate." A poster is designed to attract the passer-by, to catch his attention or the image therein. Posters exert a great influence on the observer. A poster demonstrates vividly and clearly one single idea at a glance. Its essential features are :

1. **Brevity :** Use the minimum words, *i.e.* 4 or 5.

2. **Idea or a feeling :** Idea should be put in the original form.

3. **Simplicity of lay-out :** This refers to the arrangement of the elements of the poster.

4. **Efficient use of colour :** (*a*) Use bold illustrations. (*b*) Avoid fancy lettering style. (*c*) Proper use of colour makes the poster more attractive.

Purpose of the Posters

1. Posters are used to present a single idea or a subject forcefully.

2. They motivate school and class interests.

3. They publicize important school and community events and projects.

4. They add atmosphere to the class-room.

5. They compel attention by some attractive feature and thus convey the message quickly.

6. Posters can be used in the class-room at every or any stage of presentation of a lesson, *i.e.* introduction, presentation or review.

Size and Lay out of Posters

The size of the poster will depend upon the size of the class-room

1. Large size can be of 42″ × 26″.
2. Small size can be of 26″ × 21″.

Letters should by clearly separated and proportioned.

Suggestions for Preparing a Poster

1. Decide your theme.
2. Decide words that are most suitable to provide a slogan or a title.
3. Sketch some layouts and decide on the best.
4. Gather all required material to prepare the poster.
5. Prepare the lettering.
6. Add desired objectives.
7. Give the finishing touches and erase the smudge marks.

CARTOON

Good's Dictionary defines the cartoon as "An interpretive picture, usually a drawing, intended to convey a message or point of view about things, events or situations; may make free use of exaggeration and symbolism." According to general view, "A cartoon tells its story metaphorically which carries great weight as compared with a direct statement. The symbolism of the cartoon tells its message."

Uses of Cartoons

1. A definite story is told in an interesting manner with the help of a cartoon.
2. Cartoons appeal to the young and old and arouse interest and motivate learning.
3. Cartoons are valuable materials for social studies.
4. Children can concentrate and develop their intelligence through the study of cartoons.
5. It can be used as a teaching and fixing device.

Limitations of Cartoons

(*a*) Cartoons may be wrongly interpreted and the student may get wrong impression.

(*b*) For young students it is difficult to interpret the cartoon.

(*c*) Average and below average students cannot understand a cartoon easily.

Suggestions for the Effective Use of Cartoons

1. We should be careful against wrong impressions formed and against the stereotypes perpetuating false idea.

2. The teacher should correct wrong assimilation.

3. Cartoons may be prepared by the students and can be taken from magazines.

4. Selection of cartoons should be made to make teaching effective.

5. As cartoons are either 'for' or 'against' something, they give out a black and white judgment. The teacher should explain well in either case and encourage students to make cartoons for school and children's magazine.

6. It is a good plan to arrange for a new cartoon each week to maintain the curiosity and continued interest of the students.

SCHOOL MUSEUM

Museum is derived from the Greek word 'Mouseion' meaning temple of muses. It is a place of study which specializes in assembling, protecting and showing of objects, specimens and exhibits of great variety.

Types of Museum

Museums are of many types, for example (*a*) general museum, (*b*) museum of art, (*c*) museum of history, natural history, applied science, (*d*) children's museums and (*e*) trailside museum.

Dr. Good distinguishes the following types : (*a*) National museum, (*b*) Local museum, (*c*) Provincial museum, (*d*) City museum, (*e*) College and school museum, (*f*) Class museum, (*g*) Cabinets for special research.

School Museum

School museum is a source of learning in which the material is readily available for teaching and giving instructions to the students in class-room situations. These can be developed through the imagination and initiative of the teacher and active participation of the motivated pupils. Different class-rooms or subject rooms can have separate museums. One museum can have different corners of different types of subjects. School museum should have some show cases of general interest which can be kept in corridor, assembly hall or the library.

Purpose of the Museum

1. To provide exercises in group projects and correlated activities covering various areas of the curriculum.

2. To promote sharing of experiences by group visits and discussions.

3. To exhibit materials which may be foreign to the direct experiences of the students.

4. To relate the abstract idea, concrete material and thus build clear cut understanding.

5. To integrate scattered ideas to derive a new concept.

6. To concentrate attention, to foster stimulation and to provide clarification in relation to the topics of study.

Material for the School Museum

1. Ready-made study-kits and correlated visual aids to build a display on different topics.

2. Objects and specimens collected through the resources of the students.

3. Dicarded material available from city exhibition available on request.

4. Study kits and cheap material available from industries.

5. Dolls, toys, preserved flowers, stamps, coins, ancient relics, art and pictorial materials, raw materials like minerals, food and industrial commodities can be preserved in a museum.

How to Organize a Museum

1. Exhibits should be kept clean and properly labelled. Labels should be uniform, legible and simple. Each label should have a heading and short description of the object.

2. Do not over-crowd a section. Children may get confused by seeing too many items.

3. Simplicity and clarity should be the guiding principle.

4. Let the children examine the object or model or even operate a machine.

5. Each exhibit should have a measuring for the students; for the museum is to integrate and organize knowledge.

6. Each section should have a summary of what it contains and how does it pertain to the school curriculum.

7. Exhibits should never be allowed to appear stale. These should be ever-evolving and changing with the interest and needs of the children.

8. Prepare such exhibits that may possess the power to attract the so called public appeal.

DRAWINGS AND SKETCHES

Drawings and sketches are very interesting and effective visual aids which make teaching meaningful.

Drawings

Drawings have been defined by Good's Dictionary of Education as "depicting on a surface, such as paper, with pencil, crayon, pen, brush, or other graphic means, may be free hand or instrumental, representational or purely informational or diagrammatic."

A teacher may use drawings in some sequence to make the learning process more clear.

Uses of Drawings and Sketches

1. They develop the power of imagination and creative thinking.

2. They have great story value.

3. They may be used as teaching as well as fixing devices.

Limitations of Drawings and Sketches

(*i*) They need the teacher's interest and will to use drawing.

(*ii*) Ordinary students cannot use the drawings more effectively.

(*iii*) They are costly also when purchasd in oil painting form.

Sketches

Graphic aids require some understanding of simple sketching techniques. It is not necessary for a teacher to be an artist for developing these aids. Any teacher can draw simple sketches with the help of some simple techniques analysed here.

Sketching with grid or graph lines : A picture or a sketch can be reproduced in a smaller or larger size by drawing grid or graph lines or squares on the sketch. With this technique pictures and sketches can be reproduced fairly accurately to any size.

Sketching with the help of Pantograph : A Pantograph is a convenient device for enlarging or reducing a sketch. This instrument can be fixed to a table or drawing board at one of its extremities set aside for this purpose. The Pantograph can be adjusted either to enlarge or to reduce the original to different proportions.

Enlarging with the help of transparent glass : This drawing apparatus is useful in providing proper perspective to the sketches. Sketching of the diagrams and of different elements of education are very useful for a teacher in learning teaching situations.

Advantages

(*i*) They create interest and stimulate original thinking among the students.

(*iii*) They help in clarifying the difficult parts of the lesson.

Limitations

1. Sketches are difficult to draw and to get from the market.
2. Being laborious work teachers do not take part in it.
3. They are expensive aids.
4. They are beyond the reach of the ordinary and weak students.

USE OF COLOURS IN TEACHING

Colours are very important in human life. All people use colours for pointing different thoughts and ideas hidden behind them. Colours can greatly increase the effectiveness of the visual teaching material.

Uses of Colours

1. Colour helps to classify explanations.
2. Colours help in isolating elements.
3. Colours are used to emphasise distinctions and to bring into prominence certain aspects of the subject matter.
4. It brings the vividness and reconstructs the reality in an appealing manner.
5. The use of colour makes the atmosphere conducive to learning.

Suggestions for the use of Colours

1. Colours should be used in functional aspect.

2. Use of too many colours is to be avoided.

3. Colours may be used in preparing different types of audio-visual aids.

4. The teacher should use colours in his lesson for psychological appeal.

5. A colour should be judged in the context of the subject-matter.

Colour Harmony

If we want colour harmony and to produce desired effects we must bear in mind that :

1. **Visibility in colour is the highest** : When there is strong contrast in dark and light, intensity in warm and cool colours.

2. **Intensity :** Colours of equal intensity attract quickly.

3. **Dominance :** Only one warm or cool colour should dominate in a colour scheme. Equal amount of each colour produce the dull effect.

4. **Colour advance or recede :** Red, orange and yellow are considered as warm and advance towards the observer, while blue, blue-green and violet are cool and recede from the observer. Bright colours seem nearer to us as compared to neutralized ones. A bright red or blue appears nearer than a dull red or dull blue.

5. **Contrasting colours :** Contrast in colours becomes greatly effective in the following combinations : (*a*) black on yellow (*b*) yellow on black (*c*) red on white (*d*) yellow on blue (*e*) orange on brown, (*f*) pink on black.

Colour harmony is best produced when red-voilet, red, red-yellow, or yellow-green, green, blue-green, etc. are adjoined. Red and blue-green, yellow and blue-violet, green and red-violet are opposing and unrelated colours. A black or white background always bring together discordant colours. Thus the teacher is advised to work out various combinations to produce specific effects. In every learning situation the teacher must make a judicious choice of the colour scheme to make the teaching material more effective.

AUDIO-AIDS

Whereas Visual Aids work through eyes Audio Aids appeal to ears. There are various Audio Aids which teachers can use to making their teaching effective. Some of Audio Aids are : Educational Radio and Educational Recording.

EDUCATIONAL RADIO

The use of radio to fulfil certain educational purpose is quite of recent origin but an important phase of education in India and abroad. Primarily designed to entertain the general public, the educational use of radio, both in city and rural schools, is fast gaining ground. In the words of Shri K.N. Srivastava, "The Radio is full of promise for the future of our education." Though it has not yet revolutionised the field of education, still it promises to become a potential force in educational practice and teaching procedure.

Potential Values of Educational Radio

The following are some of the important features of the potential values of educational radio in the teaching procedure.

1. **Enrichment of the school programme :** If properly used and efficiently organised, radio service can help in many ways in enriching the existing programme of the school. It is possible to bring into the class-room the proceedings of parliament sessions, some presidential addresses at some important functions in the capital or some

other part of the country, or the visit of some V.I.P. and many more such events through radio reports on them. In recent years, frequent broadcasts of prominent foreign leaders, particularly through activities at the United Nations meetings in New York, have given the school opportunities to stimulate the interest of pupils in international affairs. Again, radio broadcasts contribute to a large extent in remedying the ills of monotonous and routine class-room instructions. Alert teachers and efficient school administrators can utilize school broadcasts for educative, informative and interest creating purposes. Listening to radio broadcasts widens the range of pupils' experience, supplements class-teaching and enriches school programme.

2. **Furnishing up-to-date material :** Radio programmes and school broad-casts furnish up-to-date and correct materials on day-to-day happenings in the country and outside it. Radio commentaries on national and international events are of great help to Geography or Social Studies teacher who can keep his students well informed about what goes on in the world around them. So much so, many of the school broadcasts "attempt to supplement or correct our text-book information with the most recent developments in various areas of human knowledge and activities."

3. **Bringing the school into vital contact with the world around :** The school has tended to be isolated from what goes in on the world around. Away from the four walls of the school, there stretches a wide world which is the right place for the child to stay in. He needs understanding of the same. "The radio is one of the effective ways of making the youth conscious of the world outside and of vitally linking the school with this outside world."—its important personalities and contemporary problems.

4. **Developing critical thinking :** Radio broadcasts to which the pupils are supposed to listen carefully and

attentively help a lot in developing their critical thinking and discriminating judgement about what is being presented to them. It helps them to cast off the shadow of false propaganda and thus see things in their true perspective.

5. **Developing leisure-time interests and appreciations :** The modern world offers more leisure-time activities and opportunities than ever before. The radio seems to be a very important medium of useful and interesting leisure-time activities. The school must help the youth in learning how radio may be best utilised to the greatest advantage during this leisure time.

6. **Students' participation :** The radio offers ample opportunities for students' participation in radio-programmes. 'Radio, on account of giving opportunity for students' broad-casting, creates spirit of emulation in other children to show their histrionic potentialities."

Using Radio in the Class-Room

The class-room use of radio is a real test of the teacher. The best teacher is the one who is able to make the best use of every kind of experience—in or outside the class-room. In case of radio, it is not enough to tell the pupils, "Now close your books. Let's have a radio programme." And as the radio programme is over, the teacher is outside the class-room and the pupils have not become wiser than before.

The following are four major phases of class-room procedure in the use of the radio :

1. **Preparation :** Preparation for the experience of listening is very important if the radio is to become a useful tool of teaching and learning. Preparation involves the following aspects :

   (*a*) *Clear objectives :* The teacher should have clearly in mind the aims of a particular radio programme.

(*b*) *Gathering advance information* : All possible information regarding the programme should be gathered by the teacher before hand.

(*c*) *Motivation* : Advance information about the radio broadcast will enable the teacher to arouse pupils' interest in the subject-matter. The students should be motivated properly by telling them what they are going to listen to and how far the broadcast will benefit them.

2. **Reception** : Reception, which involves proper listening, can be facilitated by providing suitable physical conditions in the class-room. The teacher should make sure that the class-room is well-arranged, there is no overcrowding and that the radio is in perfect working condition and its volume is adequate enough to enable all the students listen to the broadcast properly.

3. **Discussion and application** : Immediately after the broadcast, a good discussion on the main points of the broadcast should follow. If possible the teacher may do well to use some other visual aids to clarify some of the difficult aspects.

4. **Follow-up** : A proper follow-up of students' understanding of the information gathered from the broadcast will serve a useful purpose in the sense that it will remove fallacies and misunderstandings, if any. The follow-up may be done in the form of a short test covering the major points of the broadcast.

School Subjects Adopted to Radio

1. **Social Studies** : Interesting programmes on various branches of social studies like history, geography, civics, economics, etc. can be broadcast on the air. Radio lessons may include past and present history, lives of great men, information about true citizenship and forms of governments etc.

2. **Science :** Science is another field of human activity which has vast scope for radio broadcast. Various scientific inventions, new developments in Physics, Chemistry, Botany or Zoology, can be programmed on the air in a most interesting manner. Interesting discussion on such topics as "Science and Better Living,' 'Science and War', 'Science in Every Day Life' etc. can be relayed.

3. **English and other languages :** The teacher of English can use the radio for several purposes, the chief among which is training in good speech. Pronunciation is the major consideration in teaching a foreign language. Radio offers excellent possibilities for inspirational material for composition, both written and oral.

4. **Music :** Radio is an effective means for promoting appreciation in music. Besides providing entertainment, patriotic songs relayed on the air are highly effective in infusing patriotic feelings in the young hearts. This is of particular importance during the days of foreign aggression.

Problems and Limitations of Using Radio

Whatever the teaching aid and howsoever useful it may be, it does have its own limitations. Likewise, some of the major limitations of educational radio may be pointed out here :

1. Listening to radio broadcasts requires concentrated attention which may at times be interrupted.

2. Radio broadcast is only one way communication and the listeners cannot 'talk back' to ask questions or clarify doubts during the broadcast.

3. It is a great limitation to adjust radio broadcast to the working hours of a particular class or even the school.

4. Radio itself is, of course, a "one shot" device. As pointed out above, through the use of recordings, it is possible to meet certain difficulties of schedule.

5. Administrative problems, particularly in smaller schools, may inhibit the proper use of the radio. Sometimes a conservative head may not fully appreciate the potential value of the broadcasts and is likely to regard the radio as "another headache" and treat it as such. Sometimes it becomes desirable to educate even the school administrators.

Future of Educational Radio

Educational radio promises bright future. Frederic Wittis has rightly observed : "I like to think of Education by radio as a timely, vital and dramatic thing; a system of learning or acquiring more information; a means of widening one's horizons or enriching one's life and breaking down prejudices through inspiration and perspiration : an education by desire and not by discipline; a moving panorama of the world in which we live." Predicting the future in educational radio, R.G. Reynolds has aptly remarked: "Some day its use as an educational instrument will be as common place as text-books or black-boards."

EDUCATIONAL RECORDINGS

Besides radio, educational recording is another sound media which can be effectively put to use for teaching in schools. The two major forms of recording for school use are disc and tape.

In the following pages, we shall describe the two types of recordings.

Teaching Potentials of Recording

1. **Recordings are two way communication :** Recordings can be stopped at will to discuss passages, to answer questions, to clarify certain points. It can be made to play over and over again.

2. **Recordings eliminate the time-adjustment problems of the radio :** Recordings can be made to play

at desire and need. The teacher can fit them into his class-room time schedule. This way even the radio material that would otherwise be lost, can also be used to suit teaching needs.

3. **Recording can be re-heard and evaluated :** The teacher can play his recording before using them in the classes and thus see how far they are suitable to fulfil the objectives for which they are meant.

4. **Recordings offer a wide range of helpful material :** The recording material can be usefully explored. The teacher can familiarise himself with the wide variety of materials available and evaluate them for his class-room use. Catalogues on recording materials can be asked for from leading suppliers.

5. **The school can have its own recording :** School's own recordings carry great potential values and advantages both for students and teachers. Disc recordings can be prepared by only those schools which can afford to spend extraordinary finances. Tape-recording is comparatively cheap and the recorded tapes can be preserved in the school.

6. **Recordings are to the ear what pictures are to the eye :** "Both, recordings and pictures reconstruct direct reality as faithfully as possible. Both enable us to overcome obstacles of time and space so that we can relive the original experience whenever we choose?"

Types of Recording

Recordings are of three types, namely: (*i*) Phonograph records (or discs recording), (*ii*) Wire recording, and (*iii*) Tape recording. All these recordings serve the same purpose, the difference is only in speed and size. Recordings can be used—

1. for introducing a lesson,
2. for illustrating some facts or skills,
3. for enriching class-room activity, and

4. for summing up a topic.

If properly exploited, this multi-purpose use of recordings can be utilized by the teacher to enrich class-room work.

1. **Gramophone records :** Gramophone is an audio-aid useful in many ways. The gramophone records offer such a range of first-class material that most teachers prefer to use them at some stage in the course. It is possible to bring high class music, rare speeches and addresses of contemporary political and socially important persons, textual materials and specific instructional lessons into the class-room. Gramophone or linguaphone records can be utilised to mend speech defects in one's own language and to teach good pronunciation in a foreign language. Besides being useful in the class-room procedures, gramophone can be used in several ways for co-curricular activities in the school. The dramatic and music club may utilise it for songs, dancing, background music in a particular scene and for many other items.

Gramophone discs vary in the speed with which they rotate on the machines that reproduce their sounds—the 'record player' or 'playback' machines. Disc or gramophone records are available in speeds of 78, 45 and 33 1/3 r.p.m. and their diameters range from 7 to 16 inches. Not an ordinary gramophone or playback but a good record player equipped for several speeds is the one most useful for the class-room.

2. **Tape recording or tape recorder :** The tape recorder is a very useful teaching device which is gaining favour with teachers and educationists. Tape recorders use a thin piece of metal, plastic or paper tape. Tape recordings are less at fault than wire recordings and have a high longevity. Educationally speaking, the tape recorder can be used to record :

(*a*) Radio programmes for class-room use.

(*b*) Pupils' discussions, debates, round table talks etc.

(*c*) Speeches at celebrations, ceremonies, political rallies.

(*d*) Interviews with workers, businessmen, community leaders.

(*e*) Extracts from disc records, with comments.

(*f*) Plays, class-room dramatizations, puppet shows etc.

(*g*) Student participations in assembles.

(*h*) Corrective work in speech.

(*i*) Documentary transcripts of children and adults at work and at play.

(*j*) Musical scores.

The above uses of the tape-recorder may be supplemented by many more according to teaching situations.

3. **Wire recording :** As the name suggests, sound may be recorded on a wire approximately 5 thounsandth of an inch in diameter. One of the outstanding advantages of wire recording is that it will not only play back the recording as frequently as desired but it may also be used over and over again for other programmes simply by erasing the previous programme. Though not a very common feature of school recording in India, not even abroad, wire recorders promise good future.

PROJECTED VISUAL AIDS

The projected visual aids are of the following types :

(*a*) The Opaque Projector,

(*b*) Teaching Slides,

(*c*) Film Strips.

THE OPAQUE PROJECTOR

The opaque projector is a wonderful teaching device with the help of which it is possible to make vivid enlarged projections of objects from the size of a postage stamp to practically that of a quarter page. In an ordinary class room, the projections can be made visible to anyone, even to a student sitting in the remote corner or on the rearmost bench. The opaque projector will project and simultaneously enlarge, directly from the originals, all kinds of written, printed or pictorial matter, in any sequence desired by the teacher.

The Opaque Projector in Teaching

The opaque projector serves many educational purposes. In procedures, the teacher may use it for the following purposes, according to his needs and teaching situations :

1. *Charts, diagrams* and *graphs* can be projected on large screen for normal instruction.

2. *Picture stories* from any source are projected and used as an approach to reading.

3. *Original drawings* are projected to the screen, to the delight of the young artists responsible for them.

4. *Written composition*—stories, poems, essays, letters—may be projected. This is an effective system of sharing a student's doubt. Darkness in the room focuses attention.

5. The fundamentals of *arithmetic, handwriting, spelling* and *composition* are illustrated by use of the opaque projector.

6. Written or typed outlines of new units of study may be projected.

Advantages of Opaque Projector

Heas and Packer have pointed out that with the help of an opaque projector the teacher can stimulate attention, arouse interest, clarify information and help students retain knowledge for a longer period of time. They have further pointed out that it can also be used to introduce subject of topics, present specific information, test knowledge and ability, review instructional problems and facilitate cooperative students-teachers participation in problem solving.

THE TEACHING SLIDE

Teaching slides, glass slides or projection slides or lantern slides carry immense value in teaching procedures. The use of a single slide can vitalize an entire teaching session. This is a successful teaching device which helps in the retention of the material taught in the minds of the pupils. A few carefully selected slides or even one pertinent slide can :

(*a*) attract attention,

(*b*) arouse interest,

(*c*) assist lesson development,

(*d*) develop student understanding,

(*e*) review instruction, and

(*f*) facilitate student-teacher participation.

A glass slide is made up of a piece of sensitized glass similar to the sensitized paper for use in photography. The slide may be in colour or in black and white. Different forms of glass slides—photographic, etched-glass slide, ink slides, etc.—may be used for teaching purposes.

Using Slides in Teaching

As pointed out earlier, slides and slide-projectors are useful teaching devices which offer huge mass of visual material. Right from the lower-primary to the high school and even at the post-school level, slides serve useful teaching purpose. Even in the programme of adult education, slides can be usefully exhibited and instruction imparted. Some of the important instructional areas in which sets of slides are available and can be used are :

(1) Reading, (2) Languages, (3) Science
(4) Mathematics, (5) Social studies, (6) Music and
(7) Art.

Though it is possible to have slide projectors on reasonable price in the market, yet every school cannot afford to have a slide projector. *A magic lantern* is a convenient device to replace the slide projector. It is not very costly and, moreover, it can be conveniently improvised for class-room use.

FILM STRIPS

A film strip is a coherent sequence of still pictures and titles on a strip of 35 mm film. It generally has 20 to 30 frames of pictures, drawings or illustrations and in size, it can be single or double frame.

A film strip is a series of related still photographs on a single roll of processed film. Taken together, the separate pictures present some product or process of learning in a step by step fashion. The average number on a film strip is thirtyfive, although the number can vary from ten to hundred.

According to Good's Dictionary of Education, *Film strip* is "A short length of film containing a number of positives, each different but usually having some continuity, intended to be projected as a series of still pictures by means of film strip projector."

Uses of Film Strips

1. It is better than motion picture because in a film strip each picture can be left on the screen for the desired length of time, thus promoting visual reinforcement which permits teacher-pupil discussion during its showing.

2. It allows students' participation.

3. It is inexpensive.

4. It is small and compact and can be stored easily.

5. Film strip projector is a very simple machine which can be operated by any teacher.

6. It can be prepared by the students as well as purchased from the market.

7. It helps in developing a group viewing situation and thus to stimulate discussion.

8. It helps to enrich background knowledge and to reinforce learning.

A good film strip ought to stir up discussion, suggest new ideas and create interest in further study of the topic. It should serve a precisely defined educational purpose and the teacher should ensure that it will have real value for the class.

Anyhow a film strip should be able to arouse interest and stimulate mental activity among the students. A film strip should be prepared by the teachers as well as the students. Audio-Visiual Aid department's help can be taken to prepare film strips in schools.

The film strip can be projected on the screen or wall or paper screen or the backside of a map etc. as the convenience and the teaching situation demands. A large number of subjects come within the range of film strips. The teacher only needs to tap the right source and the right type of strip for his teaching purpose. History, Civics, Geography, Science, Mathematics, Current Affairs are some of the subjects which have been adapted to film strips. A number of film strips are available with the Central Film Library, Government of India, New Delhi.

Suggestions for Proper Use of Film Strip

The following *Suggestions* should be kept in mind while using film strip as a device :

1. For presenting film strips in the class-room, follow the procedure outlined for *teaching slides*.

2. Determine the lessons that could be effecively illustrated with a strip.

3. Use instructional materials that are well-selected and interesting. The film strips selected should serve for the specific lesson.

4. Never miss opportunities for using the film strip in a variety of curricular areas such as Science, History, Geography, Spelling, Reading, Art, Music etc.

5. Pre-view film strips before using them.

6. Show again any part of the film strip needed for more specific study.

7. Use film strip to stimulate emotions, build attitudes, and to point out problems.

8. Use a pointer to direct attention to specific details on the screen.

FLASH CARDS

Flash cards are small, compact cards, approximately 10 × 12 inches, which are 'flashed' before a class to bring home an idea. These are very useful and provide variety and activity in the class. The cards carry brief and to the point message and may be used for a number of instructional purposes, including drill and review. The technique to be employed in the use of flash cards depends largely upon the specific problem or subject that is being presented. Used individually or in company with other teaching aids such as charts, maps, diagrams, posters etc. flash cards can render useful help to the teacher in presenting materials for subjects like languages, basic arithmetic, human relations instructions etc.

Many educational agencies like Orient Longmans, Oxford University Press and certain Indian agencies also keep specially prepared cards which can be had at price. The teacher can himself prepare such cards to suit his specific needs.

AUDIO-VISUAL AIDS

Now we shall describe those aids which combine both sight and sound. The two most important aids that fall under this category are : (1) Educational Films, and (2) Educational Television. The educational potentials of these two aids are being realized more and more now and their use as media of instruction is fully being exploited in the modern era. How far these audio-visual procedures in teaching are useful, is described in the following pages.

EDUCATIONAL FILMS

An educational film is one which contributes to the achievement of desirable educational goods by making effective use of motion picture as a medium of communication. Or by films we mean motion pictures which are produced in the standard 35 millimetre size of sub-standard 16 millimetre size. The second type is useful for educational purposes. These films are of two types :

In the field of education, the development of the motion picture as the medium of instruction has swept its way and has come to stay as one of the most potent devices in teaching. Communicating through sound and sight simultaneously, the motion picture blends pictures, words, objects, motion and even colour to make indelible impact on the children's minds. Through a series of techniques it brings reality into pupils' experience almost first hand.

Educational Role of Motion Pictures

Broadly speaking, the educational value of motion pictures may be summed up as follows :

1. Motion pictures enrich the learning process and lead to greater all-round achievement.

2. Motion pictures directly modify beliefs in desirable directions and cause students seek additional information about subject studied.

3. Motion pictures help in the improvement of educational achievement by different subjects.

4. The motion picture draws attention.

5. The motion picture makes the experience almost first hand.

6. The motion picture is an edited version of reality.

Suggestions for Making Effective Use of Films

1. Show the film first of all and then use it to develop the lesson in the class.

2. Don't explain the film before hand. Let the students find themselves the hidden aspects in the films, if it is shown for recapitulatory purposes.

3. The pupils should write notes on the film, the information received and observation made. Practical work should also be done by the students if the film gives such opportunity.

Some Precautions in the Use of Films

1. Do not use class-room films for mere entertainment.

2. Do not use films when motion is not portrayed.

3. Do not use films that are too long.

Limitations of Films

The chief defect of a film is that we cannot keep a scene for a longer time or reserve to see the previous one, for this purpose the film strips are better. Films are also very costly, every school cannot purchase a projector to use in schools. Electricity is required for it. Trained staff is needed. It is difficult to discuss points during projection.

So films should be selected judiciously and used intelligently.

EDUCATIONAL TELEVISION

"Whether you like it or not, television is going to have a far reaching effect on your life, and the life of your community, your nation and the world." These worlds which appeared in an American magazine nearly twenty years ago, seem to become a reality of to-day and revolutionary promise for tomorrow. The television is a new voice in the community and from the community at large. It is going to have its significant say in the educational set-up of the community.

The Potential of Educational Television

Educational television, though of very recent origin, is yet without any doubt, "one of the most versatile audio-visual aids ever developed." More and more teachers as well as students running with the flowing stream of progressive education are being influenced by the potential value of the television or are eager to bring it in use in the class-room. "Television has been said to the *the blackboard brought to life*. It offers a vitality and newness which attracts attention, creates interest and stimulates a desire to learn."

Educational television—"the electronic blackboard of the future" as Wayne Coy calls it, may be said to have the following most useful educational values when used as a teaching device :

1. It combines with it all the qualities of the educational radio and is an improvement on in many ways. The voice of the broadcaster as well as his figure, his movements, the illustrations used by him, the demonstrations presented by him etc. are transmitted simultaneously.

2. Educational television combines sight and sound together and thus makes the experience real, concrete and immediate.

3. Television offers uniformity of communication. In the class-room, it does not ignore any student. Even the back-bencher feels the pleasure of 'front row seat.'

4. Televising is a versatile educational vehicle. Any telecast may use a battery of audio-visual material like models, charts, demonstrations, exhibits, the chalk board etc.

5. Television, like the film, tends to stimulate and reinforce ideas, belief and tendencies already possessed by the onlooker.

6. Television offers opportunities of seeing and listening to on the scenes and events such as inaugurations, committees in session, investigations, and current happenings. Useful information can be gathered from speeches, current news broadcasts and informational lectures.

7. Television enables the viewers to profit from leisure and recreational activities by participating vicariously in sports, dramatizations of light stories and plays, pictures and accounts of travels, and musical productions.

8. Television is more effective and useful than radio. Radio is only audio-aid whereas television is audio-visual aid. But its use is very limited because of certain limitations mentioned below :

Limitations of Using Television

Like other audio-visual aids to teaching, television has some of the following limitations :

1. One way communication is the major limitation of educational television.

2. Listening to and viewing a particular TV programme in school hours would very often require the teacher to re-arrange the school schedule. And, this is not possible without creating some confusion.

3. There is the further difficulty that the subject-matter of even the most educationally profitable telecasts may have little relation to the school curriculum, or the part of it that is currently being taught, classes cannot be made to work in identical timings.

4. There is its financial aspect. Not all schools can afford to have a television set.

Arrangement of Television Programmes

Following steps should be taken while using television in school situation.

1. **Preparation for the telecast :** Students should be put in a state of readiness. The programme must be meaningful and purposeful. The students must know what to do and what to work.

2. **Actual use of television :** The teacher should guide and plan and he should give advance information of the lesson to the students at this stage.

3. **Follow up work :** At this stage topic should be discussed. Careful analysis should be done. Questions should be put by the students to remove their doubts about the contents of the telecast.

Future in Television

"Television is here. It is now upto the educator to provide the guidance and assitance necessary to bring its vast educational potentialities to fruition. The dangers of misuse, as well as the values of potential good, are the responsibility and concern of the teaching profession...Education can utilize television to open wider horizons and bring knowledge to our future citizens." As against educationally and materially advanced countries like the U.S.A., U.K., Russia where more and more schools are exploring the potentialities of educational television, its use in our country as a potent educational medium will take some time. The existing facilities and provisions in certain schools in big cities are not adequate. A network of educational telecasting stations and telecasting sets in schools will have to be established before this potent device can have its away.

8

Evaluation

We have already discussed in the preceding chapters aims and objectives of Education. To achieve these objectives we provide various learning experience to the pupils through various methods of teaching with teaching devices and audio-visual aids for the purpose.

Now to see whether the aim and objective of education have been achieved or not and how far these have been achieved, we need evaluation. In this chapter we propose to discuss Evaluation.

Every human effort is directed towards a particular end in view. These ends may be ultimate or proximate, immediate or remote, they may have instrumental or intrinsic value. But invariably there is some definite goal which determines the actions sought for acheving that goal. So every human endeavour is to be examined in terms of its outcome. Various means and methods are employed to get the desired results. But in all these trails of human activities, one is likely to lose the way until and unless a critical glance is cast at various steps and at opportune times. To seek the results of the efforts made and judge the efficacy of the means adopted, we require check-ups here and there, which is called 'Evaluation.'

EVALUATION IN EDUCATION

Education too, like other human enterprises, is directed towards particular objectives. The teacher has to adjust his approach to his work, to the kind of behaviour he wishes to ensure through his teaching. The teacher cannot assume that he has done a good job, when he has gone over a lesson in the class. Even at the planning stage, he has to ask himself, "What behavioural changes can I bring about through this lesson?" Such changes constitute his educational goals or objectives.

Educational Objectives, Learning Experiences and Evaluation

Our educational objectives therefore, are the changes we wish to bring in the child. The changes that must take place through education are represented in the knowledge pupils acquire; the skills and abilities pupils attain; the interests pupils manifest.

If education imparted is effective, then the student will behave differently from the way he did before he came to the school. The pupil knows something of which he was ignorant before. He understands something which he did not understand. He can solve problems which he could not solve earlier. He can do things which he could not do previously. He revises his attitudes towards things. Education is, thus, the process of bringing about changes in the behaviour. The fundamental test of sound education is its effect on the pupils.

An educational programme may be based on an elaborate statement of objectives and involves an enthusiastic staff. However, unless desirable changes occur in the pupils, the programme cannot be considered successful.

Learning experiences are designed to bring about pre-planned changes in the pupils. As learning takes place, teachers have to find out the extent or the degree to which changes occur.

Again the effectiveness of a learning experience can be appraised only in terms of the growth and change taking place in the pupils as a result of such experiences.

Thus, evaluation is a process of determining :

(1) the extent to which an objective is being attained.

(2) the effectiveness of the learning experiences provided in the class-room.

(3) how the goals of education have been accomplished.

From the above discussion, it is clear that there is an inter-relationship between objectives (ends), learning experiences (means) and evaluation (evidence). Objectives remain central to both learning experiences (means) and evaluation. Evaluation comes in at the planning stage when objectives are identified. Learning experiences are also planned in terms of objectives. At every point of learning, evaluation is an attempt to discover the extent of the effectiveness of the learning situation in evoking the desired changes in students.

This inter-relationship of objective, learning experience and evaluation may be symbolically represented as in the following diagram :

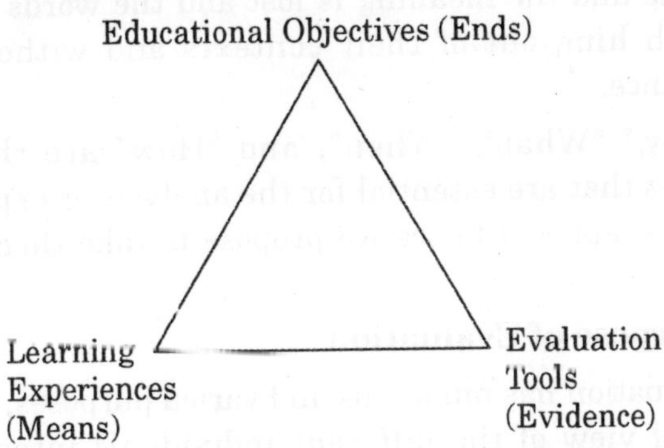

One cannot pass judgment on the students by just testing them at the end of a course of instruction. The changes occur over a period of time and therefore, no single appraisal can show us completely, these changes. It is necessary to determine the status of a student at the starting point. Then at periodical intervals, evaluations have to be made and changes identified in comparison with his position at the starting point. In evaluation :

(*a*) One has to know where students were at the beginning, if we are to determine if and what changes are occuring.

(*b*) One has to obtain a record of the changes in pupils by using appropriate methods of appraisal.

(*c*) One has to judge how good the changes are in the light of the evidence obtained.

It is only the understanding of the integrated approach to Evaluation, which can undo the harm that the old approach has done to education.

What is Evaluation?

Resisting the academic temptation of giving a well-worded definition of the term, we propose to explain its different aspects and main features. In definitions, the reader very often loses himself in the well-worded language, the sense and the meaning is lost and the words are soon left with him, out of their contexts and without their significance.

"Why," "What", "When", and "How" are the usual questions that are essential for the analysis or explanation of the concept and hence we propose to take them up one by one.

The Purpose of Evaluation

Evaluation has numerous and varied purposes, from the points of view of the different individuals interested in education.

From the point of view of students, evaluation serves a two-fold purpose.

1. To make them realise their own strength and weaknesses in respect of the subjects of the curriculum.

2. To provide them educational and vocational guidance.

From the point of view of the teachers, evaluation again serves a three-fold purpose.

1. Grading the students, is of course, the chief purpose which even the existing examinations aim at and the new ones too cannot ignore.

2. Understanding of the psychological needs of children in order to provide them with adequate education and educational and vocational guidance.

3. The teachers also can and should through evaluation, make an endeavour to judge their own success in teaching the suitability of the subject matter taught and the adequacy of the teaching technique employed.

From the point of view of parents, who, though outwardly unconcerned with education as such, do have a natural interest in the education of their own children, which lends them an inquisitiveness about their progress in school. Some of the parents do also regard themselves capable of guiding their children in regard to their choices of course in school and vocations in life.

The Contents of Evaluation

Education is a process that brings about desirable changes in children. We expect the schools to help children in :

(1) building up their personality and character so that they can take their rightful place in the nation.

(2) assimilating scientific knowledge and skills that will help them vocationally and socially.

(3) doing critical and creative thinking.

(4) strengthening their ability to converse with and write to others and thus share their knowledge, thoughts and feelings.

(5) developing healthy attitudes towards problems and people contributing to effective community life.

(6) motivating them to act according to worthy ideals in the service of the community and the nation.

(7) stimulating them into cultivating worthwhile interests in life to make life quite meaningful.

All these we expect the teacher to do, whether he is the teacher of Mathematics, Languages, Social Studies, Wood work, Pottery or any other subject. In short, each subject in the curriculum has to contribute towards these changes. These changes will form a continuous process that commences when a pupil enters the school and goes on till he leaves it and even long after that. At the end of the period of education, the child tends to behave differently. He can do many things more than what he could do before that bit of education was given to him. He can understand things better, simplify the complex things to his advantage, attempt more rigorous exercises, comprehend difficult manipulations and do everything in a way better than what he could do before. These changes, these advancements, this progress, this achievement, which affect a change in his modes of overt behaviour are what evaluation tends to measure.

When should Evaluation be done?

Whether evaluation-instruments should be employed and administered weekly, monthly, quarterly or yearly is a great problem before the educator. At the present time, he tosses between different alternatives not exactly knowing where a particular mode of action will lead him to and what information he can get out of it. The time-gap between evaluation depends upon the purpose we desire to achieve, the results of the evaluation. Evidently, from our previous discussion, the purposes of evaluation can be reduced to two basic items :

1. Guidance.

2. Grading.

If we have to employ our results to guide the students, surely we can not wait very long for it. In case of spelling mistakes, for example, we cannot wait till the end of the year, to tell the student that he is weak at spellings, or that he has committed a particular mistake in his writing. If the purpose is guidance, it should have an immediate administration. On the other hand, the case of grading the students is very different and we do not need to indulge into the luxury of grading the students every now and then. We can surely wait till the end of the year to apprise students of their standing in the class. As our purpose drifts towards guidance this gap decreases and as it swings towards grading, it increases.

TOOLS OF EVALUATION : TESTS

Following are the various tools (tests) of Edvaluation.

Psychological Tests

1. Intelligence Test.
2. Aptitude Measurement.
3. Interest Inventories.
4. Personality Tests like T.A.T., C.A.T. and Rorscha-Ink Blot Tests.

Achievement Tests

1. Oral
2. Written—Essay Type, Short Answer Type and Objective Types.

Situation Tests

1. Questionnaires.
2. Check Lists.
3. Rating Scales.
4. Teachers Observation.
5. Interviews.
6. Records.
7. Pupils' Products.

8. Home Work.
9. Sociometery.
10. Other Devices.

1. Psychological Tests

Personality tests, interest inventories, attitude scales, intelligence tests and aptitude tests are essential for assessment of different aspects of development of the student. But for all these tests, we require trained and technical personnel which are not easily available for school. As such these cannot be made use of at present to evaluate the progress of the students. However, the following tools and techniques may be used by the teachers :

2. Achievement Tests

(*a*) **Essay type tests :** These are most commonly used tools of evaluation in our prevailing system. These tests do not measure efficiently, cannot be reliably graded, encourage bluffing, have little diagnostic and prognostic value and are influenced by other extraneous factors. Nevertheless, essay-type tests have their own value regarding ability to draw up, to organise, summarise and integrate knowledge and experience. Creativity, originality, application and interpretation of facts are also better evaluated through essay type tests, so their value can not be under-estimated.

(*b*) **Short-answer type tests :** It is a free response form. The testee is called upon to, write the answers to a question and is restricted to the time limit and the response. There are many variations of this type but fundamentally such items call for recall of specific information. It demands recall instead of recognition. But these tests do not measure mental processes other than rote memory, if they are not constructed carefully. Such type of form should be used only when the question can be answered by a unique word, phrase or number.

(*c*) **Objective type tests :** These tests call for specific responses to the test items. These tests are appreciated due to objectivity and ease of scoring. These tests are good for standardisation. These may be of recall type, multiple choice type, matching type, analogy type, classification type etc.

3. Questionnaire

It consists in a series of questions or statements concerning factual information to get responses from in dividuals. It is useful to get information regarding opinion, judgment, attitudes and interests of the person concerned. While preparing a questionnaire, the following points must be kept in mind :

1. It should deal with some significant topic to make the respondent feel like reading and completing it.
2. Minimise the number of questions to get the essential data by making the items sufficiently inclusive.
3. Make it attractive, neat and clearly printed.
4. Questions should be objective and not suggestive.
5. Directions should be clear and complete.
6. Arrange the questions in psychological order.
7. Questions should be un-ambiguous.
8. Avoid long questions.

Questionnaire should be used only when the data cannot be secured through other sources, like the records, census, data etc. Its main drawback is that the respondents may not give correct information and generally the response is very poor. So respondents should be chosen carefully and a courteous, carefully constructed covering letter to explain the purpose of the study should be included alongwith the questionnaire.

4. Check-lists

The check-list consists of a few statements regarding the performance of some complex tasks or skills. These statements are given in specific and fundamental terms. Every item can be checked as either present or absent. Half-way responses are not possible. While preparing a check-list, we have to analyse the job, the task, the skills etc. into various components which should be included in the list.

For example in study of skill, we can make statements like this.

(*a*) Can I read silently?

(*b*) Can I consult disctionary?

(*c*) Can I read at a reasonable speed?

(*d*) Can I grasp the central idea of the para and so on.

Students are asked to tick-mark against the statements which suit them and cross-mark those that do not. In this way, check-lists are very useful to the students as well as the teachers for self-evaluation and self-improvement.

5. Rating Scales

It is a very useful device for evaluating a limited number of aspects or traits of a thing or a person. It gives a qualitative description of the traits in varying degrees as against the check list which merely shows their presence or absence.

Rating scale may be used :

1. **Descriptive :** When a person is rated by descriptive phrases usually from one to nine. A student may be rated for his performance in physical activities.

2. **Numerical :** In this case, a code number is given to each descriptive phrase arranged in order of degree. For example, for punctuality, number I may be equivalent to 'never'; 2 'rarely' 3. 'occasionally'; 4 'frequently' and 5 'always'.

While rating the rater places the suitable number against each.

3 Points Rating Scales

Below average — Average — Above average

5 Point Scale

Excellent — Good — Average — Below average — Poor

9 Point Scale

Out-standing — Exce-llent — Good — Above average — Average — Below average — Poor — Very poor — Excep-tionally poor

For example :

(*a*) He takes part in the evening games

(*b*) He participated in debates

A	B	C	D	E
2	1	3	5	4
5	4	2	3	1

It shows that D always takes part in the evening games while A rarely takes part. Similarly in debates, B frequently participates while E never takes part.

3. **Graphic :** A straight line may be represented by descriptive phrases of various points. To rate a subject for a particular trait, a check-mark is placed at an appropriate place with regard to his standing. For example, for co-operation, we can rate a person on a three point scale as given below :

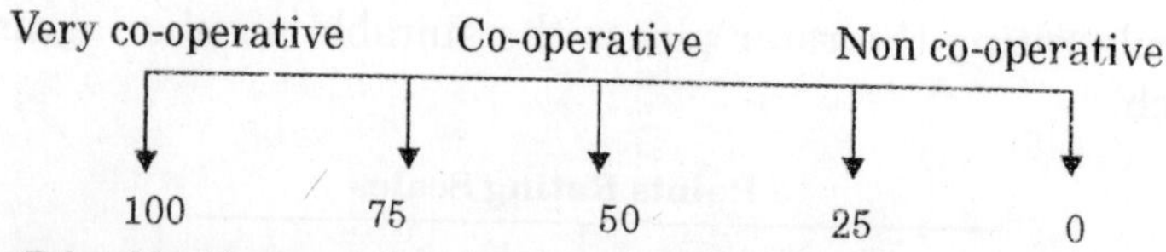

Limitations of rating scale : Rating scales have certain limitations too. It is difficult to define a trait or a characteristic. 'Halo' effect is also carried over by raters, while evaluating one aspect after the other. If a student is good in academic achievement, he is rated high in sports also. There is also a tendency in the raters to rate too generously while rating.

6. Teachers' Observations

It differs from seeing. Seeing is casual but observation is seeing with a purpose. It is specific, planned, systematic and recorded by an expert. Seeing is generally casual and is not followed by reporting or recording. Observation is thus purposeful seeing which aims at collecting useful information about a specific person, thing, situation, place, condition, object or event. For observation, instruments like thermometer, stethoscope binocular, camera, stop-watch, taperecorder etc. may be used. As this technique is mostly subjective, we can improve upon its reliability and validity by making the observation at frequent intervals and also by making observation independently by several observers at a time.

7. Interviews

Interview is based upon a face to face relation wherein the interviewer converses with the subject with a definite purpose. Interview is a good technique for dealing with young children, illiterates and others with low intelligence and poor linguistic ability. As a date-collecting device, this is good for knowing attitudes, feelings and causes of particular actions. For a successful interview, a friendly and secure relationship between interviewer and interviewee is a pre-requisite. It must be planned, conducted in friendly atmosphere, recorded immediately and interpreted cautiously. It is useful in handling individual cases with specific behavior problems. But it is a time consuming device, changed with interviewers bias and needs expert teachers to employ it.

8. Records

Records enhance the value of observations, interviews and other techniques of evaluation. These include pupils' diaries, anecdotes, records and cumulative record. Anecdotal record is a verbal snap-shot of a single but significant incident in the behaviour of students. It is a factual information regarding the growth and development of a student. But a series of anecdotes are to be recorded in order to secure a valid information about some aspect or phase of development, such as emotional stability, aggressiveness etc. The observer is to record the facts and not his opinion or interpretation. After the identity of the students, date of observation, incident and background of incident are to be noted so that proper interpretation of his behaviour may be made and suggestions for improvement be offered.

Cumulative record is another evaluative device useful to know about the all-round development of the students. If properly maintained, these records assist the teachers to evaluate the day to day progress of the students in various areas of development.

9. Pupils' Products

Things made by students provide various types of clues to the interest, attitudes, skills and abilities of students. The improvised apparatus of student showing his interest in scientific hobbies, the apparatus and also the relevant knowledge required to plant it.

10. Home Task

It is a good evaluative device to observe the study habits, industry and interest of the student in a particular subject. It helps the students to re-capitulate their lessons and visualise their difficulties. It inculcates habits of industry among the children. For the teacher, home work done by the students is a good indication of the success of his efforts.

11. Sociometry

This technique is used to describe social relationships in a particular group. This aims at knowing the likes and dislikes among a social group-whether a student would reject or accept another for a particular purpose, such as to sit together in the class-room, to work together for a project, to accept as the monitor etc. Students are asked to give their first, second and third preferences with regard to these. The choices are then represented graphically by a chart called sociogram. It is constructed by representing the various choices and persons in a definite manner. For example, the following representations are generally used.

Boy ○

Girl △

First Choice
Second Choice
Third Choice
Multiple Choice
} By different coloured pencils

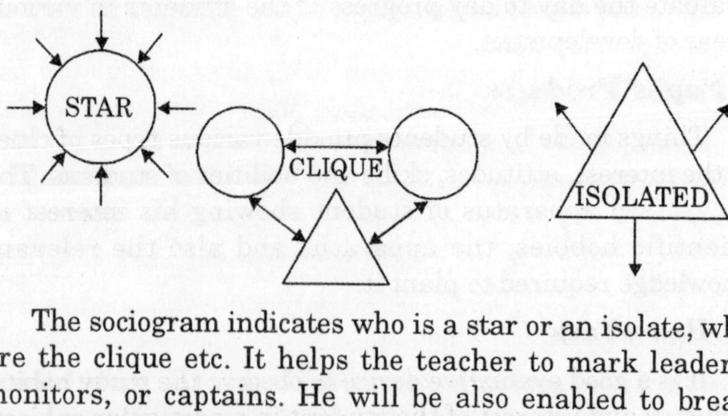

The sociogram indicates who is a star or an isolate, who are the clique etc. It helps the teacher to mark leaders, monitors, or captains. He will be also enabled to break cliques, associate more students with isolates and improve social relationships.

12. Other Tools of Evaluation

Other informal devices are socio-drama (role playing) autobiographies, compositions, discussions, projective techniques etc., which may also be used profitably in many of the situations. Informal methods are as important as the formal methods as they supplement the evidence got through the later.

MAIN FEATURES OF EVALUATION

To have a clear understanding of the concept of 'Evaluation', it is essential to discuss briefly some of the main features of evaluation. These are as follows :

1. Evaluation is a Continuous Process

Education is universally admitted, as a continuous process of growth and development. We see no gaps in the development of human beings. Changes are taking place all the time in knowledge, abilities and ideals of the individuals. One rose does not make a summer. Likewise, one bit of 'Evaluation' cannot portray the complete picture of the individual. It requires continuous evaluation in order to determine the status, the factors affecting the growth and development and also the future success of the students.

Thus external or internal annual examinations cannot evaluate the growth and development of the pupil. Even monthly and weekly tests can not do. There should be continuous evaluation based upon the observations of the behaviour of the pupil at every moment.

2. Evaluation is a Comprehensive Process

For the all-round harmonious development of the personality of the child, wide and varied types of curricular, co-curricular and non-school activities are provided to the students. To judge the harmonious development of all the aspects of the personality, we cannot limit our measuring devices to examinations that measure the academic aspect only and disregard emotional, social and physical aspects.

Since we are concerned with the totality of the child's growth and development, evaluation should be comprehensive and we should make a variety of assessments.

Fields of Evaluation

The various fields of evaluation may be :

1. Evaluation of academic and scholastic achievement: For this purpose, periodical tests-oral, essay type, objective type may be used.

2. Evaluation of child's health and physical development : For the purpose of evaluating physical development, the undermentioned methods may be adopted :

(*a*) Occasional medical inspection of the students should be held and follow-up work undertaken. A certain minimum health standard may be prescribed by the school authorities.

(*b*) The health habits of the students should be carefully recorded and evaluated.

(*c*) A periodical examination of the general cleanliness of their bodies should be conducted.

(*d*) Evaluation of games, athletics and physical exercises should be made.

(*e*) The knowledge of the students regarding personal health and hygiene should be tested.

3. Evaluation of child's participation in community work i.e. evaluation of his social development : An assessment of the work of an individual student may be made on the basis of his participation in various programmes organised from time to time. Special programmes may be arranged periodically for evaluating the capacity of the students to take part in these programmes. For the purpose of assessment, the following activities may be undertaken:

(*a*) Beautification of the school or the college.

(*b*) Dusting the furniture and cleaning the school compound.

(*c*) Staging a drama etc.

(*d*) Teaching of adults and helping the weak class-fellows.

(*e*) Doing social service in fairs.

(*f*) Participating in flood-squads.

(*g*) Organising excursions.

(*h*) Organising cultural programmes, debates, talks, discussions and exhibitions.

4. Assessment of character and personality : The problem of this type of evaluation seems to be a difficult one. It is not very easy to give a representative and balanced list of social and personality traits worth evaluating. Besides, there are no standardized and reliable rating scales and tests. There is also every danger of subjectivity playing its dominant rȯle. At the same time, it is very difficult for every teacher to possess the keen sense of observation without which character and personality of an individual cannot be evaluated scientifically. Nevertheless attempts should be made to find out a reliable and scientific way of evaluation.

The following traits should be assessed by the teachers :

(*a*) Regularity and punctuality in attending the classes.

(*b*) Honesty.

(*c*) Courtesy.

(*d*) Respect for the dignity of man.

(*e*) Respect for individual freedom.

(*f*) Sense of responsibility and duty.

(*g*) Purity in mind, speech and action.

(*h*) Truthfulness.

(*i*) Service to the sick, the poor, the handicapped and the weak.

(*j*) Followship and leadership.

(*k*) Sense of justice.

(*l*) Democratic spirit *i.e.* respect for the opponent's views.

(*m*) Patience and tolerance.

(*n*) Freedom from passions like anger, hatred, jealousy etc.

3. Evaluation takes place Inside and Outside the Class Room

The child's behaviour is the result of many factors, relating to home, school and the society in which he lives. His development is conditioned by the environments in which he lives. His behaviour in the school, home and outside is not the same. So we should evaluate him at all the places in different situations. So the evaluative process should not only take place inside the class-room but also outside the class-room. This should, even, extend beyond the four walls of the school, like home, neighbourhood, community, office etc. Under the present circumstances, the teacher should be concerned with the evaluation of at least all types of activities in the school, if not outside it.

4. Evaluation is Done by all Concerned with it

As evaluation takes place not only in the school but also in the home and in the community, there are many persons who participate in evaluation. The teacher, the parents, the neighbour, the members of the community, his play-mates, his class-fellows, he himself and others who watch him develop and grow through the corridors of time, are the right persons to evalute students' activities.

5. Evaluation is for the Improvement of Educational Process

As it has been already discussed, evaluation is concerned not only with measurement, but also with other aspects of education. It aims at clarifying the objectives, judging the effectiveness of the techniques of teaching, testing the validity of the learning experiences and serving as a basis for guidance to the teachers as well as the taught. So the process of evaluation aims at improving the whole process of education. Education envisages certain goals or objectives which bring about desirable changes in the pupil's behaviour when provision is made for suitable learning experiences. So evaluation makes a continuous appraisal of the teaching-learning process for the sake of improvement of the whole educational process.

CRITERIA OF A GOOD TEST

Criteria of a good test are as follows:

1. Validity

In ordinary language, it means that the test should be able to measure what it seeks to measure. In scientific language, it signifies the degree or the extent to which a test measures the ability, skill or quality which it is supposed to measure.

In testing History, for example, the test should measure the candidates knowledge of History and not his handwriting, spelling, way of expression etc. The nearest synonyms for this quality, in the words of Ruch, are 'goodness', 'general merit', 'worth whileness' and he has suggested the following methods of validating a test:

(*a*) By judgment of competent persons.

(*b*) By analysis of courses of study or text books.

(*c*) By harmonising with the recommendations of national education committees or other recognised bodies on curricula, courses of study, minimum essentials etc.

(*d*) By experimental studies of social utility (Such as the Horn and Thorndike) studies of the most frequently used words Ashbough and Horn Studies of spelling lists.

(*e*) The studies of the most frequently recurring errors.

(*f*) By the computation of the percentages of pupils answering each item correctly at each successive age or grade level.

(*g*) By correlation against an outside criterion.

(*h*) By combination of the above methods.

The usual method of finding the validity of a test as is evident from the above, is to compare the test with an accepted criterion and the degree of correspondence between the two will give us the validity of the test-the higher it is, the better the test will be.

In statistical language, the validity of a test is, in fact, defined as the degree of correspondence or correlation between the test-scores and the scores obtained from a reliable criterion, assuming that such a criterion exists. It should be carefully borne in mind that the criterion itself is fallible and the selection of a reliable criterion, therefore, is of prime importance, as in the absence of extremely reliable criterion, the degree of validity found out will not be authentic or trust-worthy.

2. Reliability

It signifies the accuracy of a test and refers to the extent to which it measures consistently and accurately the abilities which it does measure. The reliability of a test can be measured by giving the same test on two different occasions and if the fluctuations in the two scores so obtained are only minor, the test is reliable, otherwise not. In onther words, a perfectly reliable test will be one in which the score on a second trial will remain exactly the same as on the first trial. In case of perfectly unreliable test, however, the two scores will be un-matched and absolutely divergent. Moreover, a test which is valid must necessarily be reliable. The reverse of this, however, is not true. A test may be extremely reliable, on the one hand, but least valid on the other.

In regard to the relative importance of the two criteria, validity and reliability, Kelly's principle is of paramount importance. He states it as follows :

"If the testing time is of short, give prime consideration to reliability of the test, and if the testing time is long, give primary consideration to validity but secondary attention to the reliability of the test."

3. Objectivity

A test, the score of which depends on the judgement of the scorer, is called a subjective test and a test which is free from this bias is known as an objective test. Objectivity of a test may, therefore, be defined as the elimination of the bias or the subjective opinion of the scorer. In other words, it means that if the test is assessed by different people, the score will invariably be the same. The objectivity of a test may be determined by a mere inspection of the form of the test. If there is only one correct answer which is admissible and the personal opinon and impression of the scorer do not at all count in regard to the correct response, the test is objective, otherwise not; and the degree to which it is so is the measure of its objectivity. It is evident from it that a test in mental arithmetic is more objective than a test in History or one in English composition. It should, however, be carefully noted that a subjective test will, in all classes, be unreliable because of its very nature it will be scored differently by different socrers or by the same scorer at different times. The subjectivity of a test, in fact, is one of the fundamental conditions which affect its reliability.

4. Adequate Sampling

It implies that the samples of knowledge tested, abilities assessed or attitudes examined should be as complete and adequate us possible. It should be remembered that under no circumstances, whatever, it is possible to test everything that a candidate knows or professes to know. In order to obtain a picture of the whole field and discover the strong and weak points of the individual, the tester has preforce to select a sample of the whole and the more representative it is, the better and more reliable will the result be. The adequacy of a sample depends, to a large extent, upon its length—the longer a test is, the more adequate sample will it be on the whole. A test of 20 questions will naturally give a better and more thorough estimate of a person's ability or knowledge than a test containing 5 questions only. This principle, in fact, is not only based on common sense but can be proved statistically also. It, however, does not mean that the test should be made in-ordinately and unnecessarily long but it implies that the items tested should be so representative as to cover the entire field of knowledge or of the activity tested.

5. Ease of Administration and Scoring

It is an administrative exigency and implies that it should not be difficult for teachers to give the test and score it and then interpret the score. It not only reduces the labour but it should be remembered that if the test is so complicated, as to require the services of a specially trained examiner, teachers not in possession of that special training will not be able to use it, and if they do, the results they obtain, will not be absolute and definite in any way. The reader is, however, reminded that of all the criteria of a good test, the case of administration and scoring should be considered of the least importance. Moreover, if the test-scores cannot be easily interpreted, conducting the test will not serve any purpose.

WHAT IS EXAMINATION?

The essence of evaluation is measurement and the widely prevalent and the most usual form which it takes, is that of examinations. The word 'examination' is derived from the Latin word 'Examen' which means the tongue of a balance and an examination, therefore, signifies a systematic test of knowledge, skill or capacity carried out by a fellow worker, by a teacher or by an alien person under the authority of some public body.

Kinds of Examination

Examination may be classified in different ways. This is so because they vary not in form and conduct but also in regard to organisation, method of scoring and the interpretation of scores.

Classification in Regard to Form: Taking into consideration the form, examinations may be divided into oral, practical and written. An oral examination is individual in character; in other words, it is a sort of a viva-voce test. A practical examination is a test of skill in a performance. In it the examiner has to make or construct something. A written examination is the usual and the most common type. It involves the writing out of answer to different questions set by the examiner.

A written examination may further be sub-divided into two types—traditional type and the objective type. The traditional type consists of writing out answers to essay type questions. In the objective type examination, on the other hand, the number of questions is increased manifold but the answers expected are very brief, usually a word or a sentence is enough. The questions are such as to reduce subjectivity, both on the part of the examiner and the examinee to the minimum.

In Regard to Interpretation: Objective tests may further be classified into standardised and non-standardised tests. Standardised tests are those tests, which have been applied to a large number of pupils of the same age or grade, and for which norms have been calculated. These norms enable an examiner to have a comparative estimate of the ability of pupils. Non-standardised tests may also be objective tests but they are without any norms.

In Regard to Authority Conducting it: Examinations may also be classified as internal and external. If an examination is given by the teachers themselves, it is known as an internal examination. But an examination conducted by an outside agency, which has no direct role in the teaching of the pupils, is called the external examination. In a later section, we shall discuss the evils of the present system of examinations but it would be well to point out here that internal examinations are less liable to these evils than external examinations. It cannot, however, be denied that the external type of examination influences rightly or wrongly the form and mode of internal examinations to a very large extent indeed.

In Regard to Purpose: Examinations are also classified in regard to the purpose. If the purpose of an examination is to predict probable success, it is a *prognostic test*, if its purpose is to discover pupil's weaknesses and reveal his learning difficulties, it is *diagnostic test* : if its purpose is to measure proficiency, it is *achievement test*, if its purpose is to afford information as to how difficult an exercise a pupil can do, it is a *power test*, if its purpose is to determine the rate at which a pupil can give responses, it is a *speed test*, if it measures all these qualities with a view to giving a general picture of the whole ability, it is a *survey test*.

EVILS OF THE PRESENT SYSTEM OF EXAMINATION

The system of examination, as it prevails today, or the traditional system of examinations as we shall call it, has been carefully and critically examined and its shortcomings, weaknesses and abuses have been discovered. It is because of these that examinations have been given a number of shocking and reprehensible epithets. They have been called 'the bane of the educational system', 'enemy of true education', 'a necessary evil', 'a begetter of rivalry and strife', 'a blood-sucker', 'dead hand of education', 'an obstacle to learning', 'a growing tyranny', 'a glorification of memory at the expense of rational and creative powers', 'a presumptuous attempt to gauge the depth of human ignorance.' This is not all and quite a number of other labels of the same kind have been affixed.

The system, in fact, is certainly harmful and pernicious in its effects. In the words of the Indian Universities Commission Report (1949), "For nearly half a century, examinations, as they have been functioning, have been recognised as one of the worst features of Indian education. Commissions and Committees have expressed their alarm at their pernicious domination over the whole system of education in India. The obvious deficiencies and harmful consequences of this most pervasive evil in Indian education have been analysed and set out clearly, by successive universities commissions since 1902, by a Government resolution, as far back as 1904 and by a Committee of the Central Advisory Board of Education in recent years. With most of their criticism, we are in agreement and do not wish to dilate on the patent defects and dangers of this system. We only note that while the magnitude of the problem has been growing at an alarming rate, nothing constructive in the way of reform has happened." It would, therefore, be useful, at this stage to discuss its major defects and shortcomings and then suggest some improvements by way of reform.

Examinations are regarded as an End and not as a Means

The examinations have come to be regarded as the most important aim of education. They have not only become the main spring of the teacher's activities but success in them is considered as the be-all and end-all of the school work. The higher objective of pursuing knowledge and creating a genuine love for it are sadly ignored. The academies which prepare candidates for examinations are having a flourishing trade and their mushroom growth is a positive proof of the importance attached to success in examinations.

Examinations have Adverse Influence on School Work

This precedence of the end over the means has, in fact, cramped the atmosphere of schools and affected adversely the kind of instruction imparted in them. Teachers adapt their procedure to such a form as will secure a high pass percentage. Recourse is generally made to the exhaustive notes and guess papers, hand-books, digests, compendiums and solved exercises. Stress is thus laid on spoon-feeding, and pupils are encouraged to commit things to memory and reproduce them at will. In this way, examinations not only dictate the methods of learning but also determine the relative significance and consequence of different studies in the curriculum. *In the words of an eminent educationist,* "the value of a subject or topic comes to be judged with reference to its possibilities in examination and not by its intrinsic worth". Will this or that pay at examination, becomes the crucial question. The Government of India has also stressed this harmful aspect. When outlining their educational policy in 1904, they expressed their fear in the following words. "In recent years, they (examinations) have grown to extravagant dimensions and their influence has been allowed to dominante the whole system of education in India with the result that instruction is confined within the rigid frame work of prescribed courses, that all forms of training which do not admit of being tested by examinations are liable to be neglected, and that teachers and pupils are tempted to concentrate their energies not so much upon genuine study as upon the questions likely to be set by the examiners."

Examinations' Adverse Effects on the Health of Candidates

Examinations affect adversely the health of candidates in all its aspects. Bad methods of teaching, emphasis on spoon feeding and unintelligent rote-learning leads to mental dyspepsia and discourage formation of healthy mental habits. Moreover, they stimulate an unhealthy, competitive spirit in children and encourage them to resort to unfair and dishonest means for the achievement of success, which is highly valued. In addition to this, the stigma that goes with 'failure in an examination' is so deep-rooted that even cases of suicide are not unknown. And finally the bad methods of study and irregularity in habits of work which result in extreme over-strain immediately before an examination affect the physical health of candidates and in many a case ruin it. Physical and nervous break downs are not uncommon and marked rise in nervous and physical disorders in April and May has been attributed by an officer of the Board of Education, England (now the Ministry of Education) to 'anxiety over the examination.'

Examinations are Inadequate to Evaluate Real Education

Education, as we have repeated, in the previous pages over again, is not the same thing as memorising facts, imbibing knowledge or learning a skill. It is more comprehensive than all these and has an integrative function which permeates the whole personality of an individual and contributes greatly to its success or failure, achievement or frustration. These qualities of mind and character, which can be classified as 'attendant learnings', include amongst other things appreciation of and responsiveness to beauty, interest, attitudes, capacity of leadership, extent of co-operation, degree of perseverance or application. These attendant learnings are as important as the usual types of learnings but our examinations are deplorably ineffective in regard to their assessment or appraisal. In the words of John H. Butler, "Because of their very nature, these intangible learnings cannot be measured by the usual test techniques. To say, that, anything that exists, exists in quantity and that anything that exists in quantity can ultimately be measured, is merely to support a statement of empty logic. One can measure his material wealth in terms of units we call dollars, but what units can be used to measure one's wealth of family love and what unit of measurement can be used for a child's growth in intellectual curiosity, his tolerance of other races, his liking for scientific experimentation, his respect for the rights of others?"

Unreliability of the System

We now refer to another very significant flaw of the system. It is its extreme unreliability and the principal factors which contribute to this are (*i*) bad sampling (*ii*) changes in examinees and (*iii*) the subjective nature of the standard of marking or reward.

The sampling which is resorted to, is definitely inadequate. A question paper usually consists of 6-12 questions, and as such, it cannot possibly test every thing that a pupil knows or can do. The element of change plays an enormous part in such a bad, imperfect and unrepresentative sample. To take an extra-ordinarily extreme case, a candidate on the one hand may be knowing nothing but the answers only to those questions which have been set and, on the other hand, he may, as bad luck would have it, be knowing the entire field of knowledge in that subject with the sole exception of the questions which are asked. What a tragedy would it be in the latter case!

Apart from bad sampling, changes in the examinees are also responsible for reducing the reliability of our examinations. This effect has been called "individual variation."

There are not only certain candidates who are 'good examinees' and others 'indifferent' or 'bad examinees' but even the degrees in this respect keep on changing from one line to another.

But the most important contributory factor is the variability in marking or the subjective character of the awards. It has been conclusively shown that not only will different examiners give different awards to the same answers but that the same examiner will assess the same answers differently on different occasions. As Vernon points out, "The same script might receive a different mark if read after instead of before dinner."

Other things apart, even fatigue and mood of an examiner affect the award. It would be interesting here to refer to the vast and voluminous experimental investigation available on this point. Ketty, Ruch, Long Ballard, Hartog, Rhodes and others have put forth convincing evidence to prove that awards are undoubtedly influenced by personal bias and prejudices and that the variation in the marks given to a single paper by a number of examiners ranges from 29 to 90 percent. The accidental experiment of Wood is indeed a classic in this respect. He sent round some papers to be marked individually by six examiners. The first examiner with a view to doing the job most efficiently and conscientiously, wrote out for his own guidance, of course, complete answers to all questions. But he, unwittingly sent his own set of answers also to the other five examiners, and surprisingly enough, their awards to that particular script ranged from 40 per cent to 90 per cent. The crucial reason for the discrepancies in awards as Vernon points is, "that different workers conceive differently the desirable or undersirable characteristics of examination answers." In other words, they attempt to assess many diverse type of abilities. One examiner, for example, may give credit for comprehensiveness, another for accuracy, one may look forward to originality, another to faithful reproduction, one may value clarity of expression, whereas another may be searching for emotional qualities and so on. Sometimes, the items valued are even contradictory and the fact that "each script manifests an extreme complexity of features" makes the difference in the opinion of the examiners inevitable.

Lacking Definite Aims

Finally it must be mentioned that the lack of definite aim of examinations is also a prime short-coming of the system. The examiners are seldom sure of the function, an examination has to perform and they, therefore, in the words of a well-known writer, "examine for examination's sake and are naively taken to serve all possible purposes." One instance in this connection will suffice. The present Matriculation examination which in the state of the Panjab is still conducted by the University, is not only an examination which provides a gateway for admission to a university but it also marks the completion of a specific course of general education. This is not all. It serves the purpose of selecting candidates for scholarship besides being a passport to all sorts of jobs. On the top of this, the same examination serves as a test of efficiency not only of teachers but of institutions also. In this way, it is used to perform the function of a qualifying examination, a competitive examination, a prognostic examination and so on. This is extremely undesirable. The function of each examination should be clearly defined—the examiners as well as the examinees should not only be familiar with its purpose but they should also have a knowledge of the qualities that are being tested. Moreover, it should be carefully borne in mind that an examination with more than one aim is bound to be a bad examination. This is so, because the multiplicity of functions will not enable it to perform any function efficiently or effectively.

NECESSITY OF EXAMINATIONS

We have discussed in the above pages, the weaknesses and the shortcomings of the examination system. It would, however, be too far-fetched to conclude from this criticism that we, in any way, whatever suggest counsel or advocate their abolition, examinations, it should be remembered, are not only vital to the process of education but occupy such an essential and consequential place in any system of education that they must stay. We have laid down elsewhere the various functions that they have to perform and doing away with this instrument, altogether, though it is admittedly defective, would be tantamount to throwing the baby with the bath water.

What is, therefore, required is to bring about reforms in the system. Ending will not do, what is needed is mending. This point has been very ably emphasised in the report of the Indian Universities Education Commission where it is stated as follows :

"We are convinced that if we are to suggest one single reform in university education, it should be that of the examinations. We advisedly say reform although we know that in India as elsewhere in the world, dissatisfaction with examinations has been so keen that eminent educationists and important educational organisations have even advocated the abolition of examinations. We do not share that extreme view and feel that examinations rightly designed and intelligently used, can be useful factor in the educational process. If examinations are necessary, "thorough reform of these is still more necessary."

SUGGESTIONS FOR THE IMPROVEMENT OF PRESENT SYSTEM OF EXAMINATION

The reform and refinement of examinations has engaged the best attention of educationists and many suggestions have been made to reduce their harmful and pernicious effect to the minimum. We, therefore, proceed to discuss these now.

1. **To be regarded as means and not as ends :** Examinations should be regarded as means and not as ends.

They should be so conducted as to be effective instruments of education. They should enable the pupils to learn new facts, gain new experiences, discover weak points, stimulate learning and estimate progress. This will result in casting off the unfavourable attitude which pupils generally have towards this important and useful device of education. In the words of Yoakam and Simpson, they should not be "regarded as hurdles to be surmounted or as trials to be undergone", but should be considered as valuable exercises leading to a variety of educative experiences.

2. **Warning against undue multiplicity of aims :** Examinations, as has been stated in the previous pages, have to serve many purposes and fulfil many functions. But it would be wrong to conclude from it that the same examination can serve or fulfil all these purposes. It should be carefully borne in mind that an examination which aims at fulfilling many aims is certainly a hard and ineffective examination. The traditional instrument available for the purpose is crude at the present stage of development and to imagine that the same measurement can serve many purposes from incentive to prognosis is to make the instrument worthless and the measurement vague and meaningless. The purpose of each examination should, therefore, be clearly defined and there should be no mincing up in this regard. The exact purpose should be understood clearly and distinctly both by the examiners as well as by the candidates.

3. **Improve the type of questions set :** The questions set in the examination deserve a very careful consideration. They should be such as will discourage craming on the one hand, and encourage thinking and integration of ideas on the other. They should be evenly distributed over the entire field of the subject and should not only call for originality of thought processes but also stimulate the interests of the examinees. If questions of this type are set, they will have a very healthy influence on the methods of teaching and the

quality of work in schools and colleges. Consequently this improvement in the system of examinations deserves a most careful and immediate attention on the part of the examining authorities.

4. **Have experienced examiners :** The improvement in the type of questions to be set necessarily implies better examiners for the job. They should have plenty of experience in this field and should be selected with great care and thought. They must understand and appreciate the exact purpose of examination and must have a vision to realise its significance for the candidates taking it. Marking should be done under carefully controlled conditions with a view to increasing its objectivity. This will enhance the reliability of the examination system. The results will become more accurate and as such more reliance could be placed on their findings.

5. **Avoid numerical marks :** Awarding of numerical marks should be given up and candidates should be grouped in different divisions according to their ability. There may be three or five such divisions but if a still greater refinement is desired, the three point scale may be converted into a nine point scale and the five point scale may be converted into a fifteen point scale by the use of 'plus' and 'minus' signs.

This switching over to group system is suggested because examinations are usually assessed on a percentage basis, and keeping in view the limitations of the system, it can hardly be defined that it is not only extremely difficult but well-nigh impossible to discriminate between 32 per cent and 33 per cent or between 50 per cent and 52 per cent. This kind of classification enables us to distinguish about 30 or 50 degrees of merit in a group of 50 pupils, but this is just ridiculous. In the words of Professor Mial, "We can readily distinguish four or five degrees of merit in the candidates, few examiners can certainly recognise ten, and it is ludicrous to profess that we can distinguish a hundred." Moreover, this sort of classification tends to promote unwholesome competition in the class and develops anti-social qualities especially selfishness and jealousy etc.

In case of objective tests, however, where the answer is definitely right or wrong numerical marks are all-right but in case of the traditional examination, grading of pupils into various groups will be much more honest than the awarding of numerical marks.

6. **Introduction of internal examinations :** Internal examinations should be given precedence over external examinations because the teachers who have done the actual job are in a better position to know the scope and limits of the tests to be applied to their pupils and the standard of answers to be expected of them. Moreover, it is comparatively easier to interpret the results and the scores correctly in case of internal examinations than in the case of external ones. It cannot, however, be denied that the danger of these awards being subjective is inherent in this system to quite an appreciable degree because the personal knowledge of the examinees generates likes and dislikes and they affect the scores.

7. **Introduction of new-type tests :** Another far-reaching and useful suggestion which has been made to remedy the event of the traditional examination is to replace it by the objective or new type tests. This type of examination has a very strong foot-hold in the United States but is little known in this country. The recent report of the Universities Education Commission has, however, drawn pointed attention to it and it is hoped that in the very near future, it will be made more use of and will be a popular feature of our examination system. But it should be remembered that the new type of test is not an unmitigated blessing and as Vernon states "Americans, however, realise now that these (new types tests) are also liable to certain

defects when used indiscriminatingly and that there are still functions which can better be performed by the old or essay type of examination."

DIFFERENCE BETWEEN NEW AND OLD TYPE TESTS

These are three fundamental differences between the two kinds of examinations, the traditional or the essay type examination and the objective or the new type examination.

1. In the first instance, the questions in the old type tests are usually of the essay-type *e.g.*, 'write short notes on', 'compare and contrast', 'explain', 'give resons for', 'summarise' etc. New type tests, on the other hand, contain short questions where some words are to be underlined, absurdities have to be discovered, true statements have to be identified or selected from among false ones or corresponding statements have to be matched.

2. Each question in the old type test involves a number of mental processes and operations to be performed, whereas in the new type test, the number of operations involved in a question is reduced to the minimum. These questions are, therefore, short questions which admit only of one correct response.

This brings us to the second difference between the two tests. In the old type test, usually half a dozen questions are to be answerod in a couple of hours or so, whereas in the new type test, a hundred or more questions are to be answered in about half an hour. In this regard, it has been estimated that whereas in the old type examination the average examinee, as a rule, expresses less than one idea or fact per minute, in the new type test, he can easily and conveniently deal with 3 to 6 questions during the same time. This is so, because in the latter system, writing is practically eliminated; words have usually to be underlined or numbers stated etc.

3. Finally it should be remembered that it is very easy to set a question paper according to the old type test. Just a few questions have to be thought and included in the question paper. In the case of the new-type test, however, the setting of paper is a labourious process and needs careful preparation, through acquaintance with the subject-matter and a deep insight into the working of the human mind. It has been suggested that in the old type examination, the examiner has an easy time, when setting the paper and his headache begins when the answer papers are received. In the new type test, however, the headache is practically over when the question paper has been set, their marking being easy and mechanical. In the words of Ballard, "the motto of the new examiner seems to be, look after the testing and marking will look after itself."

Advantages of New Type Examination

The chief advantage of the new type test is that marking in the system is objective. The questions, as has been stated above, admit of only one response, and hence the chances of the disagreement between different examiners or in the case of the same examiner at different times vanish into thin air. The immense reduction in the amount of writing in the new type examination automatically leads to the elimination of irrelevant factors as handwriting, speed of writing, general lay-out etc. which blur the view and consequently distort the examiner's awards. This elimination of the subjective element in assessment increases not only their reliability but their validity also. The large number of questions included in the test, moreover, permits of a very adequate and comprehensive sampling of the whole field of learning and that also adds to the confidence and trust that can be reposed in their results. Another advantage of these tests is that they can be scored very easily and in a very short time. This naturally provides the teacher, with an opportunity of discussing the tests and their scores at a time, when the interest of the pupils in the test is at its highest. The scoring, in these cases, may even be done by mutual exchange of papers. This is so because all that the scorer needs is the key to the question, there being very little occasion for him to exercise his own skill or his own judgment. In this way, these tests can be turned into useful and effective devices of learning.

In addition to these advantages, the new type tests discourage cramming and encourage thinking and observation, scrutiny and reflection. These tests, moreover, can be standardised and then they can be used as effective and reliable instruments of measuring the standard of a school or its efficiency in comparison with other schools of the same area. The results of such tests can also be expressed in the form of percentages which are much more exact and precise estimates of an individual than any percentage mark of his work and ability.

Shortcomings of the New Type Tests

These tests, as has been remarked in the foregoing pages, do not bestow unmitigated blessings on the teacher. They have their own short-comings and defects. The foremost of these is that they encourage guessing. This point is made out in those tests especially where only two opinions are possible *e.g.* the true-false test. But we have to draw the attention of the students to the researches of Gray and Marsdon in which they tried to discover the extent to which children actually guessed and answered instead of answering only the questions which they knew. Their finding was that the amount of guessing was almost negligible. But even if it is admitted that it does take place, we can counteract its evil by subtracting the number of wrong responses from the number of right responses and by considering this difference as the final score. This will eliminate the chance factor and will give the pupil credit for his genuine knowledge only and not for his guess.

Apart from this, however, it is generally asserted that these tests measure only fragments of knowledge and the trival or superficial aspects of the ability of the examinees. Without going into the validity of this criticism, we must, however, admit that there is a greater opportunity of displaying higher mental processes in the essay type examinations than in the new type tests. In the new type questions pupils miss the valuable experience of making comparisons or giving explanations, and are denied the opportunities of evincing their abilities, of organising their thought processes. Finally, the new type tests can even be diagnostic in their function. This is because they can never enable a teacher to find out where a pupil makes a mistake in consecutive thinking or where his reasoning process goes wrong. Moreover, the line of demarcation between ceasing to think and starting to guess cannot be drawn.

The Place of New Type Tests in the Examination System

The new type examination, therefore, does not give us the magic formula which will solve all the ills of the traditional system of examinations. The latter has its own merit and these in the words of Symonds are "sufficient to guarantee its continued existence." The proper place which should be assigned to these tests has been admirably assessed by Evans. He syas, "All the evidence seems to point to the conclusion that it (the new type examination) is the most accurate method of testing students' knowledge of the subjects, that we have yet discovered. It does not, however, in my judgement, test sufficiently the students' powers of accurate and cogent expression, and his ability to organise his material. I should, therefore, feel that in an examination adequate time should always he given for at least one or two questions of the essay type."

LONG TERM v/s SHORT TERM EVALUATION

The Long Term Evaluation

Long term evaluation includes annual examination and the promotion of students thereby. Usually this type of evaluation forms the basis of promotion in most of the schools. Evaluation is made annually after the completion of the course of studies prescribed for the session.

Advantages: The long term evaluation has the following advantages :

1. It is easier to administer. A lot of time and money is wasted in organising short term tests.

2. It is economical in cost.

3. The students spend one year with the teachers thus giving them sufficient time to understand them and work accordingly.

4. It is in conformity with the plans followed in higher grades of education.

5. The year is quite a long time and it is very easy to organise and divide the subject matter of instruction into units.

6. The students can devote themselves to social service and co-curricular activities during the whole year as the examination is conducted at the end of the session.

7. The scope of long term evaluation is very comprehensive.

8. A student who could not do well due to certain reasons, can make up the deficiency by working during the last two or three months before the examination.

Disadvantages: The long term evaluation has the following disadvantages :

1. The student who fails in one subject has to repeat the whole course, and this imposes unnecessary burden on him.

2. The loss of one year means a good deal of money to the parents.

3. As the time for promotion is the same for all, the progress of the superior students is checked.

4. As the progress of the students is judged only by the annual examination, they do not work throughout the year. Just near the annual examinations, they burn the mid-night oil. Habits of regular work are not developed in them.

5. It leads to cramming and memorising. The students depend upon chance element. They lay emphasis on the subjects and the portions, which are useful and important from the examination point of view.

The Short Term Evaluation: The short term evaluation includes :

1. The weekly, fortnightly tests—oral or written.
2. The work done in the class.
3. The written work.
4. The practical work done in various subjects.

Advantages: The short term evaluation has the following advantages :

1. This helps in developing habits of regular work in the pupils.
2. A systematic regular work is assured.
3. In the light of this evaluation, necessary modifications may be made in the teaching process.
4. It minimises cramming.

Disadvantages : The short term evaluation has the following disadvantages :

1. Much of time is wasted in organising tests.
2. Students neglect one subject at the cost of the other.
3. Students take these tests lightly.
4. There is the possibility of copying and using unfair means on a larger scale.
5. As the subject matter is not much, it is easy to get through in such tests.
6. The integrated study of the subject suffers.

Synthesis of the Two

Even though the short term evaluation has got some minor drawbacks, it is essential and is acclaimed as an integral part of any system of evaluation. The long term evaluation, in spite of their drawbacks cannot be abolished altogether, as these provide a common yard-stick for all teachers and all schools. Hence, both supplement each other. What is required is the synthesis of the two. The promotions may be made not only on the basis of the annual examination, but also on the basis of internal assessment. The system of internal assessment is an innovation. It has not yet received a practical shape. There are yet a number of problems concerning short-term evaluation or internal assessment, which remain to be solved.

Problems concerning Internal Assessment

The problems concerning internal assessment or short term evaluations are as below :

1. **Lack of scientific basis :** The first problem is how to work out a scientific basis of short-term evaluation. Generally teachers are ignorant about the factors to be counted under it. It is suggested that the following factors should be counted under a comprehensive programme of internal assessment :

   (*a*) Oral activities such as debates, declamations, recitation, dramatisation, discussion etc.

   (*b*) Written activities, such as wall magazine, school magazine, paper-reading, preparing charts etc.

   (*c*) Class work, such as text book reading, class discussion, dictation, composition and other written work done in the class.

   (*d*) Home work given by the teacher in the form of usages of vocabulary, preparing summaries of chapters, answering questions given at the end of the chapter, translation, composition etc.

(*e*) Periodical tests—oral and written.

(*f*) Some qualities should be valued for the purpose of assessment *viz* :

Regularity and attendance, Comprehension of subject matter, Hand-writing and spelling, Expression and originality.

2. **Ignorance of the methods of evaluation :** The teachers are ignorant of the methods of evaluation. They adopt the same method of evaluation in internal assessment which is adopted in external assessment. It is suggested that the method of evaluation may be as under :

(*a*) Observation and recording the achievements of the pupil in his diary.

(*b*) symbolic marking of the home-work.

A+	Excellent	I Class
A	very Good	
B	Good	Second class
C	Fair	III Class
D	Failure	Failure

(*c*) Finding the average of the above.

(*d*) Permanent recording of the marks should be made in the examination register and cumulative record card. Besides, a class will be prepared for purposes of guiding the pupils.

3. **Lack of competence of teachers :** There is another problem of lack of competence of the teachers. The teachers need a thorough understanding and appreciation of the system. For this, special refresher courses or training camps may be held by way of in-service education. The duration should be at least one month. To begin with periodic conferences of teachers and headmasters must be held so that the objectives of internal assessment are clarified.

4. **Lack of co-ordination of standards :** There is another problem of co-ordination of standards among different schools and school subjects in internal assessment.

DIFFERENT WAYS OF EVALUATION

There can be following three ways of evaluation :

1. As it exists today; in the context of external examination mentioned above.
2. As it exists in some of the states where partial internal assessment has been introduced to supplement external examination.
3. As it may come up in future, if the states decide to shift over to total internal assessment.

External Examination Alone

The external examination, in a way, appears to provide a measuring rod to maintain uniformity of standards in all the schools by having common papers. Standards of marking differ from examiner to examiner and scientific procedures have to be developed to make them as uniform as possible. The following steps should be taken :

1. A meeting of examiners may be held, where the head examiner may explain clearly with the help of typical answers what he actually expects under each question. He may also define clearly good average and poor answers to each question and fix up the range of marks for each category. He may also point out what mistakes are to be taken into account and which are to be ignored. Besides he may fix up the range for the total marks in the whole paper, subject of course, to honourable exceptions on either end.

2. Detailed uniform instructions to all the examiners, both with respect to the scope of the answers and the distribution of marks for each part may be issued. Samples of examined answer-books may be checked by the head examiner and random samples of examined answer books

may be checked, after the examiners return the answer-books to the examining bodies.

3. Each answer-book may be subjected to examination by more than one examiner.

Internal-cum-external Assessment

In some of the states, partial internal assessment has been introduced to ensure uniformity of standards in external examination and the same procedures as suggested under (*a*) above may be adopted. To ensure uniformity in internal assessment some or all of the practices may be adopted:

1. Teachers may be given short term training courses in the techniques of examination.

2. Teachers' estimates may be against the results of scaled external examination.

3. Standardized tests concerning objectives and subject areas for which the teachers are to assess their pupils may be used as the measuring rods against which teachers' estimates may be scaled.

4. Assessors to check the teachers' estimates may be appointed and their identity may be kept confidential. They may compare assessment from different schools and also check them against other criteria which may be decided upon.

Total Internal Assessment

One of the essential pre-requisities of introducing total internal assessment is freedom to the teacher and the school. In such a case, it may not and shall not be found necessary to create any outside agency to impose upon the teacher the uniformity of standards. He will be free to compare his own standards with those of others, he may be provided with standardised tests (objective or essay type or both) but these tests shall not be compulsorily imposed upon him :

In this situation uniformity of standards may be ensured indirectly in the following ways :

1. Advisory bodies of experts in different areas of knowledge may be appointed. They may issue suggestions to different institutions from time to time and also inform them about relevant articles from magazines and books for the guidance of the teachers.

2. A complete change in teacher's attitude will be necessary. It shall have to be brought home to them that these experts are not official supervisors but only advisors to whom they may refer their problems in time of need.

SUGGESTIONS FOR RELATING INTERNAL ASSESSMENT TO THE EXTERNAL

Examination Marks

The following suggestions are presented :

1. Internal assessment should be in relation to various aspects of the pupils' growth, such as his scholastic achievements, his interests, attitudes, personality traits etc.

2. There should be some minimum standard of passing prescribed for both internal and external examination in academic subjects and the result should be announced on the basis of pupils record of achievement in both, mentioned separately.

3. To make the results comparable, it may be desirable to bring total marks of both internal assessment and external examination at par, so far as academic subjects are concerned.

4. It should, however, be noted that internal assessement may be in symbols and grades or in qualitative description for assessing the pupils' achievements in some fields, and therefore external and internal results may not be always comparable.

5. Certificates showing the achievement of students both in the external examination and internal assessment

will provide better scope to the employee for making his choice.

This type of certificate will provide the opportunity to carry on some studies to find out whether the internal or external result is more valid and reliable in respect of a particular school. This will also help in developing criteria for classifying and accrediting schools.

The Problem of Recognition of Internal Assessment

The importance of internal assessment has been recognised by all. But teachers are reluctant to prepare regular records as long as the public examination continue. When the University authorities, the employers and the general public recognise and give weight only to the certificate bearing the stamp of the University, the School Board or any other Governmental examining body, the teacher's internal assessment does not get any recognition at all. Then what for should all this labour be? For this reason, it may be asserted that internal assessment should receive due recognition. This is possible if some weightage (at least 25%) be given to internal assessment in the final public examination also. The examining bodies must demand the record of pupils about the periodic tests from the Headmaster, and must strike the average of the marks obtained during the whole course. These marks should be added to the marks obtained in the external examination. The teacher's labour will thus be rewarded. It is for the examining bodies to see that uniformity is maintained in different schools in the scores of the internal assessment. It might be that a particular school is too generous or too strict in awarding marks in internal assessment. A comparison of the scores in the internal assessment and external examinations of all the candidates of the school can be made *viz.* divergence in the two averages can be removed. In addition to it modification must be made in the internal scores in order to bring these nearer the external scores. The internal scores of scholarship cases should be verified properly. The 25% weightage to be given to internal assessment is suggested only for the present, when we make a beginning in this direction. As the internal assessment is found more and more reliable, more and more weightage can be given to it. An ideal state of affairs would be, when honesty and unformity prevail to such an extent that each headmaster would test his students himself even in the final class and would issue his own certificate. For the present, it would be in the fitness of things, if the University authorities or the examining bodies would issue their own certificates containing alongwith the external scores, summary of the results of the internal assessment attested by the Headmaster. Or else, the headmaster should be allowed to issue certificates containing the scores of the internal assessment, as well as general remarks about the pupils. This certificate should be given equal recognition with the certificate issued by the public examining body.

The Problem of the Work Load of Teachers

The system of internal assessment demands extra labour on the part of the teachers in maintaining the records and holding periodic tests regularly. At present, the teachers are already burdened with all sorts of teaching and clerical work. Besides delivering lessons in the class-room, and working for about 36 to 40 periods a week, the teacher is also required to supervise games and other extra-curricular activities, correct piles of note-books, complete registration work, write diaries, conduct correspondence regarding the school, meet parents and attend to special school tasks assigned by the Headmaster—library work, admissions, scouting, school project, school clubs and societies etc. Besides all these activities, he has to realise dues from the students. Under these circmustances, when the work load is so high, he is reluctant to accept another huge task of maintaining records of internal assessment.

To solve this problem, all clerical work hitherto assigned to the teacher should be assigned to a whole time clerk to realise the dues, maintain accounts, keep a record of the attendance of the pupil and do all sorts of clerical work, where no technical knowledge, teaching work is required. Being rid of all clerical work, the teacher's work load is minimised, so as to enable him to attend to the most important task of internal assessment. Each teacher should be responsible for maintaining regular records of internal assessment of the subjects he teaches to various classes. A teacher may be kept over-all incharge of the house tests and internal assessment. His teaching load should be lessened, to compensate for the additional labour involved.

CONCLUSION

Various Commissions have given suggestions for the improvement of Examination System or Evaluation. But till now there is no improvement. Lot of research is required to develop a fool-proof system of Evaluation keeping in view the Indian conditions.

Bibliography

Adam John, Sir : Modern Developments in Educational Practice

Adam John, Sir : The New Teaching

Anderson : Practical Problems in Teaching

Austin : Questions in the Class-room

Barnard, H.C. : An Introduction to Teaching

Bayles : The Theory and Practice of Teaching

Boardman, J.A. : Practical School Method

Barbara Priestman : Froebel Education To-day

Burnett : Essentials of Teaching

Catty Nancy : The Theory and Practice of Education

Catty Nancy : First Book on Teaching

Cole : The Method and Technique of Teaching

Davis Valentine : The Technique of Teaching

Dhiman, O.P. : Principles and Techniques of Education

Dhiman, O.P. : Foundations of Education

Dumville & Benjamine : How to Teach.

Dumville & Benjamine : Teaching : Its Nature and Varieties

Dougles, H.R. : High School Curriculum

Daiken Leslie : Teaching through Play.

Elliot : Film and Education.

Engelhardt & Oven : Secondary Education : Its Principles and Practice.

Fern & Robbins : Teaching with Films.

Flemming, C.M. : Research and the Basic Curriculum.

Frasim : Principles of Teaching.

Granles & Inverson : Modern Methods in Secondary Education.

Gilbert Hight : The Art of Teaching.

Harper, A.E. : Introduction to the Project Method.

Hughe & Hughe : Learning and Teaching.

Harrold Spears : Principles of Teaching.

Highet : Art of Teaching.

Heitland : How to Conduct a Discussion Group.

James : Talks to Teachers.

Krug, E.A. : Curriculum Planning.

Mander : Class-room Teaching.

McKnown & Roberts : Audio-visual Aids to Instruction.

Melvin A. Gordon : General Methods of Teaching.

Morrison : The Practice of Teaching in the Secondary School.

Montessori Maria : Education for a New World.

Mecnee : Instruction in Indian Secondary Schools.

Panton, J.H. : Modern Teaching Practice and Technique.

Pinset, A. : Principles of Teaching Method.

Polham : Handbook of Suggestions for Teachers.

Raymont, T. : Principles of Education.

Raymont, T. : Modern Education, Its Aims and Methods.

Ryburn, W.M. : The Principles of Teaching.

Ryburn, W.M. : The Progressive School.

Ryburn, W.M. : The Creative Education.

Ryburn, W.M. : Play-way Suggestions.

Salmon, D. : The Art of Teaching.

Smith & Harrison : The Principles of Class Teaching.

Sumner, W.L. : Visual Methods in Education.

Struck F. Theodore : Creative Teaching.

UNESCO : Visual Aids in Fundamental Education.

Word & Roscoe : An Approach to Teaching.

Welton : Principles and Methods of Education.

Ward : An Approach to Teaching.

Yoakam & Simpson : Modern Methods and Techniques of Teaching.

Index